D0098454

FOUR DAYS
TO GLORY

FOUR DAYS TO GLORY

WRESTLING WITH THE SOUL OF THE AMERICAN HEARTLAND

MARK KREIDLER

HarperCollinsPublishers

FOUR DAYS TO GLORY. Copyright © 2007 by Mark Kreidler. All rights reserved. Printed in the United States of America. No part of this book may be used or reproduced in any manner whatsoever without written permission except in the case of brief quotations embodied in critical articles and reviews. For information, address HarperCollins Publishers, 10 East 53rd Street, New York, NY 10022.

HarperCollins books may be purchased for educational, business, or sales promotional use. For information, please write: Special Markets Department, HarperCollins Publishers, 10 East 53rd Street, New York, NY 10022.

Designed by William Ruoto

Library of Congress Cataloging-in-Publication Data is available upon request.

ISBN: 978-0-06-082318-4
ISBN-10: 0-06-082318-6

07 08 09 10 11   ID/RRD   10 9 8 7 6 5 4

For C.M.T.C.-K.
with love and missing flowers

Contents

FOUR DAYS
TO GLORY

CHAPTER 1

Locating the Enemy

Jay doesn't plan on his headgear ricocheting across the wrestling mat and spiking against one of his teammates' legs, but he won't be racing over to do anything about it, either. You can hear the slap of plastic on skin from across the gym when it makes contact, but since the teammate caught in the crossfire is both an underclassman and a varsity wrestler in the state of Iowa, he does not so much as throw Jay a look. The boy instead sits there in his chair alongside the mat, hunkered down, the hood of his sweat top pulled around his head to shadow his face. He does not move. There is, his posture suggests, no sting from the spiked headgear, no red mark on his leg from the point of contact. Nothing has happened. And Jay need not apologize for—well, for what is essentially nothing.

But Jay means it, of course—not the ricochet, but the rest of it. He wants his disgust fully visible to anyone inside the gym, which is why he yanks off the equipment and fires it downward in the first place. Let there be no question about his mood after another forfeit. He has sat with the rest of the Linn-Mar team on a yellow-and-black school bus for two solid hours while it shuddered and skidded along the icy rural roadways from Marion to

Dubuque, and has done it because he desperately wants the moment that now eludes him. He wants to get out there and beat somebody to death. He wants to wrestle. He needs it. There's no sense in pretending anything else.

This quest is impossible without getting in his work, and that's the thing. Jay cannot become a four-time state champion unless he is in the best shape of his life when the time comes to go for it, and now, in January of 2005, that time is barely a month away and Jay cannot get a freaking match. Opponents run from him, even when they're on the mat. Coaches try to wrestle around him. They all know about Jay Borschel. They'd sooner forfeit the weight category than waste one of their decent wrestlers in a match they figure Jay will win easily. And so they run.

From his place in the bleachers above the gymnasium floor, Jay's father, Jim, sees the forfeit signal and suddenly has had all he can take. "Oh, come ON, coach!" he bellows over the heads of the other Linn-Mar parents and fans, his foghorn voice easily carrying the distance across to the Hempstead High coach, Chuck Hass. Hass never moves, never glances up; he keeps his gaze fixed upon the mat itself. He knows what he's doing.

Hass has just finished ducking Jay by moving away from him a good 171-pound wrestler, a boy named Dan Chmelar, who is ranked among the top ten in the state in Class 3A. But 171 is Jay Borschel's weight, or at least his current weight; in the past, Jay has won state titles at 103, 125 and 152 pounds. Jay already defeated Chmelar once this season, and it wasn't close. Sending Chmelar out there again would have been, for Hass, a points sacrifice straight down the line. The smart move was to skip Jay, concede the forfeit at 171, and save Chmelar for a better matchup, even though it would mean asking him to wrestle at a heavier weight.

And that's exactly what Hass has just done. As soon as Linn-Mar coach Doug Streicher made his move to send Jay to the mat, the avoidance plan went into effect. From the Hempstead side came no activity, no one rising from his chair or loosening up or pulling off his sweats. After checking in at the officials' table, Jay had walked out to center mat, popped from side to side on the balls of his toes and cranked his head from shoulder to shoulder, waiting for the opponent who was not coming. After a few seconds, Jay had seen that his pre-match suspicions were realized—that he would stand alone. After a few more seconds of inactivity from Hempstead, the referee had raised Jay's hand to signal the forfeit.

After the match, Chuck Hass says that as soon as he won the coin flip that forced Streicher to send out his wrestler first, he knew he wasn't going to be letting any of his kids face Jay. "Everybody knows Jay's the hammer," Hass says. "He's going to beat whoever you send out there—and we've got a good kid at that weight. I'd rather take my chances that Dan can get me points at 189 than just give them away against Jay.

"I know it frustrates Jay," the coach says. "We've got a kid at 119 pounds who goes through the same thing. In fact, I think Linn-Mar forfeited to him last year. It's just a part of the game."

And it is the right move for Hass's team. Chmelar shifts to 189 pounds, since wrestlers are allowed to move up in weight classes without penalty, and he wins a decision over the Linn-Mar wrestler there. Hempstead's usual 189-pounder, Justin Whitty, subsequently goes up to 215 pounds and wins a major decision. Those two victories are worth a combined 7 points for Hempstead, and the Mustangs ultimately win by 4, 31 to 27. Linn-Mar, meanwhile, gets the same number of points (6) at Jay's weight for the forfeit as it would have received for a pin, but is denied the emotional lift that comes with seeing Jay manhandle someone from the other team. The Lions get the forfeit, but not the blood.

And Jay? He gets no closer. No closer to the dream at all.

"That's awful!" Jim Borschel thunders, turning away from

the mat in disgust. Jay's mother, Carol, who isn't apt to sit still under the best of circumstances, is unable to contain herself any longer; she pops up from the bleachers, trots up the steps in her Linn-Mar-red sweat suit, and begins pacing the concourse above the sunken courts and mat area. She appears to have as much pent-up energy as her wrestler son. "I just can't believe that," she says repeatedly. "That makes me so mad. How can you not let two Top 10 wrestlers face each other?"

"You can't hide him at State!" Jim yells to the Hempstead coach, but it doesn't matter now. Both Jim Borschel and Chuck Hass know the deal. Both wrestled in high school. By the end of the evening, in fact, both men will have acknowledged that there aren't really any hard feelings, at least not between them. Jay is too good. It's a standing issue.

Slamming through a set of double doors, walking down a hallway that leads to the Hempstead High workout room, Jay feels the blood pounding in his temples, the pre-match adrenaline still coursing through his system. He will have to lift weights and ride the stationary bike and run the halls until he begins to feel his body coming down to earth again. It could take a while.

"God, I hate when they do that," Jay says. His blue eyes go flinty for a few seconds. "I came to wrestle. I mean, that's why I'm here."

He looks off down the hallway for a moment. "I hate it," he says again, almost to himself this time. "But it happens."

Lately, it happens with regularity. These episodes are becoming familiar to Jay; they infuriate him even as he recognizes the truth: He thrives on exactly this kind of angry energy. It is the essential contradiction of Jay Borschel that he wants to be respected for the champion he is—by everyone, everywhere—and yet he feeds on the notion that such respect won't quite come his way, or that, if it does, it will be in an unpalatable form like this. It is, in the end, what drives him. He's better when he thinks the people out there want to see him fail.

"That's just the way it is," Jay says later, calmer now, looking out over the emptying Hempstead gymnasium after his team's defeat. He sounds more definitive than the situation really is. On the one hand, Iowans may really want to love Jay, to see him crush the odds and become an immortal—to do this sacred thing and join the giants. On the other, hardly anybody in the state feels like actually getting on the same mat with him. Go figure.

"Man," Jay says, "I was ready to go tonight." He shrugs, picks up his bag and heads for the school bus. It is mid-January, barely a month before everything is supposed to happen at the State Tournament, the center of the wrestling world for those four days in February. Barely a month away, and this is Jay: all geeked up and nowhere to go.

By the next day, you're hard-pressed by Jay's demeanor to believe that anything seismic has occurred the evening before. He is back in control, back in wrestler mode. He will not go on railing against his inability to get some competition, because wrestlers do not complain in such a way. Wrestlers, Jay says, believe in action, not words.

"Just have to keep doing it on the mat," he says, "and let the rest take care of itself."

And it would be tempting to accept that, that Jay is all about the action. It is only the note that seems to suggest otherwise.

The note is hardly hidden; in some ways, it appears that Jay wants it seen. It is taped against the wall of Jay's little bedroom at the end of the hallway, in the house on Larick Court in the subdivision in Marion, just north of Cedar Rapids in the eastern part of the state. The note, placed a few feet from a Dave Matthews poster and near a light switch over which a piece of paper with the words 4-TIME STATE CHAMPION has been affixed, is blotting out a significant part of an elaborately hand-lettered and framed bracket. The bracket illustrates a time, two years before, when Jay won it all. The note says he won't win it again.

Well, it doesn't say that, exactly. What it says is that Jay Borschel is about to get his ass kicked by a better man, en route to getting his ass kicked all season.

Well, it doesn't even say that, really. If you read the post, it's actually fairly respectful, considering it is something offered by some anonymous writer, which Jay yanked off an Iowa high school wrestling message board on the Internet. It suggests that Jay may have trouble against a particular wrestler in an upcoming match and, beyond that, he may find that moving up so many weight classes each year—as he has done regularly since winning a state title as a skinny 103-pound freshman—can present its own unique set of challenges.

The note reads, in part: "It just might be a little different when he's wrestling with the big boys. Which is the whole idea I think. He WILL be pushed at 171."

It is a reasonable enough sentiment. For that matter, the note-writer goes on to say that he expects Jay to become a state champion yet again, this time in historic four-title fashion. But it is enough for Jay. It is everything he needs to hear.

The opponent mentioned in the note is a great wrestler and a friend of Jay's, a senior from Lisbon named Ryan Morningstar. Ryan has a chance to become a three-time champion if he can win state in February in Des Moines. His dad is one of Iowa's gods, a four-timer. The thought of Morningstar and Borschel, these two defending state champions, going after each other in a sanctioned high school match is enough to get any real Iowa wrestling fan to talking. God, it would be a titanic thing. And Jay knows how much people would love to see Morningstar knock his block off.

All in all, it sets up as a fantastic match. One hitch: It will never actually happen.

Jay and Ryan have met once in their high school careers, during their junior seasons, in a match won by Jay that was about as close as a competition can be. They won't meet again. They now wrestle two full weight classes and 19 pounds apart, and while Jay's Linn-Mar team wrestles in Iowa's 3A high school division, Ryan's Lisbon team is a 1A school, in the same classification as Jay's friend Dan LeClere's North-Linn team out in the country. Although Ryan, the lighter of the two, had at one point mentioned the possibility of meeting Jay at an early-season tournament, he never came close to gaining enough weight to do it. As great as the match might have been, Ryan was—like Jay—already focused on his larger goals for the season, namely, winning the big one at the Barn.

So the note on Jay's wall is old and inaccurate, which has nothing to do with the issue of whether Jay will ever remove it. He has taped it there with a sign above it, which he printed out, a sign that blares the words NO RESPECT in huge capital letters. What matters to Jay is not whether the note is relevant, but that the note conveys doubt. It is the doubt upon which he feeds, exactly the disrespect he requires to get his emotional engine warmed. He has lost once in his high school career, and still they doubt. State champion three times over, and they doubt. He's the closest to a sure thing in the history of the state in wrestling. People are lining up not to wrestle against him. They forfeit in droves, send jayvee kids out there to take one for the team—and still somebody doubts. And so the thing stays up there on the wall for as long as need be, doing its job. It might even do better if Jay had the slightest idea who wrote it.

"I don't know, some guy," Jay says when I ask about the note. "Just some guy."

Jay looks at the words again, shakes his head dismissively. "He's got it all figured out, doesn't he?" he says.

Oh, man. It's just so perfect.

Carol Borschel is setting out steak and shrimp, and Jay is prepared to eat all of it as many times as he can fill his plate. After years of starving himself, he has achieved a sort of wrestler's nir-vana: He can eat what he wants, more or less, and still maintain his lean, strong 171-pound weight with relative ease. For a wrestler at any competitive level, that is a rare condition, and inherently a temporary one. Jay has no illusions about what awaits him during his college years. It won't be pretty. For now, this will do fine.

Along one windowsill in the kitchen lie the bottles of sup-plements that make up Jay's daily regimen. There is a standard multivitamin, and ginkgo biloba, and Siberian ginseng root, and the muscle-enhancer Creatine, and a raft of Advocare products: POS 1 and POS 5, something called Catalyst that combines glu-tamine, leucine, isoleusine and valine, and Advocare Performance Gold, to be used only on competition days.

"All mine," Jay says. "They think it makes me better."

"They" would be mostly Jim. And Jim, really, is advocating nothing unusual for an elite athlete. Though Jay's regimen of pills and powders is impressive, it is hardly unique; the closest he comes to any-thing controversial is Creatine, a product often mentioned as part of the routines of some of America's most prominent athletes, many of whom (Barry Bonds, Mark McGwire, Jason Giambi) have gone on to become associated with or implicated in steroid scandals. Creatine itself is an amino acid produced naturally in the kidneys, pancreas and liver, and a supply of it in one's body can aid in high-intensity work-outs by allowing extra energy to be stored. The long-term effects are yet unknown, but the product is legal and has become a staple in high school locker rooms and workout facilities.

Beyond all that, though, the enjoyment for Jay lies in the consumption of actual food. And the accompanying dinnertime entertainment on this evening takes the form of an ongoing teas-ing of Carol, who is attempting to tell a story.

"I remember the weekend in Waterloo . . ." Carol says.

"That wasn't Waterloo," Jay immediately interjects. "That was somewhere else."

"Are you sure?" Carol asks. "I thought it was Waterloo."

"Mom, it wasn't," says Jay's sister, Hannah.

"Anyway, Jay and Mitch were running around in between matches—"

"Mitch wasn't there," Jay says.

"That weekend?"

"No."

"He was there," says Carol. "I know he was there."

"You're thinking of a different tournament," Jay says. "Mitch wasn't there. You can't remember the weekend?"

Across the table, Jim eats his steak and smiles to himself. The dinnertime give-and-take suggests to him that his family is functioning normally, and after all the winters when Jay was either viciously cutting weight or just generally in crabby-wrestler mode, Jim can live with the goofing on Carol. Carol can live with it, too. She waits patiently for her children to stop interrupting her, throws a look of classic motherly exasperation toward Jay's sympathetic girlfriend, Jillian, then continues with her story about a tournament at which Jay had overheard some people doubting his ability to win. Inspired by their skepticism, he pinned his way through the ensuing weekend.

"They don't understand," Carol says, a finality in her tone. "That kind of stuff just fires him up."

Sitting one chair away from her, finished for the time being, Jay appears unfazed by having his mother speak of him as if he weren't in the room. He stares off into the darkened backyard, waiting for Carol to finish. This, too, is not new: The Borschel family has made it through a few waves of interviews over the past couple of years, as Jay's victories piled up and local writers began coming around to learn more about him. By now, Carol knows to come prepared. She carefully brings out three large, red-jacketed photo albums, one for each of Jay's first three state-championship seasons. Tucked inside are stories, photos and memorabilia from those years, many of the articles bearing the bylines of the two writers from the *Cedar Rapids Gazette*, K. J. Pilcher and J. R. Ogden, who have most closely followed Jay's progress since he came to Linn-Mar High. The albums draw the arc of Jay's wrestling existence to this point, from his lone loss in high school (in ninth grade, to his friend Joey Slaton) to his current status as a three-time winner. Included is Pilcher's account of Jay's riveting 4–3 victory over Morningstar in January of 2004, a meeting of then-unbeaten defending state champions, which Pilcher described as "arguably the most anticipated prep wrestling match in years."

As Carol presents the albums, Jay retreats to a couch on the other side of the family room, as if to create some distance between himself and his past.

"That's kind of Mom's thing," he says. "I don't look back too much."

Not at the victories, anyway. Jay's past success doesn't resonate with him in the way that the public questions about his future do. There is a reason that the old championship bracket on the wall of his room is partially obscured by the message-board post. He's just better at processing the doubt than the praise.

"And that's funny," Jim says, "because the one bone of contention between us is that Jay thinks I've never been able to give him full credit for how good he is. Maybe he's right."

Or maybe he just needs the friction.

As he comes out of the locker area the next afternoon and heads for the practice mats in the Linn-Mar wrestling room, Jay could be just about anybody. He doesn't look like a champion, at least not in terms of carriage. He seriously lacks a strut; he almost slouches his way to the mat. He isn't the most chiseled guy in the room—solid-looking, certainly, but not as muscle-bound or obviously defined as some of his teammates. Through his headgear, his deep-blue eyes make him look soulful, not menacing. Rather than chatting up his teammates, he sits quietly among them on top of the rolled-up mats that rest against the far wall of the room. He is no more or less riveted by Doug Streicher's pre-workout speech than anybody else, and as the minutes pass, he grows restless and bored. As Streicher issues instructions, Jay amuses himself by tucking up his shorts so that they resemble an adult-sized diaper.

"He does that sometimes," Jim says drolly, gazing across the mats at his son. Jim has stopped by after work to watch a little of the practice. "Jay walking into a wrestling room does not instantly command the respect of others."

But as soon as Streicher needs a wrestler to help him demonstrate the takedown move he wants to teach, he motions to Jay, and Jay bolts off his perch and rushes onto the mat. Suddenly he's alive, in motion. He runs to get into position to be driven to the surface by Streicher as he illustrates the move, and as soon as the coach does so, Jay bounces back up, ready to go again. After a few tries, Streicher lets Jay take the offensive, and the pleasure is evident on the senior's face as he tries to force his stockier, heavier coach to the mat while Streicher explains to the Linn-Mar team how to defend the move.

Again and again the two go at it, always in control but with gradually increasing energy between them. Streicher suited up for Dan Gable at Iowa, and he wrestles mercilessly, because that's what Gable taught—that only the merciless can succeed on the mat. Jay has no problem with that. Among the Linn-Mar coaches, he has always been known as an exceptionally hard worker; he puts in his time in the weight room and does his running, and for three years he has managed his weight with no issues. But those are the mechanical aspects of wrestling, achievable by anyone with either a carrot in front of him or a stick behind. It is only on the mat itself that Jay's wrestling character is truly displayed.

During this practice, Jay is repeatedly thrown in against the assistant coaches on the Linn-Mar staff, who wrestle him in alternating turns of a few minutes at a time. It's a necessity; Streicher says there is no one on the roster capable of wrestling Jay at his required level of intensity for any length of time. The competition is fair; Streicher has insisted upon hiring only assistants who wrestled in college. It comes in handy here, with Jason Haag and CJ McDonald and Kevin McCauley all trading off against Jay, CJ and Kevin with a huge weight advantage and Haag with his wealth of experience and trickery. Jay allows a brief smile each time a new coach comes on to face him, but when the whistle blows to begin the one-on-ones, he begins scrapping fiercely. Several times during the hour of almost nonstop work, Jay and the coaches go tumbling out of their designated area on the mats, cutting out teammates' legs from underneath them. But Jay won't give it up, and he won't come off for a break. Longtime Iowa wrestling fans would find that scenario familiar: It is, the legend goes, how Gable used to get ready for his matches, by basically wrestling everyone in the room until there was no one left to go against him. Jay isn't in Gable's league, of course. No one is. On the other hand, Dan Gable never had a chance to win four straight high school championships.

When the practice finally ends, Jay quickly dresses and comes out to see his father, and there are no hellos exchanged. Instead, it is as though the two have resumed a conversation they were just having a minute before.

"So how much money have you got?" Jay says.

"Sure, now I'm the bank," Jim jokes, but he is already reaching into his wallet. Jim pulls out a $10 bill and hands it to Jay, who takes it between his thumb and forefinger and walks away, holding his new money in the air as though it were an artifact.

"He's already thinking about food," Jim says. "You'll want to make a note of that. It'll come up fairly often."

CHAPTER 2

Merely Really Good

They didn't grow up together; it only seems that way sometimes. Jay Borschel is, at heart, a city kid; he has grown up either in university towns or the suburbs of Cedar Rapids, where his parents settled when he was four. Dan LeClere, though he knows his way around the city, has spent his life to this point largely on the farm, on land that has been held in the LeClere family name for a century. Jay goes to the big high school in Marion. Dan will graduate from North-Linn High School with a senior class of fifty. They are separated by perhaps a twenty-minute drive, but radically different lives; put the two in a room together and, other than wrestling, you wonder what they'd even have to talk about.

But there is wrestling, of course. There always was. And it is what draws them together, now as it has drawn them for years. It brings them together now because of what they are after, because going for four state titles, as each of them is, is such a profoundly lonely thing to do. They both could succeed; they certainly both could fail. And that success or that failure will be played out in front of a state's worth of people who know their sport almost as well as they do, and who don't mind passing immediate judgment upon it. It is a pressure none but the two of them will feel, and that's the part about being brothers.

"Put it this way," Dan says. "It's a lot better going through something like this with someone you feel like you've known your whole life."

Only Jay and Dan can understand. This is no ordinary quest. One cannot be an ordinary person and attempt it.

There are many ways by which to measure oneself as successful in Iowa, but only a couple by which to be loved. In the eighty-plus-year existence of the Iowa State High School Wrestling Tournament, easily the largest event of its kind in the United States, there had by the winter of 2005 been exactly fourteen people who, through a combination of determined will, outrageous fortune and the ability to go for years without enjoying an anxiety-free meal, somehow found themselves in the possession of four individual state championships—four titles, all to themselves. Only once during that eight-decade span had two wrestlers achieved "four-time" status in the same year.

Consider the odds; they're astounding even by athletic standards. In the late fall of each year, somewhere north of 8,600 wrestlers begin the journey that will take them around the state and right on through hell, an extended stay replete with wind sprints and projectile vomiting and blood and contortionist acts and stinging, salty sweat. By February, 632 of these wrestlers will have earned the most sought-after placement in Iowa, a spot in the four-day State Tournament. In the end, the tournament will produce a winner in each of the sport's fourteen weight-class winners, and it will do so in each of Iowa's three high school wrestling classifications, Class 1A, 2A and 3A. That makes for a total of forty-two state champs, or roughly .005 percent of those who began the season.

That is the math behind doing the unimaginable, taking your

school and the town or the rural communities that surround it on a wild, emotional ride, and winning it all—one time. Now factor in the truth of the adolescent body, which is that no matter what you do (and wrestlers have pretty much tried everything), it more or less refuses to stop growing and changing shape. Factor injuries and luck. Factor the potential of everything else going right, only to result in an inexplicably terrible draw at State—getting an enormously difficult first- or second-round match, for example, because of the tournament's history of not seeding the wrestlers in any sort of pecking order.

Factor nerves and slippage. Factor, let us say, a severe week-long case of bronchitis that robs a superior athlete of one of his greatest advantages, his conditioning, and returns him to the land of the merely mortal at precisely the worst time. (We'll get to that.) Factor the sport's enduring truism, which is that even the great ones are usually one false step removed from being put on their backs by some kid they've never heard of.

And most of all, understand the stakes, because to become a wrestling champion in Iowa is to be changed. The history of the State Tournament is rich in stories of kids who brought to communities the only glory they've ever experienced. They still play football in Iowa, sure, and it matters intensely. They play basketball, and the basketball players generally still get the good school bus on game nights. But on the larger scale, there are only two things for which Iowa is internationally known: (1) It produces corn; and (2) It produces wrestlers. Everybody there understands the difference between a good wrestler and a champion, and everybody—just everybody—understands the difference between a champion and a four-timer.

A champion rattles a community. A four-timer shakes a state.

Jay understands that, and he understood it on that night two years ago, when he abruptly jerked up his head in the middle of his sophomore state-championship match in order to take in the full roar from the crowd inside creaky old Veterans Memorial Auditorium, the place known as the Barn, in downtown Des Moines. It was applause aimed not at Jay but at a senior named Mack Reiter, who on an adjacent mat was putting the finishing touches on his own victory—his fourth title in four years. It was just so huge, that moment. Reiter was joining the ranks of people whose names wind up in the annual program. They would talk about him forever, maybe. And Jay soaked in that moment, the one that belonged to the other guy. He let the atmosphere fill him up for perhaps a two-count; and then he remembered why he was there on the wrestling mat in the first place, trying to win his second title. But before he did, he said to himself, "That's me in two years." Only to himself did Jay say it. Only inside himself did he carry it. No one else needed to hear. No one else needed to know. No one, when you get right down to it, could do a thing about it, anyway.

And when the moment came, it would arrive with company, with Dan LeClere, in some ways the kid Jay really did grow up with. The two had shared wrestling rooms and road trips for years, summers on end, as part of the youth wrestling fanaticism in the state. They had known for years that they were different, a little special. Dan was more pronouncedly so, the son of a wrestling coach; it was a given, knowing Dan's father, Doug LeClere, that Daniel would be brought into the sport and kept there, even if no one realized back then how much he might achieve.

It would never occur to Dan that he might find himself, at the moment of approaching that kind of greatness, in a position to suddenly lose it all. It would never occur to him to think that way, because there's no future in it, and that makes it impractical, and wrestling, like farming, is just not the sort of thing one can do and be impractical at the same time. And it would certainly never occur to Dan that his path might carry a personal cost beyond the physical, beyond exhaustion and mere pain. He would never see the dark side coming. Only gradually would it become apparent that Dan had other opponents to deal with before he could try to become the wrestler that he and Doug wanted him to be.

Jay and Dan have known each other since elementary school, began wrestling at about the same time they got any good at walking. They are the ones who grew up in the shadow of the Iowa Hawkeyes program, becoming Little Hawks themselves, dreaming of their futures with Gable in Iowa City. They are the ones who gradually shunned other sports, casting them off one by one, year by year, advancing upon this singular pursuit. They will join with six or eight other athletes from the eastern part of the state to form arguably the greatest senior class in the annals of wrestling in Iowa. But without that fourth title, Jay and Dan will join a long list of people who won a bunch but didn't really get it all—respected wrestlers, who had periodic bouts of excellence without quite ascending to heaven. Merely really good, is all.

By essentially winning everything in sight for as long as anyone has been taking notice, Jay and Dan have made it clear what the expectations should be of their talent. You don't leave your talent lying around in a sport like wrestling. You tend it.

They will tend their talent, then, because nobody else can. They will ultimately do it on their own, because the sport is wrestling, and the thing about wrestling that makes it so perfect is the fact of there being no easy way to approach it.

You want to become an immortal? Listen, everybody does. It's the part about actually getting there that makes this such an Iowa tale.

CHAPTER 3

The Family Business

In the dead nighttime quiet of the farmhouse out in the open land beyond tiny Coggon, Dan pulls a blanket around him as he curls in tight against one corner of the couch in the TV room, and you are reminded what a compact person he is. He wrestles at 140 pounds as a senior, and he wrestled at 119 pounds as a freshman. He has been the same size throughout high school, basically. He long ago mastered the art of maintaining his optimal weight. He knows the difference between a pound of meat and a pound of chips, put it that way. On this night, he makes do with a small bowl of chili and, for a treat, a miniature Tupperware cup of Froot Loops. It's a cup you might normally see used to keep Cheerios on hand for a toddler—enough for a taste but not really an experience.

Doug LeClere sweeps into the house through the back door, having made his rounds on the farm and changed the cattle's water, testing to be sure it wasn't frozen solid. Although "farmer" is just one of at least four jobs Doug carries, it is easily the one with the most insistent and immediate demands. As he puts it, "It's not the kind of thing you can ignore for very long at a time."

Inside the house, Mary LeClere, Dan's mother, having cleared the table and washed the dishes, pads off quietly to another room, carrying a little dessert with her. Mary long ago learned that if she wanted to enjoy something sweet, she needed to do it out of the sight of her wrestler children.

As Dan and his younger brothers, Nick and Chris, lounge on the couch, putting off homework, Doug reaches for a tape and pops it into the VCR. He is looking for some old video of Dan to show, something from when he was a mite wrestling in little-kid competitions, but what appears on the screen instead is relatively new footage, taken within a year or so—and it is not of one of the LeClere boys. It's the dad.

"Where'd that come from?" Doug asks, but it's clear he is not bothered. He is seldom embarrassed by anything, least of all something to do with wrestling, even if it's a video of a 40-something adult scrapping around in a weekend all-comers competition. Wrestling is Doug's identity, more so than farming. Wrestling is his family's calling card. He was good enough at it in high school to earn a ticket to State, and when you're a true wrestler, the season never ends. At least that's what the tape suggests.

As Doug describes the location and the opponent, Dan slowly takes notice. At first he appears bemused, maybe even slightly annoyed, that his dad has dragged out one of his own matches; but as the moments pass, Dan's eyes never leave the television screen. At one point, he shifts slightly forward on the couch, looking intently at the images until he sees Doug's opponent stumble briefly on the mat, appearing to lose his footwork.

"There," he says. "That's where you had him. See his balance shift?"

"Yeah," Doug agrees. "I didn't get him then, though."

"It's OK," Dan says. "Here comes your other chance."

Sure enough, a few seconds later Doug's opponent wavers again on his feet, and this time Doug gets the takedown and scores the points that eventually stand up for his victory. Dan saw it coming because, clearly, he has seen this video dozens of times already, on dozens of nights, after dozens of workouts, in advance of dozens of matches. But all the fun's in seeing the thing as if for the first time.

"He wasn't bad," Dan says of his father from the couch, a little smile playing across his face. He could mean the match he has just seen, or he could mean Doug's high school career in general. Dan doesn't completely mind the fact that his father's wrestling life came before his. Doug set the bar, was part of the first real group of North-Linn wrestlers to bring an identity to the school in the sport. He did good things. Dan is pretty sure he can go them one better.

At the North-Linn gymnasium the next evening, Dan is doing the work before the work. Someone has to get the place ready to host an invitational tournament on the weekend, and Dan and his team- mates are the ones. They spend an hour or so rolling out the large wrestling mats, taping their edges together and then down against the floor to prevent them from peeling up during competition. The junior varsity kids, the ones with no real standing in the pro- gram yet, draw the duty of disinfecting the mats with ammonia spray and swabbing them with towel-wrapped push brooms.

When the other wrestlers aren't sure where something should go, they ask Dan. He ought to know: This is his backyard. He is familiar with pretty much every inch of the North-Linn gym, because he has either run, wrestled on or cleaned all of it a hundred times over. On this night, he works easily, quietly. "It's a little like home," he says.

Funny, then, that in so many ways Dan—only his coach, Brad Bridgewater, gets away with calling him Danny—already has prepared to leave. From up there in the empty bleachers, with a few wrestling-team members still down on the floor scooting chairs and scorers' tables into place, it is clear that a part of Dan has moved on, that some of him has gone ahead to college already. "I think it's easier for me this way," he says. "I know I still have something to go on to. This isn't the end of the road for me. In a lot of ways, I'm just getting started."

And it is more complicated than that, of course. Dan may feel (or presume) that his wrestling career is only beginning, but there is no question that what he is attempting to accomplish at North-Linn—*for* North-Linn—is historic. He already is the first student at the school ever to receive an athletic scholarship to a Division I university. Now he is attempting to cement the area's reputation as an Iowa sports success: North-Linn, the place that produced a four-timer.

It is no mystery to Dan, not any of it. "I grew up in the wrestling room," he says. "I've basically been a wrestler my whole life. I'm not really that good at other sports. I'm pretty terrible at ball sports—I get teased about that pretty good. Wrestling comes easier, I guess."

What it comes from is family—from Doug, the first prominent LeClere wrestler, and from Dan's older brother Michael, the first of Doug's children to attempt to take the torch and run with it. No one in the family disputes that Michael eventually blew up, but before that, he logged solid years in the pipeline, coming through the kid programs and the junior-circuit tournaments and long weekends of wrestling. Now Dan has traversed much the same path, with the added benefit of seeing where Mike went wrong and what Dan needed to do to fix that, and he patched things up as he went, and here he sits, the best wrestler anyone has ever seen at North-Linn. He is the hope.

Dan sees that, sees it in the looks of the wrestling parents and fans when they wish him luck, sees that those people aren't just rooting for him but for the program. They're rooting for the town. As Mike Hageman, a longtime supporter of the program, puts it, "Dan's the face of the program. Who wouldn't be excited about that? It says the best things you could say about North-Linn."

"I know they want me to do good," Dan says. "I want to finish strong. But I can't think about it that way. It's better for me to think about this just being the start of things. I think there's better days ahead for me."

He needs all of thirty seconds to record the pin, and probably the first twelve of these are the traditional staging and dancing around, looking for an opening. The rest is fury and certainty, a story that has already been written. In other words, this is exactly how Dan expected things to go.

The kid on the other side of the mat inside the North-Linn High School gymnasium has heard of him, but by now, in mid-January, that is more or less a given. Probably 75 percent of the people Dan wrestles anymore are beaten before they step into the gym; it's an emotional surrender to the bearing of a three-time champ, nothing less. This particular opponent isn't prone to such surrender. He's a tough kid from the town of Cascade, and though he knows whom he is facing, the boy is ready to wrestle. He thinks aggressively during the short match; he does most everything right; he looks like he wants to attack. It isn't hard to imagine that he is on his way to some real success in this sport. It just won't come this evening. Or, to put it another way, he's not Dan.

Sitting in a little folding chair set out at one corner of the wrestling mat, Brad Bridgewater looks on expectantly, not anxiously. Bridgewater knows that Dan will arrive ready to wrestle, that it would take an act of God to knock him off his feet. He knows that Dan would barely come out of his position on the mat if the building were on fire. He knows that Dan is almost impervious to either pressure or pain, or at least that he appears that way during a match. Bridgewater has the right horse in this race. He's got the boy who, with no more apparent athletic ability than anybody else in the room, has worked himself to a level of performance—and expectation—that most of his contemporaries will never know.

Walking onto the mat, Dan feels the comfort of the gymnasium around him, the place where he has wrestled every one of his home matches. His folks are there, with his mom in the stands and his dad down on the gym floor as Bridgewater's assistant. His younger brothers are there. Bridgewater is the same coach he has always had. The families of his teammates are there. The LeClere farm is maybe a ten-minute drive from here in Dan's 1994 Trans-Am, the car he won't give up no matter how often people tease him about getting a new one. Dan's girlfriend, Leah, whom he has been dating since ninth grade, is there in the stands, too. He is a person who sticks with what works.

Dan has won so many times under these familiar lights and before these same faces that it would be difficult to conjure the thought of any outcome other than victory. In particular, on an evening like this, against good but inferior competition, a pin is what is supposed to happen. As often as not, it does.

Dan and his opponent would appear at a glance to be evenly matched. Both are chiseled. Both have low centers of gravity, making them harder to move around on the mat. Both weigh somewhere between 140 and 145 pounds, depending upon who ate the most recent bite of food. Both look totally capable. There is almost no such thing, after all, as a middle-weight varsity wrestler who looks like he's about to get manhandled—that is, unless you know something about the person on the other side of the mat.

As the referee blows his whistle to signal the beginning of the match, Dan and the Cascade wrestler move warily, in starts and stops, a step toward each other and then one back away, in search of a place on each others' bodies that may suddenly make itself vulnerable to attack. In the stands, the North-Linn parents and fans watch at something approaching a low hum, with almost modest interest. Their years spent in the sport have led them to a clear understanding of when to get excited over something in a match, and this is not the time. The time, traditionally, comes a few seconds after Dan makes his first move.

When he does finally initiate that strike, the first jolt of realization is that Dan is working with a set of skills entirely different from his opponent's. It's the quickness you notice first—funny, since Dan is not generally regarded as the fastest person in a room of wrestlers. Still, he uncoils like a snake. In one instant he is standing, hunched over, in a wrestler's crouch, looking for an opening like every other opponent who ever started out a match. An eyeblink later, Dan has dived to the mat, grabbed one of his opponent's ankles, sprung back to his feet and lifted his boy's leg into the air. A quick cheer goes up from the North-Linn stands, a cheer of recognition as much as anything else. This, from Dan, the North-Linn fans have seen before. The Cascade wrestler is going down. The rest is just marking time.

With the gymnasium lights dimmed and a single spotlight trained, theater-style, down upon the wrestling mat, Dan goes to work, quietly enforcing pain and selecting an angle of attack. The years of experience flow through him. He blocks every other thought from his mind, becoming in the moment an object of almost pure focus. That first move feels comfortable and familiar to him—an "outside single" in the vernacular, meaning Dan goes to the outside of his opponent to grab the ankle and is already moving halfway behind the Cascade boy before he knows what is happening. Now, in his vision of the match, Dan sees what comes next. He knows precisely what it feels like to take someone's leg and use it as a weapon against him, lifting up and then ramming down on the limb, burying his shoulder into his opponent's hip to drive the boy down to the mat. In the relative calm of the gym, Dan works almost expressionlessly. The Cascade wrestler, writhing and flailing, only thinks he is going to find a way out of this. Dan already is working through the sequence of the pin in his mind, clicking visually from one move to the next reaction, then to the following move, and then beyond. It is chess with body parts.

"Turn him now, Danny," Bridgewater says from his chair, but his voice remains even, not rising to the kind of full-throated shout he reserves for other members of his North-Linn team. A few feet away, Doug frets as he normally does, but Dan's father says nothing. Both men know that vocal instruction is only marginally necessary where Dan is concerned. Dan is on it.

When the Cascade wrestler tries to jerk his leg away from Dan's grip, he unwittingly provides the opening Dan had foreseen. The boy's attempt to pull his own limb free has caused his body to lurch a little to the right as he lies, stomach to the mat, on the wrestling surface. Dan allows that momentum to gather and then adds to it, slamming his head into the boy's left side while taking the wrestler's left arm and wrenching it behind the boy's back. It's a simple enough levering maneuver, devastatingly effective when it is done well. The combination sends the Cascade wrestler into spasms of hurt, and even as he tries to resist being turned over onto his back, he is already close to being done. His choices, essentially, are to roll over or risk something cracking or tearing in that arm.

And Dan knows it. He has used moves like this ten thousand times. They worked for him as a kindergarten-age wrestler, and they work just as well now. The basics of the sport never change, never, and in this case, it is but a matter of seconds before Dan's opponent has to yield. Wrestling is substantially about managing pain, but it is also about torque, body mechanics. There are only so many ways a human arm can move. "Now," Dan says to himself, with one more fierce wrenching of his opponent's arm. The Cascade boy is on his back in another flash and then pinned almost as quickly as he gets there. Dan uses the power in his arms and shoulders and torso, the accumulated strength of seventeen summers on the farm and in the wrestling room, to prevent the boy from rolling further. The Cascade wrestler goes from his stomach to his back and then gets locked there, as Dan covers him with his own body. The match referee immediately throws his own body down onto the mat near the wrestlers, in order to verify for himself that the Cascade boy's shoulders are being forced into contact with the foam rubber, even as he arches his back in desperation, trying to somehow wriggle himself free. Two seconds later, the ref slaps an open palm against the mat. It is a pin.

In the stands, Mike Hageman applauds and hoots, validated in his judgment of how the match would go. "Sometimes he makes it look so easy," Hageman says with a broad smile, and then he shouts out to Dan, "Nice work!" But Dan scarcely hears him. He has successfully created a distance between himself and those around him, not just in wrestling but in his life, and it is this distance that allows him to take in the moment of a victory without getting bogged down in the details. They can clap for him, but they can't get close to him. It is Dan's secret for wrestling and staying sane at the same time.

For Dan, this victory is a training session, laying a foundation for what is yet to be built. Dan is immersed in the future, in trying to gain bigger victories. It is what he works for—not the cheer, but that flash of an instant in which it suddenly becomes clear that he has planned it all perfectly, that his vision will be made real almost to the last detail. He will have won in exactly the ways he saw himself winning, and even if it is difficult to take any real joy in a thing so expected, the satisfaction is enough. It is worth the sweat and the hunger and the sleeplessness, the time spent in that little box of a training room, the brutal place where Dan's championship ideal is honed to its sharpest edge. It is, all of it, including the vision and the expectation and the victory, the path itself.

CHAPTER 4

Stick with What Works

The wrestling room at North-Linn High School measures 26 by 46 feet, or about the size of an extra-large garage, which figures, seeing as how it used to be the school shop. There is a garage door at the far end, mounted on a roller system, covered in pads, which presumably could be pried open in a heatstroke emergency to allow in a blast of cooling air. The catch, of course, is that no self-respecting wrestler would ever admit to needing relief. And this place must hold everything that the varsity and junior varsity teams require: the heavy bags, the medicine balls, the exercise bike, the heavy and light jump ropes, the wrestling mats, the stereo, the bulletin boards, the wall space where the wrestlers have taped up their lists of personal goals for the season: "Stop eating junk food." "Listen more to my coaches."

It must contain two dozen or so high school boys, who range from Ben Morrow, wrestling at 103 pounds, to Kirk Schmidt at 275 or beyond. The coaches figure that Ben, on most days, probably has to jump up and down on the scale to hit triple digits, while Kirk, still just a ninth-grader, will be fighting a constant battle to convert his girth into wrestling strength. But the two will go to the same place as Dan each day to be weighed: the tiny storage closet that also holds the ropes and jackets and pretty much everything else that needs to be out of the way most of the time. It's the only spot in the room that Bridgewater could find to stash and plug in the digital scale.

It isn't much of a wrestling room, but then North-Linn wasn't built as much of a showplace. It is a school that works, set out on a rise in the cropland along the paved road that runs between Troy Mills and Coggon, maybe fifteen miles north of the most northern reaches of greater Cedar Rapids. When they say the LeClere family lives in Coggon, what they mean is that the LeClere family farm lies within the general vicinity of Coggon (population 752) on the map, and the same is true for many of Dan's classmates. The school itself was built not in order to accommodate anybody in particular, but rather to inconvenience everybody just about equally. The kids from Coggon and Troy Mills and Walker, the rural communities that comprise the district, each make more or less the same daily journey in terms of miles covered to get to class. A few years ago, a middle school was grafted onto the high school. It didn't take that much space.

The walls of the wrestling room are painted in the school's colors, white and red and silver. The mats are mostly red, which covers the stains and blood and such. They look like they've already given their money's worth to the program. On the first day of practice in the third full week of January, the tournament almost exactly a month away now, Dan walks into the room and glances around, sees the mats with their silver trim and the drawing of the Lynx lion mascot. He spies the beat-up stereo that is set on a shelf whose gray metal L-brackets have been hammered into the cinder-block wall. Dan reaches for the light switch. The lights click on with a sharp glare and an audible hum.

"This place sucks," Dan says, an affectionate smile thinly crossing his lips. It is, in fact, a world of wonders. And today, like most days, he's the first one in.

For most of his waking life, Dan has been padding down the cool tile hallways of North-Linn, down the steps past the lockers and the vending machines, through the scarred metal door on the left just before the southeast exit from the building, and into this unique torture chamber. He tumbled around in here as a kid. He wrestled in the youth programs—the Little Lynx, the kids were called, a takeoff on the high school's nickname—at a time when his dad was the North-Linn head coach.

Dan watched Michael work out in this room, and burn out, and give up wrestling altogether after his sophomore year, and break his father's heart. Dan stood here, as well, to see his own name painted onto the far wall that runs the length of the room, the same wall upon which his father's name was painted a quarter-century before, for having reached the State Tournament as a wrestler. All the State qualifiers' names wind up on that wall eventually. They'll have to figure out some way to take the thing with them when they move.

This is a cold little room when empty, and it gets hot too fast when it's filled with wrestlers, and Bridgewater already is in the midst of a fund-raising drive to build an entirely new work-out space that is going to cost something like $150,000, which, strictly speaking, is the kind of money nobody has. "We're getting there," Brad says. Considering the memories that have been built in here, it is probably just as well with the traditionalists of North-Linn if that all happens later rather than sooner.

By the winter of 2006, the workout room, wherever it is, will contain three LeCleres: Dan's two younger brothers and his father. Dan himself will be the latest memory, gone on to his next phase, a college wrestler. In fact, even as he pursues the greatest prize of his sporting life, it is apparent that a part of Dan already has left. It isn't the part that wrestles; it is the part that finds the future. And it won't be long before the future arrives.

Doug sees that moment of separation coming; in his mind's

eye, perhaps, it is already here. Doug knows the drill. He is a farmer and a wrestler and a coach of young men, and seasons change. Doug has experienced loss here and there, beginning with his first son Michael's baffling decision to quit the sport. Doug already has had the recurring dream in which he walks into the wrestling room, looks around and asks, "Where's Kyle?"— searching for Kyle Burkle, one of his favorite former wrestlers. In the dream, it is either Bridgewater or assistant coach Larry Henderson who finally comes over and says quietly, "Coach, he's gone," and only then does Doug begin to realize that Kyle has actually moved on a year ago. It is time for Doug to start measuring his loss.

And perhaps it will be that way with his own son. A year from now, Dan—and his success or failure in this final push—will be one more brushstroke of paint on the wall. In some of the important ways, Doug already has braced himself for that reality. Whether Dan sees it or not, Doug is slowly but inexorably shifting his emotion and his passion over to Nick, a tenth-grader and the next LeClere in the wrestling bloodline. Doug pays his attentions to Nick now, reserves his fury for Nick's mistakes and his occasional sloth. He fiercely hangs on to Nick's triumphs and openly worries through Nick's injuries and setbacks. Chris, an eighth-grader, is waiting in the wings. Michael is long gone. Dan is next. But for now, the North-Linn wrestling room is his. When Dan enters it, he is in his world.

It's a small one. Bridgewater studies my expression upon looking around the North-Linn wrestling room, smiles and says, "You're used to a bigger space if you've been spending time at Linn-Mar." He's right. Compared with this, the Linn-Mar High School wrestling area, the place where Jay does his thing, is a wing at the MGM Grand. And it represents the difference, or at least one of the differences, between Class 1A and Class 3A in wrestling in Iowa.

School classifications are based primarily upon school enrollment, but the bucks don't stop there. They carry on through the ability of programs to fund-raise and lay out capital expenditures that help make coaches' and athletic directors' dreams come true. Linn-Mar is a solid 3A classified school, the largest class in Iowa for wrestling. There is money flowing into the school system, but also flowing around it. You can feel the surge; things are happening. Malls have been constructed up and down Collins Road, the delineation of North Cedar Rapids and Marion. Swing past Barnes and Noble and Taco Bell and the new sixteen-screen, stadium-seating multiplex, and you know you are traveling along a path where developers figure significant future growth to occur.

That growth doesn't ensure a waterfall of money into coach Doug Streicher's program at Linn-Mar, but it at least affords the opportunity. Out in Troy Mills and Coggon, though, the school enrollment is not growing, because the district as a whole is not growing. Farmers often consider themselves fortunate if any one of their children, once grown, is willing to return to the land to take the place of a family member who is moving away or retiring. Basically—if it all works out—they are looking at something close to a zero growth cycle in the area itself. The LeCleres have lived on various parcels of family land for a century, but already the modern heirs are beginning to fan out. By the fall of 2005, Dan will be in college, and Michael will be contemplating a move to California, gearing up for graduate school while taking a job to establish residency and lower his tuition bills.

Bridgewater, who wants a new wrestling facility for his very tough, very good program, is going to have to fight like hell to get it. He already has raised something like $50,000, and the school board is trying mightily to come up with matching funds, and the other $50,000 will have to be gotten somehow. Things like locally hosted wrestling tournaments are drops in the bucket—a few hundred dollars of profit, maybe more if the snack bar has a good day—but it is by dribs and drabs that the project is coming together.

Until then, this will have to do, a place so small that more than half the wrestlers can be found standing against the walls, waiting for their turns on the small mat area. But what the facility lacks in amenities, it makes up for in volume and effort. The stereo cranks, the workouts ratchet up quickly, and Bridgewater, a slender, bespectacled, unassuming person away from the mat, becomes a commander upon it.

Bridgewater wrestled at a small-town high school and then went on to Division III Simpson College in Iowa, one of a number of highly regarded programs in the state. He has essentially been teaching and coaching wrestling ever since. He spent a few years as an assistant on the North-Linn high school team, then took over the middle-school program during a time of rough transition, and finally was pulled up—some seven or eight years ago, now—to run the show. In person, on the phone, meeting parents, counseling kids from his computer science classes, Bridgewater is polite, funny, calm and friendly. But on the mat he is transformed. Like so many former wrestlers, he is in his element here, not so much reliving a past as continually forming a present and future that still has wrestling at the center of it. In Iowa, such is still possible. The state's continued fascination with the sport acts as a blinder that prevents the people here from seeing the truth, which is that wrestling is in trouble in so many other places around the country where it once thrived.

Bridgewater's voice carries in a hoarse growl, and because it is a Monday in mid-January, barely six weeks away from the State Tournament, this won't be a workout for the meek. As Bridgewater puts his charges through their paces, it becomes evident that what you are seeing is the kind of effort and dedication that other sports don't often—or, depending upon your view, ever—demand. Again and again, the wrestlers throw themselves at each other in a series of one-on-one drills that soon leave everyone hacking and gasping for air. As the kids fatigue and lose their edge in the foggy sweat of the room, Bridgewater begins increasing his rhetoric. As a coach, Brad saves himself for the moments when he's needed, and right now the wrestlers are getting close to the point of wanting to ease up.

"This is it! It's time to get after it!" Bridgewater shouts across the room, his words slamming into the matted walls on the far side and being absorbed into their thick material. "Third period, both wrestlers tired! Who's got more? Who wants it more?"

His kids hunch there, doubled over. They struggle to regain a normal breathing pattern. But they haven't stopped listening.

"You have to start wanting it right here, guys," Bridgewater says, a little more quietly now. "You can't wait for conference or sectionals to decide to turn it up. It's gonna be too late then. You have to do it here, now. Now turn it up right here!"

Like all the other high school wrestlers in Iowa, Dan and his North-Linn teammates are on the clock. Only a couple of weeks of the regular season remain, weeks to prepare for the great push that follows. The first weekend in February, the Class 1A teams vie for their conference titles. A week after that, the sectional championships will qualify wrestlers to districts; the district tournaments, held on February 19 all over the state, move that precious thimbleful of winners on to the State Tournament. By the following Wednesday, the last Wednesday in February, seemingly half of Iowa will have descended upon Veterans Memorial Auditorium in Des Moines for State.

It is, in other words, coming fast and going fast; and as if on cue from Bridgewater's speech, the wrestlers suck it up for another try. Over in the far corner, Kirk, the young heavyweight who is doing almost all his learning on the job, picks up his bulky mass one more time. In the middle of the floor stands the rangy 152-pound junior, Tyler Burkle, the brother of former North-Linn state qualifier Kyle and himself a veteran of the tournament, having made it last year. Tyler dances back and forth on the balls of his feet, shifting his weight from one wrestling shoe to the other as he gets ready for another roll. The kid is all edginess and force, ready to spring upon whoever it happens to be who is sent out there to face him.

And opposite Burkle, just now, is an old man wearing a bandage around his head that makes him look like a drum-and-fife member of a Revolutionary war corps. As usual with things involving Doug LeClere, there is a story to be told.

Just 44 in human years but with a lifetime's worth of farm work behind him and enough other jobs—firefighter for the city of Cedar Rapids, inspector for the American Soil Conservation Service, assistant wrestling coach—to have made him mature before his time, Doug walks with a slight limp. The parts of him that aren't yet broken look like they're starting to wear thin around the edges. Or, as Doug later says in a typically blunt self-assessment, "My body's shot to hell."

None of which keeps him out of the wrestling room. Doug fell in love with the sport early on and never fell out of it, savoring the sacrifice, finding in its demands and its seasonal domination of his time an almost perfect philosophical complement to the farming life. In the end, Doug is a wrestler. He just ran out of teams to wrestle for.

And so now, after decades of wrestling competitively and then head-coaching the North-Linn High team himself for a while, LeClere is back to assisting Bridgewater, which keeps the job at something approaching part-time status, which is mostly a joke, since the in-season demands on wrestling coaches are the same as the coaches of other sports at the high school level. There are workouts almost every day of the week, dual matches on Thursday evenings, duals and tournaments on Saturdays and some Sundays. Being an assistant only allows Doug to occasionally miss practice because, for example, he's on one of his 24-hour shifts at the fire station. But missing the practices kills him a little bit at a time. This is his passion, the thing he wants to do the most. His wife, Mary, says that Doug was crushed when Michael abruptly stopped wrestling in high school and never picked up the sport again. Doug simply couldn't understand why anyone who knew as much about wrestling as Michael wasn't interested in continuing the education, because Doug is still as vitally interested in that education as he ever was. He never gets tired of it, never wearies of talking about it. As Mary figures it, this may occasionally be the problem.

In the meantime, that is Doug out there going against Burkle, bandaged up but refusing to (a) come off the mat or (b) go anything less than all out. Burkle has inadvertently opened a cut on Doug's right ear—could've been a head-butt, could've been a hand swipe or a knee—and Doug is bleeding profusely. A few random attempts to stanch the flow have failed, and so Doug finally grabs a wad of toilet tissue, jams it against the ear and resumes a ferocious scrap with Burkle, a kid for whom the coaches have high hopes in the State Tournament despite the fact that Burkle's Class 1A weight, 152, is the one at which Ryan Morningstar wrestles.

Doug and Burkle go at each other repeatedly, and you see at once where the LeClere boys get their wrestling prowess. Doug is all power and leverage. He's still quick on his feet, good with a low shoot-in to grab one of Burkle's ankles, and he is virtually impossible to move around on the mat with his low center of gravity and almost perfectly balanced wrestling stance, two traits that Dan clearly carries.

The wrestling goes on. And on. For what feels like an hour without a significant break, the wrestlers continue in two- and three- and five- and seven-minute periods. There will be pounds and blood lost today that may never be found. And Bridgewater isn't close to being done. Before this practice is finished, he will send his wrestlers on a series of suicide sprints back and forth across the width of the room—twelve sprints and a break, then ten, then eight, then six, then four, and then two. It's the old-school approach to fatigue, like a lifter going to a lighter weight with each repetition until the point where he is working with almost no pounds, yet is so exhausted that his arms and shoulders can barely function anyway.

After the sprints comes the jump rope, and after that—the end of perhaps two and a half hours of nonstop practice—it is hoped that some or all of the wrestlers will stick around for extra work. Both Doug and Larry Henderson go through the entire workout, even running the sprints with the kids, and they refuse to leave until every wrestler who wants something extra—a partner for stomach-crunching sit-ups, someone to work with on constructing or practicing moves on the mat—has been served.

Doug can't help it and long ago gave up trying to. He is not a halfway person. That, ironically, explains why he had to quit being the head coach at North-Linn those several years ago: He was so completely involved with the program that, among it and his other jobs, he was driving his own homelife into ruin. "It about split me and Mary up," Doug says, "and so that was that." Doug once had a friend tell him that the friend's wife had demanded a choice: It was wrestling or her. The divorce, Doug says, came quickly, and the man later told Doug the story with something approaching pride. "I told him, 'I'd never do something as stupid as that.' If I kept the coaching and it broke us up—there was no way I was going to do that."

Still, it is hard for LeClere. He knows how he wants to teach wrestling, and to coach it. His sons are really the products of Doug's coaching more than anyone else, in the same way that Morningstar is the product of his four-time state champion father Scott. Doug says that at the State Tournament, "I won't coach Dan much in the early rounds. I let everybody else have their time with him. Then, when it gets to the finals, that's when I'll get in there." Of course, by that point the father will be infinitely more nervous than the son. But that doesn't mean he won't be coaching.

On this day, the post-practice news is not good. Nick, still just 15 years old, has been battling a hyperextended elbow, and it has gotten to where it throbs and hurts even when he tries to jog lightly. An MRI has been scheduled to see if there's any further damage. For Doug, though, the news represents nothing so much as time lost in trying to prepare for the huge upcoming month of wrestling: the conference tournament, sectionals, district, and state tourney on consecutive weekends.

"If Nick don't get some practice time, he's not going to be able to do anything," Doug says, sitting at a table in the school library, sipping a Gatorade after his pounding workout with the kids. Seated next to him, Mary looks over in quiet amazement. She can't believe he's even talking about Nick wrestling, considering the news on the elbow. Mary is no softie; she is a girl from the farm country who understands that a certain amount of pain or discomfort is to be expected of life in general and wrestling in particular. She isn't the kind to turn her head when a wrestler is getting beat up on the mat. But when she looks at Nick, she sees a boy who's a little bit scared of hurting himself even further, a kid who already has dealt with a hip-flexor injury earlier in the wrestling season after coming straight to the team from his job as a running back on the football squad.

When Mary looks at her sons, she sees not merely fine athletes, but boys who have been brought into the other family business—the one on the mat. They may not grow up to take over the farm, but, in the meantime, Doug figures they most certainly can be molded into champion wrestlers. The question in Mary's mind is whether they want to be so—whether, for example, it is really Doug's dream that Dan is fulfilling when he goes out there and takes opponents apart with such utter dispassion. Doug qualified for the State Tournament himself as a wrestler at North-Linn in 1978. He didn't place, but he did stick around long enough to watch other wrestlers be crowned champions. The day he saw the looks on the faces of those champions and saw the great love and affection that rained down on them from the farthest reaches of the Barn, he told himself that someday he would make it possible for his own children to have that experience. It has been driving him, for better and for worse, ever since.

*Bridgewater blows his whistle or sounds a horn at predetermined inter-*vals, the better to shuffle some kids over to the side and get others out there on the mat, but nobody is really resting. At most, they're recovering their breath from the intense series of one-on-one simulated matches they're undergoing—drilling, so-called in a wrestling practice—in time to go again. And they will go with full intensity, even though they are matched against their own teammates. It is a sport with no collegiality attached to it until after the work is done; two kids on the mat are two kids trying to inflict pain and suffering on one another, and the fact of their wearing the same-color singlet is irrelevant in that moment. They will go until they drop, and then they will get up and go again until they perhaps need a break to go vomit or spit, and then they will get up and go again, because to do anything less would be to admit that, when it comes right down to it, you just don't want it badly enough to work for it.

So Bridgewater keeps it going, round after round, interval after interval. Sweat flows in rivulets down the wrestlers' faces and falls to the mat every time they look down. But Dan's expression never changes. He looks intently in at whomever he happens to be paired with at the moment, body calm, breathing controlled, waiting for Bridgewater's whistle to blow. Waiting for another chance.

Nearby, Doug bleeds. He is a few weeks away from that 45th

birthday, which almost certainly means he should be coaching the sport instead of doing it. But Doug wants to be out there on the mat—and, besides, it's the most effective teaching method he can figure. It just makes more sense, sometimes, to be able to show a wrestler what you want instead of telling him, the same way an offensive line coach in football demonstrates a blocking technique or a hitting coach in baseball gets in the batting stance himself. The difference here: At some point Doug stops coaching and becomes a full-bore wrestler again, another guy on the mat trying to win. That much is just ingrained. It is impossible for him to pretend otherwise.

And so Doug stands there, "bleeding like a stuck pig," by his estimation, but it is still the middle of practice, and he is not done. "Wrap it up," he says, and he jams some fresh cotton and gauze near the earlobe where the blood is. One of the kids brings another roll of gauze, which he helps the coach wrap round and round the circumference of his head to keep the bandage in place. And then Doug, the old man with the kids who wrestle—like all the other old men with kids who wrestle in Iowa—gets back out there and starts thundering away at Tyler Burkle once again, because time is short. Tyler is good, and he needs the competition. The state tourney is coming, the big show at the Barn, and there's no time for pussying around. Anyway, Doug's head will be all right. You give anything enough time, it'll clot.

CHAPTER 5

A Specific Desperation

One does not go to the wrestling room at Linn-Mar; one descends upon it, down the stairs from the main floor of the school to the locker-room area and Doug Streicher's office, which evidently doubles as the school's electrical room. It says so on the sign bolted into the wall just outside his door, at which one can stand and take in the wall-to-wall overlap of blood-red-colored wrestling mats out there on the floor, the concrete beams along the ceiling that bear the names and signatures of wrestlers past, and the sign painted along the far wall that reads, PAIN IS TEMPORARY. PRIDE IS FOREVER.

Streicher is the real deal from a real program, in possession not only of a known wrestling team but a corner view of history. Streicher won it all twice in high school (his brother, Kent, won three titles) before going on to wrestle for Dan Gable. His is a lifetime in the sport, and he knows the goods. Jay Borschel, the most significant thing ever to happen to wrestling at Linn-Mar, is the goods. "We know," Streicher says, "how important this can be—not only for Jay, but for our program."

The coach's office is a comical mish-mash of items crammed

into the room. A brushed metal air duct, perhaps four feet wide, runs the length of the ceiling. Along one cement wall are set the circuit breakers that appear to control a significant portion of the school's lighting systems. A few feet from Streicher's desk stands a transformer, bolted into the ground, on top of which has been hand-scrawled a sign warning interlopers not to set anything on top of it, least of all themselves. The room itself is jammed with every imaginable thing, up to and including the crimson-colored sofa that Streicher somehow managed to get through the door. A television sits on a cheap metal shelf, with a VCR and an old-school Nintendo 64 game system attached. An unfinished cabinet holds rows of videos, the ghosts of Linn-Mar teams and matches past. On one shelf sit bottles of bleach mixed with water and sprayed out on the mats to be wiped down before each practice. (True to the wrestling ethic, it's the junior varsity team members who draw most of the disinfectant duty each day.) Fallen off to one side of the couch, lying angled on the floor, is a worn copy of Gabriel García Márquez's *One Hundred Years of Solitude*.

Sitting on top of one shelf is another homemade product, this one a crude trophy atop a wooden base that reads, LINN-MAR WRESTLING. EATING CHAMPION #1. Glued into the wooden base are a fork and an empty 20-ounce bottle of Mountain Dew. It is a gag gift with a ring of truth: the diet of champions.

On the eve of a junior-varsity tournament, Streicher has specific instructions for his younger wrestlers. "Don't come in here weighing spot-on," he tells them. "You want to be at least point-three, point-four underweight, because you don't want to take chances with the scales." The difference of an ounce or two can be enough to disqualify a wrestler in his weight class, forcing the coach to choose between sitting him down altogether or moving him up to the next-highest class. Most coaches deactivate the wrestler for the night. It is a simple lesson: You miss your weight, you hurt the team. You hurt the team, you sit.

And how easy is it to miss weight? As easy as a few extra bites from the plate.

There is, of course, no such thing as a satiated wrestler. To live with hunger, to go to bed with a gnawing feeling in the stomach, is to live the life. It is the season of an athlete who spends most of his waking hours, and some of those when he's supposed to be asleep, contemplating calories expended and calories consumed, and the long-term cost of eating that French fry, and what is the smallest amount of liquid he can take in and still partially replenish a dehydrated body, and so on. It demands of high school students a kind of self-imposed discipline that is both excessive and wildly unreasonable, yet routinely met. It requires the wrestlers to deny their bodies the basis of a more natural physical growth pattern. They're actually stunting themselves, and they do it on purpose and in the sort of vague half-knowledge and general industry reassurance that, sooner or later, they'll be able to get it all back. Maybe they will, maybe they won't. This much is clear: In his senior year, Jay Borschel is sure trying.

This is the winter, after all those other winters of self-denial, that Jay gets to eat. He can pile on food and still qualify each week to wrestle, because of his ferocious workouts, extra time in the gym, routine long runs. He has had the happy experience of waking up lighter than he was when he went to sleep, the result of his having done some weight work late in the evening—calories burned without new calories being consumed. He has got it down to a science.

He considers himself unremarkable in this regard. In fact, though, Jay's weight progression is unprecedented in the history of wrestling in Iowa. He won his first title as a freshman at 103 pounds and is now attempting to win his fourth at 171, and no one has ever done that, gone up that many weight classes and still won. None of the previous four-timers gained anywhere near that much weight over the course of their high school careers.

(Dan LeClere's special distinction is that he is trying to become only the second wrestler ever to win four titles without winning his first championship at 103 pounds, the lightest weight class available at the high school level and usually the easiest to win because it's so often filled with freshmen and a few sophomores.)

Later this winter, Jay will find himself embarrassingly asked to pose for a photograph while holding 68 pounds of beef by a hook at a local meat locker, one newspaper's attempt to show its readers exactly how much weight he has gained over the years without sacrificing a title. Staging aside, it's an impressive truth. When Jay moved from 103 to 125 in a single year as a sophomore, the widely held assumption was that he would struggle to keep up with the bigger boys. Instead, he beat a brilliant wrestler, his friend Kyle Anson, in the semifinals on his way to winning it all. (Two years later, Kyle is still wrestling at 125 pounds.) When Jay moved from 125 to 152 as a junior, there was again talk that by skipping everything in between—130 pounds, 135, 140, 145 pounds—he was setting himself up for failure by pitting himself against much, much bigger and stronger kids. And it wasn't simple jealousy. There is history in such a claim.

The weights in wrestling are an elaborate shell game with human consequences. Todd Conway, a Marion physician, former wrestler, father to current wrestlers and author of a book about sensible weight control in the sport, notes that almost every piece of available evidence suggests an unfortunate but undeniable truth: The wrestlers who cut their way down from significantly higher natural weights do indeed perform better, albeit hungrier and generally with more personal torment, than their counterparts in the weight classes for which they might qualify more naturally. "It'd be great for the sport if that weren't the case," says Conway, "but that's what the evidence shows."

In other words, it's better to weigh 167 pounds but wrestle at 152—assuming one can get from 167 to 152 every single week, a constant roller-coastering of weight that in itself is problem-atic—than it is to weigh 156 and lose only a couple of pounds to get down to that same 152 class. The time-proven weight-cutting practices, some of them reasonable and some of them insane, al-low the larger athlete with the naturally bigger frame to retain his musculature while essentially shedding water and otherwise starving himself down to the lower weight. There, if he's any good technically, he dominates. It is a crappy truth, but the truth is the truth. Even Conway, who hates the practice and the horrible (and occasionally dangerous) habits it encourages, accepts the ba-sic premise of the evidence.

And so, with Jay, the feeling each year was that he was sud-denly taking himself into the Land of the Giants, that this was the year in which he would finally have risked too much by follow-ing his body's natural progression up to the higher weights. Not necessarily his fault, the detractors would say—but it's hard, in wrestling, to grow a lot and still win a lot.

"I heard that every year," Jay says. "I couldn't make the jump to 125, and then everybody was gonna tear me up at 152. Same this year."

"Does that bother you?" I ask.

Jay shrugs. "People like to talk."

Wrestling, as Doug Streicher often says, is a motivate-yourself-any-way-you-can kind of a sport. They don't stay up nights inventing cool new cheers for the wrestling team. It isn't a lonely existence so much as a select one, and the wrestling coaches and parents and fans use that fact as a sort of proof of vir-tue: wrestlers are better than other athletes because their drive is so pure, because their pursuit is so solitary. So few people outside their closed circle of fellow wrestlers could ever even begin to understand the sacrifices they make in order to simply get on the mat, much less compete and win.

It is on Mondays that wrestlers who've allowed themselves a

little of the good life over the weekend begin getting back down to their target weight—and by "good life" I mean an actual Saturday night, post-tournament dinner that isn't missing any of the fun parts, and by "getting back down" I mean the energy-sapping, soul-diminishing art of cutting weight. It is the tradition-bound practice, the most delicate balancing act that any of these athletes may ever attempt, walking the line between light enough and strong enough. It does not separate the men from the boys; it reveals who has the slightest business even being out there in the first place.

Dan LeClere's mother, Mary, long ago accepted the fact that during wrestling season, she has to cook differently than she might like to. Her menu consists of a fair amount of lean meat, lots of green vegetables and not many potatoes, which "don't get a big reception at our table," Mary says with a smile. It is the way of the world for any wrestler cutting weight, and Dan made his peace with it some time ago. For Dan, hunger equals anger, and anger, the kind of anger he might never express any other way, is almost perfectly suited to his role on the mat. "You get used to being hungry," he says. "I can live with that." In fact, what Dan does is control it, harness the hunger. He thinks about dominating his opponent on a Saturday afternoon, and he thinks about the nice meal—controlled portions but good food—that he will allow himself on Saturday night. After all, Monday, at that point, feels like a month away.

The greatest shooter on a basketball team has four courtmates, and those players need to produce something of at least distraction value while they're out there. Otherwise, it's just Allen Iverson scoring 43 points for Philly in a loss. But wrestling, like swimming or tennis or cross-country, is one of those disciplines in which the way to help one's team is—almost exclusively—to win for oneself at the same time. When Jay Borschel pins somebody, as he has done almost a hundred times in his high school career, his team gets 6 points. If an opponent forfeits to him, it's 6 points. A technical fall (a win by more than 15 points) is worth 5; a major decision (by 8 points) is worth 4, and a decision 3. It is not tangential; most of the time, in duals and tournaments in which every point is counted, it matters. But there is nobody on his team who can help Jay get that pin or that major, unless screaming hard from a nearby metal chair counts. (Most wrestlers say they hear almost nothing but the white noise ringing in their ears during a match anyway). The sport just doesn't function that way. No one can make a move for Jay; he has to make it himself. No one can roll Jay off his back; he has to escape himself.

He is, at the end of the day, responsible for his own self, the wrestler. And, as Jay has learned the hard way, he cannot help his teammates, either.

He cannot help them become people who want to get better if they aren't. He can't help them work harder if they won't. He can lead, and he can exhort, and he can do all of the things that he does from time to time in the Linn-Mar wrestling room to try to create an atmosphere of fiery effort and great results. But if, in the end, most of his teammates just don't give enough of a damn to get better, well, that's where the line gets drawn. And so, this year, it has been.

Jay's wrestling teammates also used to be his closest friends and most admired classmates, but, looking back, he sees that he was living a dream. The Linn-Mar teams of his first couple of high school seasons were almost a mirage, they were so good; Streicher, just a few years into his tenure, had imposed such a change on the program by the time Jay arrived that the Lions were producing state qualifiers and tournament and dual winners at an impressive rate. In Jay's freshman year, he not only won the state title at 103 pounds but was part of a winning team. Linn-Mar sent a raft of wrestlers to Des Moines, finished third overall in Class 3A, then went on to wrestle the State Duals. Streicher, himself a former state prep champion and an NCAA All-American for Iowa, was named Coach of the Year. It felt like the best time in the world to be a wrestler at Linn-Mar.

And it was illusory, or at least temporary. Those early teams were loaded up with juniors and seniors who had come of age and quality together, part of the first real wave of talent that was shaped and molded by Streicher. Back then, Jay, despite his obvious command of the sport, was almost along for the ride. He surfed the waves of enthusiasm of his older colleagues in the practice room, drafted off their effort until he developed his own sustainable ethic. It was easy to want to go for it, because so many other guys—older guys, wrestlers worth respecting—were going for it at the same time. What they lacked in Jay's natural affinity for the sport they compensated for by their willingness to brutalize themselves for the sake of improvement. They had fun by working hard. Their idea of a great weekend was to send more than half the team to State. It was cool to be wrestling for the Linn-Mar Lions.

Then it ended. Trickled down, really. From that gusher of performance in Jay's freshman year, the numbers began, very gradually, to dwindle in the wrestling room. Many of the football players began to view wrestling as too much commitment for their "off-season," as though they were National Football League elites who needed their rest after a rigorous year in the trenches. The football coach didn't particularly sound the call to the wrestling room once his season ended. "At other schools, kids from football will almost be directed into wrestling, and vice versa—they feed us, and we feed them," Streicher says. "For some reason, that doesn't really happen here."

Linn-Mar's heavier-weight classes began to suffer, as kids who might normally have gravitated toward wrestling after the football season instead skipped the sport's Spartan demands, choosing to hit the weight room and the Creatine and basically make their own schedules for a few months. It wasn't a shocking development, exactly—even in Iowa, football has a way of making itself king—and it was hardly unprecedented in the annals of prep sports. But it had its effect. Wrestling, even at Linn-Mar, was bound to struggle now and again.

"My first couple of teams were so good," Jay says. "I thought that's what it would be like." Now the issue isn't merely the number of athletes who won't come out for the team, but also some of the athletes who do—the ones who have enough interest and ability to make varsity but who, for whatever reason, just won't sell out to the sport.

"They're just not into it," Jay says curtly, and what he means is that they're not into it the way he is into it. It is evident in their three-quarter-intensity workouts, and in the early-morning sessions many of them never attend, and in the afternoon practices they occasionally skip or beg out of with vague injuries, and in the way they sometimes simply accept getting beat in a dual. When Jay was coming up, a little freshman watching the veterans take control of the place, he saw that huge numbers of the junior varsity squad would show up for Streicher's six a.m. varsity workouts, on the theory that they wanted to learn the techniques the coach was teaching the starters. Now, here in the final winter of Jay's high school career, the jayvees are all but invisible early in the morning. Jay sees them in the hallways later on at school and finds himself almost involuntarily blurting out, "I was here two hours ago. Where were you?"

"It's like they don't get it—they *need* to be there," Jay says. But the reality is that they don't need it, at least not the way Jay needs it. That's life.

Even those with whom he remains close on the team, like heavyweight Shawnden Crawford, with whom Jay has been traveling to wrestling tournaments seemingly forever, don't feel it the way he feels it. But Jay reserves judgment on Shawnden; he likes him too much personally, and feels about his situation too closely, to be fully critical. Shawnden came into the Borschels' life because his mother moved him out of a bigger town, worried about his surroundings. Shawnden is black and came from a family with little money, and the town of Marion is mostly white and pretty solidly middle class. But Shawnden shared with Jay a common interest in wrestling, and Jim began bringing him along on Jay's early forays to local and regional tournaments, sometimes paying Shawnden's entry fee so he could compete. Shawnden has kept a hand in wrestling all the way through. Jim would like to believe that the involvement helped keep Shawnden—and Jay, and most of the other wrestlers, for that matter—out of trouble as he grew up, and in that he shares a sentiment with many other parents, the ones who seek out sports for their children as a way of keeping them busy. But the young ones grow up, and, as Jay and Shawnden will later suggest, they cannot be protected forever.

Now Shawnden has grown to a heavyweight's class, 275 pounds and beyond, but wrestling for him has always remained something more fun or enjoyable than really critical—not a passion so much as a welcome release. He likes to win but refuses to be devastated by a defeat. He has qualified for State twice with the talent and strength he already possesses, and thus appears in no great hurry to find another level of performance. A current knee injury, here in January, will keep him out for weeks, and the one thing evident is that, though he wants to wrestle again and attempt to reach Des Moines one final time, there is no severe urgency attached to the effort. He gets there if he gets there.

As much as Jay likes Shawnden, he just can't grasp that thinking. Even in the case of his friend, the mention of his comparatively easygoing approach to wrestling elicits a shaking of the head. "It's just not right," Jay says, setting his jaw. He can't handle the mentality. He cannot abide the idea that people like Mitch

Benfer and Bryan Telgenhoff could be better, but just aren't—that they could win the matches they're losing, place in the tournaments in which they're failing to advance. These are his friends, people whose company he is generally glad for—and yet, when it comes time to flip the switch and really get after the work of becoming great wrestlers, Jay finds himself alone.

The thing they don't tell you is that it's lonely being great, that it can be a separating existence. It can be ludicrously difficult to come to grips with the mere fact of one's difference—in this case, the fact that Jay wants to excel so much more desperately than so many of the people around him, even though they're ostensibly wrapped up in the same general pursuit. And it takes a very specific desperation to get there. In some ways, that inner drive has become Jay's companion to the exclusion of his other relationships. It is Jay who reaches for that next level—and sometimes Jay alone. He has his friends. He has his teammates, and certainly his coaches. He has his family. But, in the end, most of them will wind up doing the watching, not the acting. And that's the difference.

It may explain why, as the season wears on, Jay becomes gradually closer with Matt McDonough, a freshman wrestling at 103 pounds. Matt may be a braces-wearing mite, a classic ninth-grader in his first year wandering the halls of the high school, but he is also a true athlete getting almost everything possible out of his developing body. He pushes hard. He transcends pain. He shows up for more. He has the ferocity on the mat to realize his potential, and Jay taps into that, because that is what Jay needs—what they both need, really, if either one of them is going to do something great.

This is, of course, the other way in which Jay stands in possession of the elite athlete's conceit. To Jay, Matt McDonough is only doing exactly what he is supposed to be doing: working his ass off to get better, and thus to avoid wasting the wrestling talent he has brought with him to this point. Matt, the son of the former University of Iowa wrestler Mike McDonough, wants to capitalize on his experience, not squander it, and Jay recognizes that drive in his young teammate. He loves Matt's approach, because it is the same as his. He remains baffled every time one of his teammates fails to see the equation in precisely those terms. Even if he understands on an intellectual level that people just aren't hard-wired the same way as he is, emotionally, physically—as a wrestler, that is—he can't make peace with it. Absent peace, he creates a distance between himself and the teammates around him who just don't get it.

As the winter continues, Jay will become more distant in the wrestling room, communicating with and engaging the coaches more often than his teammates, slowly submerging himself in the underworld of his own goals and the things he needs to do to achieve them. He remains friendly and by all appearances open, but his frustration comes to the surface more often—he's more prone than ever to barking out at teammates for lagging behind on sprint drills and the like—and he tends to clear out of the room faster and faster at its conclusion. He wrestles against coaches like Jason Haag and CJ McDonald partly out of a practical need and partly because he is already ascending to that higher level of athletic performance, a world of far more complicated thought patterns and much, much harder pushes against the body's willingness to be extended beyond its supposed limitations. Jay needs to be wrestling against people who know how to anticipate his moves; he needs to work on new attacks and new countermeasures. And he needs to wrestle against the kind of athletes, like Jason and CJ and Curt Hynek, who went on to the college level and wrestled there. This is the season for reaching higher, and there may not be a high school teammate at Linn-Mar who can really process what that entails. The coaches know what it takes to win, and how it feels to lose. It is amazing to Jay, and so frustrating, that some of the kids wrestling for Streicher cannot make the same connection.

CHAPTER 6

Saturday in Wyoming

He sets to pacing maybe twenty minutes before it is time to rock, because that's how Dan has always done it. If you looked in from the entrance to the claustrophobic gymnasium in Wyoming, you'd probably assume at first glance that he were a young man in a hurry to get somewhere. He paces fast and turns on a dime to come back pacing fast the other way; and at some point over the years, the people around him simply have come to believe that this is his way of getting his legs warm for a match, getting the blood going, something like that. Even Doug, who has coached his son from the cradle, never really asks.

But it's not the legs; it's the vision. Tramping around trying to find some space along the wrestler-cauterized walkways in between the mats, Dan only looks like a guy trying to get warm. In his mind's eye, the match is already over.

What happens is that Highway 151, which isn't dominating to begin with, eventually crosses little Highway 64, which passes the mid-size equipment sale and the farmers' market and goes on into town, to the Wyoming Drug and Variety Store on one side of the street and Ted's Swinging Door Bar and Grill on the other. But it's the absence of sound in the town of Wyoming that you notice, an almost eerie kind of noiselessness, really. The snow has laid down a thick sonic blanket over everything it touches, but that's not it entirely. There are no cars whizzing by, save for a time like this, when twelve schools' worth of wrestlers and cheerleaders and parents and coaches converge on the pint-size gym. Normally speaking, there is no traffic. There also is no anticipated traffic. There is, further, no traffic being contemplated. If there's a growth plan in Wyoming, population not quite 1,200, they're not letting on.

That fits. From 1990 to 2000, Iowa's population grew by slightly more than 5 percent—a virtual holding pattern when compared with the overall U.S. growth rate of roughly 13 percent during that time. As it stands, the state comprises fewer than 3 million people. Almost all of them, nearly 94 percent, are white. According to the 2000 U.S. Census, barely 2 percent of Iowans identify themselves as either black or African-American—one-sixth the national average. When Iowans speak of diversifying, they could just as easily mean rotating soybeans for corn as anything else.

The land is open. Entertainment is scarce. Cultural sophistication is the exception rather than the norm. The work is hard, the winters harder. Perhaps unsurprisingly, the *Los Angeles Times* reported in February of 2005 that from 1995 to 2000, Iowa saw a higher percentage of its young, college-educated, single adults move away than any state except North Dakota, with nearly twelve thousand of them vacating the premises. Some state legislators were sufficiently alarmed to consider asking for a law giving the young adults a straight-up tax break—something on the order of $600 per year—if they agreed to continue living in Iowa, but the kids already had fixed their gazes elsewhere. They headed for places that were more happening, with greater job opportunities and, inevitably, more people. It is why school districts like North-Linn face such an uncertain future. It is why people like Doug LeClere wonder about the long-term prospects for their slices of the rural life. It is certainly why a place like Wyoming, Iowa, can look like a ghost town on a snowy Saturday in the middle of wrestling season.

But, of course, that it outside. Inside, it feels like all hell is breaking loose. This is no ordinary wrestling weekend in Wyoming: The tournament, a thing called the John Byers Invitational, appears to have grown to a size cartoonishly beyond its capacity. People spill out of doorways and jam into bleachers, the wrestlers themselves form a blur of constant motion and clashing school colors. The place radiates a dense, moist heat. It is the last weekend in January, not even a full month before the State Tournament itself, and Iowa's severe weather over the past fourteen days has forced so many postponements and cancellations that teams everywhere are scrambling to get their wrestlers enough matches to stay sharp. An even dozen teams have sent wrestlers to Midland High School, which, judging by the size of the gym, is at least half a dozen teams too many. They're going to wrestle from early morning until late in the evening, and they'll need to, since Midland's space can productively house only two mats. In order to plow through twelve teams' worth of athletes and wrestle all the way out to sixth-place finishes, this day is going to require a solid ten hours. That's a long time to sit on a wooden bleacher, first of all, and God knows it involves an astonishing amount of downtime for most of the top wrestlers, who may hit the mat only three times over that ten-hour span. But it is absolutely critical, considering what is coming over the next few weeks.

Over in one corner, Dan sits among his teammates, a row above Leah, staring off into space. Already thinking. He is two matches ahead, envisioning his moves, how the day is going to unfold, the feeling of hooking his opponent and slapping him down onto the mat, putting a shoulder just about through the guy's body entirely. They will raise his hand in the end, and he will have seen it coming, which may explain why he won't smile when it actually arrives. Nine-thirty in the morning, and Daniel's mind already is fixed on what happens at seven p.m.

At the Class 1A level, an extra layer of postseason wrestling—an extra step in the weeding-out process, basically—is included in the form of sectional tournaments. They're essentially an elaborate first round, out of which only the top two wrestlers in each weight class are advanced to the district tournaments, the events that will determine who gets to book passage to State. It's a device set in place to reduce some of the overwhelming numbers of 1A schools before the district competition begins for all the classes in Iowa, a brutal thinning of the herd. This is, after all, a state full of small towns and small schools. So, while wrestlers at the higher school classifications are able to push hard and then enjoy one open, recuperative weekend before attempting to qualify for the state tourney, Dan LeClere and Ryan Morningstar, among others, must go through the conference, sectional, district and state tournaments on successive weekends. It's a hell of a month's work, a grand tradition of pain and elimination.

And, this winter, Dan won't be the only member of the North-Linn team trying to cover that distance. He is the undisputed headliner, but there are several other Lynx wrestlers who, even in a tough district, have a shot at finishing in the top two and moving on to State. The *Predicament*, an Iowa-based publication more or less considered the Bible of area wrestling, has at this point installed the Lynx as the No. 2 team in 1A overall, behind only powerhouse Don Bosco High of Gilbertville. Brad Bridgewater, never one to overreach, understands that he has got a roster with some real possibilities.

There's Ben Morrow, who despite being very young may

have a shot at making some noise at 103 pounds. Ben is a ninth-grader on the upswing, and he has been wrestling well lately—and confidence, for a young wrestler, sometimes outstrips savvy and technique. Madison Sackett, from a wrestling family, has a shot at 112 pounds. Ryan Mulnix, also from a wrestling family, is healthy enough to go at 125 and has a high state ranking despite dealing with a balky shoulder that keeps popping out of joint, even after a surgery that was supposed to fix it. The thing finally has become so chronic that Ryan wears an interlocking series of Velcro-secured stretch wraps to hold the uncooperative append-age more or less in place.

And then there is Ben Fisher, the most fragile good wrestler imaginable. By the time of the Midland tournament, Ben has already compiled a 24-1 record as a senior at 135 pounds, has achieved a state ranking, and is considered even by his tough-to-please coaches as a strong candidate to see Des Moines for the first time since going there as a freshman. But all of that assumes that he won't self-destruct along the way—and that, really, stands as an open question.

Ben is dark-haired, compact, muscled from top to bottom. A good student, he already has made his college plans: He'll at-tend Iowa State University as a premed student, then set his sights on Nebraska University's medical school—going back home, in a way, to the state where he lived before his family relocated to Iowa when he was in elementary school. (It also may be, his mother, Kathy, says with a chuckle, the affordable option for his family.) Ben's grandfather is a doctor, and Ben plans to follow in the business, as it were. In the meantime, he stands as a classic example of the kind of athlete that schools like North-Linn must have in order to survive, which is to say he can play just about any sport to varsity status (in his case, just as long as it doesn't require him to be tall), and quite usually does.

Then again, things haven't been usual for a while. It was

during Ben's sophomore year, the year after that exhilarating first trip to the Barn, that the muscles in his back began to feel like guitar strings that were being tuned way too high, and the feeling grew and grew, and then one day at a wrestling tournament in Marion he landed harshly on the mat after being thrown and he couldn't get up for a while, and that was pretty much that. The back never felt right again. It was like having a corkscrew turned down around the lower lumbar area, and turned again, and then again. It hurt like hell. It hurt that way for a long, long time. And Ben Fisher did what came naturally, which was to try to play football the next fall anyway.

And why? Well, of course, because this is North-Linn, not some student body–larded school district. Kids at North-Linn with any aptitude are not only warmly encouraged but, in ways both subtle and obvious, politely expected to play multiple sports, as many as the overlapping seasons will allow. When I ask Ben what his sports are, he replies, "Well, football in the fall, and then wrestling. Oh, and I golf." He offers this as a fact, not something to be surprised about. The truth is, it happens all the time.

The coaches all make their peace with this, because it is what it is. As Brad Bridgewater says, "At a school this size, you've got to have kids playing two, three sports, because we just don't have the numbers. I want Nick [LeClere] and Tyler [Burkle] in the wrestling room, but the truth is they were probably the two best players on the football team this season."

What does the wrestling coach do about that?

"Wait," Bridgewater replies with a smile. "And hope they don't get hurt."

Or that when they're already hurt, a season spent colliding with other people on the football field doesn't do too much to exacerbate the damage. But the reality is not only that the school needs its athletes to play multiple sports, but that the kids can enjoy the relative luxury of being able to make the team in whatever sport happens to be in season. For many schools at all different levels, of course, football often flows naturally into a winter wrestling schedule for some of the stronger players. But from wrestling to golf? That's a kind of a Class 1A thing to do, and it's very cool.

Still, injuries don't always heal on schedule. After resting over the summer before his junior year, Ben went out and did what was expected of him (and, to be fair, what he wanted to do himself) and jumped back onto the football team, hoping for the best and taking care of himself as well as he could. He nursed his back through most of the season, but he knew he wasn't completely right; and, sure enough, the bulging disk finally went on a rampage of its own, a little bodily mutiny. Ben's football season ended late in the fall, on the spot. His wrestling season was a complete cancellation. He was going to have to shut things down, because the disk was going to have to be dealt with. Ben went into physical therapy and intense rehab, and waited. And slowly, with difficulty, his patience tested straight down the line, he got better.

He went back onto the football field in the late summer of 2004, because he was a senior and it's football. "The doctors told me the deal," Ben says quietly, standing just off the wrestling mat after winning his first match of the day. "If I hurt it again, I might be done with all contact sports—and I might not be able to play golf."

And on the other hand, this is the North-Linn school district in small-town Iowa in sports-honoring America. There is an unspoken code at play. You don't quit in high school when your teams need you just because your back hurts, and especially not if this is probably the best opportunity of your life to be so involved in so many different ventures. Iowa State won't be offering Ben a wrestling or football scholarship, put it that way. Add to this the traditional wrestler ethos, which is that you're not hurt even when you are (and even then not so much), and it is easy to comprehend Ben getting himself back out there.

It worked out—as of this minute. Ben went back on the football field, resumed his spots as a running back and cornerback and kicker, and got through his senior season more or less whole. He will win his weight class in Midland on this day. And he will go on with a straight shot at making the State Tournament, because he is a good wrestler, and because the State Tournament is the place to be.

Ben's family lived in Nebraska until 1997, when it moved first to Marion and then finally out to the country, about fifteen minutes beyond Troy Mills. In Nebraska, he says, they wrestle, and they're not bad at it at all, and pretty much nobody ever follows along, and that's that. But Iowa is different. "In Iowa, if you're on the football team, you'll get some attention for sure," Ben says. "But if you're a wrestler and you go to the State Tournament, the whole town will go there to follow you. That's the way they treat it. They all want to be there."

So Ben is out there, working past the alternating senses of thrill and concern; and he is taking his risks being there and asking his body to contort into shapes that only the most nimble of human beings could even ponder. Even then, it doesn't always look quite possible. And some days Ben feels good at it, and some days Ben feels like the most worthless fool to ever pull on a singlet. Some days the doubt crushes him, and you can see him backing off in the middle of a match. Some days he rolls through the competition and looks like he'll never lose again. "When he wrestles the way he can," says his father, Mike, "he can be very hard to beat." But you can't depend on that. It's a provisional life in wrestling for Ben Fisher.

With Nick still injured, Dan will move up and wrestle at 145 pounds in Wyoming. If you're a knucklehead about the sport—if, in other words, you are me—then you look at the brackets and see that, theoretically at least, Dan could have moved up one more weight class to 152 and wrestled in this tournament against Morningstar, a match that would've had the mat community clucking for weeks. LeClere versus Morningstar is the stuff of Iowa wrestling dreams, just as Borschel versus Morningstar was the most talked-about match of 2004. Had Dan shifted up one more weight class, he could have had that shot. That's the knucklehead train of thought, though. In reality, doing so would knock Tyler Burkle out of his spot at 152, and that makes no sense for North-Linn as a team. Together, Dan, Nick and Tyler—when all are healthy and all are wrestling—make for one hell of a tough middle of the order for Bridgewater. In fact, Brad can go from Ben Fisher to Dan to Nick to Tyler in four successive weight classes, with Mulnix just two weights below Ben at 125 pounds, and there aren't many schools who can boast of five potential State entrants in such short succession.

But that presumes the health and vitality of each wrestler. Dan is by now a given. Burkle has been good all year. Ben's hanging in there. Nick is a different story, and so today he will sit and watch, waiting on that elbow to heal in the same way that Ben Fisher once waited for his back to stop killing him. Any other time of year, Nick would have shut things down entirely, but this is the season. This is the time. He isn't angling for full health, just for the hurt to go away long enough for him to scrap.

Thus, this becomes a day for watching Dan work, which is not necessarily the same as watching him be challenged. He will barely break a sweat in squeezing off his three victories, pinning his first opponent, scoring a technical fall against the second and winning the tournament title with a 22–9 major decision in the final. (The technical fall is a handy device for stopping the madness when a match is out of hand; if you build up a lead on the other guy of 15 points, no matter when it occurs in the match, the thing is over.) Likewise, Dan's final at 145 pounds, against a senior named Luke Bader from North Cedar High in the northern part of the state, is never in question. Luke, who has lost only once all season to this point, does a fair job of avoiding the pin, but he's on the defensive from the moment the match begins. Dan stalks him around on the mat, constantly shooting in low to grab a leg and drive Luke down; all of Luke's points come from Dan voluntarily releasing him, thus allowing repeated escapes to occur. It is a fitting end to a dominating day.

But that's not to say that the day is without note. In Dan's semifinal, he appears to have his opponent pinned several times, but doesn't get the call; eventually, he piles up a 15–0 lead and the match is halted. Although most observers I later speak to agree that Dan had the pin more than once, there is a pronounced lack of conversation or surprise about the fact that it was never called. Only then do I realize that Doug, who has been all over everywhere all morning coaching the North-Linn wrestlers, hasn't come down to sit matside for Dan's match.

"That ref doesn't like us," Mary explains candidly, as though she is simply reciting the fact. "Dan wasn't going to get the pin. The guy doesn't like Doug. It goes way back."

The LeCleres' view of the situation is straightforward: Doug once loudly insulted the ref for calling a lousy match, one of the many occasions in many places in which Doug has spoken first and considered the implications later; and it was not the kind of conversation an official forgets. And in one of those Iowa things, this ref has been around ever since and likely will be around for as long as the LeCleres have kids wrestling, because most of the officials never do leave the sport, in the same way that timers and scorekeepers and such have been showing up to the State Tournament in Des Moines for fifteen and eighteen and twenty years.

So this gentleman will continue to be on hand. And for as

long as he is, Doug LeClere will mostly avoid the mat when he referees. It's a lot of small towns.

When I ask Dan about the non-call later, he replies with the full diplomacy of a skilled senior. "Well," he says, "with some refs you have to bury the guy four feet under the ground before they'll give you the pin." What's interesting here is that, although both Mary and Doug have taken note of the outcome and processed it through the context of their memories, their son is over and done with it. He wrestled well. He wasted no time. It should've been a pin, perhaps, but then he isn't trying to set a state record for falls. He wins; he moves on. And in that sentence, you have just learned everything about Dan LeClere's approach to his final high school wrestling season.

Away from the mat, Dan is one of the great energy-conservers of his time. Between matches, he sits in the stands quietly, with almost no movement, sometimes interacting with Leah, sometimes not. (Their friends like watching them together; as one said, "They're almost like a little old couple the way they take turns looking out for each other.") Dan turns slowly when spoken to, takes his time in thinking before he replies. He walks very deliberately around the gym, if indeed he finds it necessary to get up and move around at all.

But LeClere in the moments leading up to a match, and in the match itself—that's something else again. To borrow the old expression, he appears to flip some sort of internal switch. When Dan wrestles, there is the distinct impression of watching a stage play rather than a game with a significant degree of chance involved. It is an exercise in prearranged endings. Dan betrays virtually no emotion at any time during a match, neither surprise nor frustration nor elation nor any damn thing. He looks like a guy packing lunch for a long day job. He could be repairing fence-line or unloading sheet metal. It looks like a job because that is exactly how Dan intends to make it look. He loves it. He says so. But wrestling itself is not unlike work.

Out on the mat, in the final at 145 pounds of the Byers Invitational, Luke Bader circles but mostly backs up, sensing Dan near him the way one might sense a snake along a walking path. Dan approaches and approaches. He just keeps coming. It's not a question of Luke fending him off. You are witnessing the arrogance of the blessed, and Bader is merely the person on the other end of the exchange today. For all the talk of the crucial difference a weight class can make, that difference is often neutralized by the truly great wrestler. Dan is no less a load at 145 pounds than he would have been at 140. He will win again. It is the pool of candidates to finish second that has changed.

If you were going to draw up a blueprint for the construction of a wrestling body, Dan's shape would be one of the first you would reach for. He is squat; with the same low center of gravity his father has, Dan is virtually impossible to knock off stride. His muscles are in all the right places, with tremendous strength through his legs and hips and a chiseled upper body. He is big enough to hold off other 140-pound wrestlers who occasionally appear at first glance to outsize him. His forearms are taut, thick ropes of strength. And his neck, while not a thing of artistic beauty, is of itself a brilliant wrestling tool. Dan sometimes pummels opponents into submission almost strictly by using that neck strength to drive his chin into their backs or threaten to puncture that vulnerable soft spot between the shoulder and the clavicle. (Try it sometime. You'd be surprised how quickly you can make somebody cry uncle.)

And yet he is not invincible. As a freshman, Dan suffered his one defeat to a fellow Iowa high school wrestler; he was beaten fair by a very good opponent named Cory Kalina, a kid from Belle Plain. Dan can tell you about that match today, in detail, at the slightest prompting. He was just starting out in his high school career, and Cory was a senior; and it hurt like hell to lose. Dan remembers vividly the feeling of losing and the rare sense of being outmaneuvered on the mat, the flushing of his cheeks at the defeat, all of it. And yet that match, the loss to Kalina, was the match at which it first really occurred to Dan that he could compete at the high school level—"compete," naturally, meaning "win." He was a punk ninth-grader losing to a senior—he barely knew what he was doing, in hindsight—and yet he was mixing it up with the older boy, staying close. "Once you go to the next level, from junior high to high school—I was good in junior high, but what am I in high school? I didn't really know until I wrestled that match," Dan says. "It'll probably be the same way in college. I really won't know where I'm at until I wrestle in competition somewhere."

Dan's first title, at 119 pounds, came later that freshman year only after he had defeated a brutally tough wrestler in the championship match at the State Finals—Cory Kalina. Dan had been right: The boy from the farm could wrestle with these guys.

No, the Kalina defeat Dan can live with; it is the only other loss on his high school record that really eats at him, the one he suffered in his junior year to a kid from Minnesota during a tournament. It was an overtime defeat, 4–3, during one of the scads of tournaments Dan entered and usually won over the years. Dan remembers very clearly that he was simply off all day, just not all the way there. He felt, he tells me, like he was losing from the start of the match, even though he had every chance to win, and even though his opponent never did go on the offensive. The kid stayed back and hunkered down and waited for Dan to make a mistake, which Dan finally did, in overtime. It never happened before, and it hasn't happened since.

"He didn't take it very well," Brad Bridgewater says. "He was pissed—and he should have been. We took about ten or twelve shots and couldn't finish anything. The thing goes to overtime and we try the same move we've been working all day, and the kid gets around him and scores two, and that's it.

"We did all the work, and at the end they raise the other guy's hand," Bridgewater says. "But nobody's unbeatable. Ask Dan Gable."

It is that message that Bridgewater wants Tyler Burkle to understand, but on this day, Tyler is up against two-time state champion Morningstar. And although Burkle wrestles with great energy, it's clear early on that he does not want to take too many risks with Morningstar; he is almost afraid to go in and attempt a takedown, and he gets punished for it. Ryan wins the 152-pound championship with a 13–1 major decision, and he looks completely in control doing it. Tyler knows he's got his work cut out for him if he is to make a run at the state title.

By the time they get through the heavyweights and the consolation matches, the day has given way to evening; it's going on twelve hours since many of these high school kids first arrived at Midland-Wyoming, and a rare full dinner—or at least as much food as their shrunken stomachs can hold—awaits many of them as soon as the tournament titlists are all awarded and the crowd dispatched into the black night. But for the families and wrestlers of North-Linn, there is one more piece of theater to be staged.

As the team standings are compiled, it becomes apparent that North-Linn may tie North Cedar for the team championship, an almost freakish thing considering how many different ways points can be compiled here—by advancers, by place-winners, falls, technical falls, all of it. Still, the murmur through the crowd is that the teams will fall exactly even and have to share the crown. The North Cedar head coach, a man who wrestled for the Lynx under Doug's tutelage and who himself was a place-winner at the State Tournament, comes over to Doug to joke about the possibility. "Hey," he says, slapping Doug hard on the shoulder, "tell you what, if it's a tie we may have to wrestle for it. You and me, for the trophy."

He says it in jest, surely. The gentleman outweighs Doug by at least 75 pounds and probably much more than that. Doug is certainly thicker than when he wrestled, but he wrestled at 132 pounds. Giant he ain't. At the same time, Doug doesn't much care for being slapped hard on the shoulder, much less challenged—however jokingly—to prove up for his program with a trophy on the line. Some guys never do stop competing.

"You think?" Doug shoots back at the North Cedar coach, and already I see the fire in his eyes.

"Yeah. You and me," the coach replies. He's chuckling now. It only raises Doug's ire all the more.

Finally, the coach makes his way back across the mat to his own team, and Doug and I resume talking about something else, about how Dan wrestled or whether anybody can take Morningstar this year or something like that. We've chatted for a few minutes when Doug looks back across the gym, turns back to me and says thoughtfully, "I think I could take him, though."

"Who?"

"North Cedar guy. I think I could take him."

Fabulous news: Doug is about to get that chance. As the announcer booms out the team totals, he comes to the top of the list and, sure enough, pronounces North-Linn and North Cedar the co-champions of the Byers Invitational for 2005. Since the Midland coaches will be seeing North Cedar again during conference and sectional tourneys, all parties agree to present the one trophy on hand today to the Lynx, who may not be coming back anytime soon, and give out the other one later. Hands are shaken, cheering is commenced, and we are done for the day—except, that is, for the North Cedar coach who is now sneaking up behind Doug as he chats up some friends just at the far edge of the mat.

The coach laughingly grabs Doug around the waist and lifts him into the air, but Doug hasn't lost his reaction time; he quickly spins around, lands on his feet and squares up to wrestle. And although these two adults are smiling, it suddenly becomes clear that they may actually do this thing. Around them forms a circle of friends, who assume the two old acquaintances are mostly kidding. And that would be mostly underestimating the once-a-wrestler-always-a-wrestler vibe that has just this moment enveloped the gym, which is to say, you can only smile for so long while in a mutual headlock.

It's just such an amazing moment: Doug and his former pupil going at it in their street clothes, their faces still trying to keep the mood light, as if to convince the onlookers that neither man cares about the result and both are out there in a sort of mock indignation at having to share the team title. But as they continue to circle and grip each other, and the scab over Doug's right ear— the one he originally cut while wrestling Tyler in the practice room—finally and predictably tears open, the gymnasium grows a little less lighthearted. It gets quiet for just a few seconds, and it appears that even the longtime wrestling folks aren't exactly sure what to think. Doug is by now dripping blood down the right side of his face and onto his clothes, which he doesn't even realize. He is completely outmanned by this extra-large human, Doug trying to stay upright while wearing jeans and a collared shirt and beat-up tennis shoes, and before long what began as a joke takes on the proportion—just very briefly, mind you—of something personal and rooted in grudge. When the huge coach finally uses his bulk to throw Doug to the floor, there is an audible "Ooooh" from the crowd, but even before Doug can spring up, the nervous laughter and friendly calls of "Okay, boys, that's enough" have begun to circulate. You can tell the people want this thing to end before it actually does get personal. And though Doug and the coach both leave the mat smiling and pretending friendliness, the

truth is that Doug is burning inside with the fury and embarrass-
ment of being tossed to the mat—even here, now, with nothing
on the line, having been snuck up on by a former student who
earlier had spoken of his genuine appreciation for what LeClere
taught him in that wrestling room back at North-Linn.

Someone hands Doug a towel to wipe off the blood. Most
of the observers, knowing nothing about the situation, will walk
away under the impression that the blood is a product of a wound
inflicted by the North Cedar coach. It is a likelihood that only
adds to Doug's seething sense of humiliation—a sense not simi-
larly shared by anyone around him—at being "beaten" by the big
guy with the bear hug. It puts an odd, disquieting spin on this day.
And it is something that will gall Doug for weeks to come.

CHAPTER 7

Only Warm in the Room

On the same final weekend of January, Doug Streicher already has sent his junior varsity to a meet across town. The rest of Linn-Mar High School looks deserted; the mass of students have long since piled their stuff in their lockers and gotten the hell out. The hallways are empty up there. One level below, down in the wrestling room, it's learning time.

For Streicher, having the varsity and nothing but the varsity is an unimaginable luxury. He likes having the JV around for the afternoon workouts, it's true; he likes having the numbers, and being able to find a workout partner for every wrestler in the room, and getting a crack at teaching so many kids a basic move at the same time. He likes the noise and the energy that a crowded room brings. Still, there is something so team-building and binding about a varsity-only workout, especially a lonely one at the end of the week. The big dance at the Barn is coming, and this workout, late on a Friday, with the whole world gone on to easier things, is for the ones who are still willing to believe they might get to Des Moines somehow.

Certainly, Shawnden, the heavyweight, would be on track for

State were it not for his injury. He got his leg twisted the wrong way during the overtime period of a match against the Hempstead wrestler that night a few weeks before in Dubuque, and although a subsequent MRI has showed no severe damage, the swelling was immense and Shawnden has obviously been in pain. At the time of the injury, a couple of people close to the program wondered if he might have been feeling more hurt than he really was, because he was about to lose the match; after all, he has lost very few times all year and was a returning state qualifier. But time has proven Shawnden's injury real, and now all he can do is lightly ride the stationary bicycle, wait for things to get better, and hope.

But Streicher has hopes for other wrestlers as well. One is Matt McDonough, the freshman who is becoming a better wrestler by the day. In street clothes, Matt looks like the worst he's capable of is sneaking an extra piece of cake off the cafeteria food line. He is funny, goofy and humble enough to withstand the taunts and jokes of his teammates about the fact that he spends so much time with Jay's sister, Hannah, who, following Jay's athletic lead, has made Linn-Mar's varsity softball team as an eighth-grader. But in the wrestling room, Matt is the real deal. Like Jay, he is a product of the little-kid wrestling club system, one who has spent most of his formative years attending meets and learning the trade, from his father and from the people who would in time become his coaches. By late in his first high school season, Matt is beginning to take over matches, to see the combinations he wants to put together to knock off his opponents. He can finish.

Streicher sees the possibilities with McDonough, and with a handful of other candidates. This isn't his strongest team, but there are some fair chances for individual success here. For one, Doug has Wes Shetterly, an obviously gifted all-around athlete and acrobatic gymnast. After missing a huge chunk of the season due to injury, Wes is returning to the team just in time to be ready for conference and district competition—but to do so, he needs a place on the roster. Wes most likely could make weight at 103, but instead he has chosen to move away from Matt and go up to 112. For Streicher, it's the stronger team move, but there is a consequence: Wes must challenge the current placeholder at 112, his teammate and fellow sophomore Spencer Jordan, for the right to start on the varsity.

The challenge is straightforward, and it happens in wrestling rooms all the time. It is also one of the most bloodless events in any sport: If you seek the other guy's spot on the varsity roster, you must go and wrestle him for it. Beat him, and the spot is yours. The next week, that teammate may challenge you for the spot right back, and if you're not good enough on that day, you can lose your varsity status as quickly as you gained it.

Practically speaking, this isn't going to happen all the time, because in some cases it makes no sense. In the same way that Wes has chosen to bypass Matt at 103 pounds, no one is going to challenge Jay every week, because it's out-and-out stupid to think you could take away a three-time state champion's spot. At any rate, no self-respecting coach would want two of his better wrestlers vying for the same place on the team. That's one of the things weight-cutting is for, to help slot wrestlers in the right positions to do good things for the team as well as for themselves.

In this case, Wes has the right instinct. He has defeated Spencer before in matches at 112, and now the two have become involved in a drawn-out, best-of-seven series—spread over several practices—to determine who will represent the school at districts. Spencer has been carrying Linn-Mar at the weight class for the better part of the season while Wes nursed his injuries and got ready to come back. For most of the winter to this point, 112 pounds has belonged to Spencer. The problem is this: Wes is better.

The other wrestlers have been sent out on a run through the school's hallways, and so it is just these two underclassmen and their coaches. Jason Haag referees and keeps the score while Streicher and Kevin McCauley look on and run the clock, and the only sounds in the wrestling room are of the movements on the mat and the desperate exertions of the two boys. You are reminded how quiet a struggle wrestling really is most of the time. It gets hard to tell under those layers of coaches bellowing instructions and parents going nuts and cheerleaders pounding the mats and referees blowing whistles, but at its heart, the sport is almost eerily silent. The two boys work their way around the mat, one or the other occasionally grunting with effort or surprise, and Wes's superior speed is apparent. He is able to get around Spencer for the first takedown in an instant, slipping behind Spencer to grab one of his ankles and trip him down to the mat. Jason Haag raises two fingers to signal Wes's lead.

Every once in a while you hear an arm sliding off the opponent's body, or Wes or Spencer shifting around on the mat to get a better grip. Otherwise, it's quiet, just the sound of Spencer's body as it hits the mat. Wes is able to put together a couple more takedowns and easily outpoints Spencer for his second straight victory in the best-of-seven. Spencer can barely bring himself to shake hands with his teammate before he hurries away from the mat, taking his wounded pride and bolting out of the padded room. Wes is going to take the spot on the varsity roster, and everyone can see that now. It's as clear as it is heartbreaking.

Wes is better. It doesn't matter that he hasn't come back until now. He was a member of the team who got hurt, not some kid who suddenly decided he'd like to give it a shot—although, under the basic ground rules of the sport, even that kid bursting through the doors for the first time would have as much right to vie for a position as anyone else. But at the end of the week, it comes down strictly to who is good enough to take the job. Right now it is Wes, and there's just no getting around it.

So, now Doug Streicher has Matt, and Wes, and Jay, and 165-pounder Kyle Minehart—and perhaps Shawnden—for the district tournament set to begin in three weeks. He has maybe fifteen days to get these wrestlers into peak condition, and Streicher is making the most of the time. Drill after drill goes off in the room, the stereo thumping out the strains of Tom Petty's "Last Chance for Mary Jane," coach McCauley stalking the mats giving instruction, Streicher leading the workout, barking commands, urging his wrestlers on to a greater effort. Jeff Nelson, the father of promising sophomore Jason Nelson, once said that Streicher's approach is very straightforward: His team might not always be the deepest or most technically elegant, but by God it will be the best conditioned, because in wrestling, superior condition is a survival tactic. A conditioned wrestler, if he can get to the third period, has the edge over the opponent who might have a few more slick mat moves but is rapidly depleting his oxygen supply and beginning to burn in his legs and arms and shoulders. Wrestlers deal with enough pain on a good day. That pain is compounded and magnified if they're not in shape enough to go full speed for six minutes of a match (plus one minute of overtime, which is why so many of Streicher's straight-up wrestling drills force his kids to go for seven minutes without a break).

Jay wrestles one of the heavier kids. From every corner of the room come the exhalations and grunts of the gradually exhausted. Outside, the sky is growing dark and a cold wind slices through the south parking lot at Linn-Mar High. When Jay comes out later to look for his car, it will be standing there under a sheet of ice that has blown in and covered the thing like a shell. Up by the edges of the lot, near the road, the streetlamps switch on. The lot itself is empty save for this tiny little band of cars, all parked together, down by the doors that lead to the locker rooms. It is the start of the weekend just about everywhere you look. Down in the wrestling room, the music thunders and the sweat glistens, and the coach intones, and Jay and his teammates pant and listen and get a drink and check for blood, and then they get ready to do it all over again.

CHAPTER 8

The Ghosts of Gable

Iowa's total area ranks it 26th among the United States. The state, bordered by the Mississippi and Missouri rivers, has the 30th-largest population in the country. You could hardly be more center of the pack. It rests, in the words of the writer Joseph Frazier Wall, "in the middle ground, a Mesopotamia lying between the two great rivers that drain the continent, bisected by the 42nd parallel . . . the line that was roughly followed by the first transcontinental railroad and then later by the transcontinental highway, so that for over a hundred years the constantly moving Americans have had to cross Iowa from New York and Chicago to San Francisco."

To much of the nation, Iowa remains exactly that: a flyover. It has little to distinguish it from the other states of the Great Plains, either topographically or culturally, and it becomes newsworthy perhaps only once every four years, when, as if on cue, those reporters who cover politics for a living come crashing through the gates, intent on revealing Iowa's true agrarian nature and man-on-the-street ordinariness, as suggested, naturally, by a presidential primary.

Generally speaking, Iowa is a place that rests on the shoulders of people who don't mind the work and don't mind the weather—people like the LeCleres, who for a hundred years have farmed the land outside of Coggon in economic and social conditions that ranged from reasonable to ridiculous, or like Jim and Carol Borschel, who bounced around the country as a younger couple only to discover that what they hungered for was courtesy, character, security. Iowans were once jokingly described by a national reporter as "terminally civil," but it isn't that. They simply lack the pretense to act too busy for you. They move forward, but never at a pace that precludes you from coming along.

Wrestling long ago became a surrogate for many of Iowans' perceptions of themselves, particularly those who spent days working the land. It was basic and it was predicated on strength of body and strength of mind; and just about anybody could learn to do it. Iowa got better at it than anybody else. And over time, that became a calling card in itself, something that did distinguish the state. It became a thing to be cherished and appreciated and bragged upon, and one generation of wrestlers gave rise to the next until a century had flown by and such a thing as the legend of Dan Gable had been created, and wrestling was simply the thing that was done. And even today, as wrestling finds itself pushed to the brink of irrelevance at so many colleges and universities, Iowans cling to it more fiercely than ever. It is, for lack of a more benign way to put it, their heritage. Or, as former Iowa Olympian Tom Brands says, "It goes back to the roots, goes back to the rural. These are hard-working people. Give them a reason to come together and celebrate and get behind something. And it might as well be something as grueling and hard-nosed and tough as this sport."

And you understand, knowing this, why Jay is wrong, why Iowa isn't secretly pulling against him or gathering together in a mass conspiracy to deny him his rightful due. He does have some detractors, no question, but he is also a towering figure even now.

A little controversy is simply part of the deal. Jay is a three-time champion in a pocket of the world that debates his particular sport with real passion.

It isn't as though wrestling in Iowa exists unchallenged—this is still America, after all; the cheerleaders are still going to go for the football players first—but it is one of the truly enduring conversation pieces available. It has a history that traces almost through the entire arc of Iowa's statehood, through the days of Frank Gotch, America's first legitimate world champion wrestler, back in a time when professional wrestling wasn't an oxymoron. In the early 1900s, Gotch was Dan Gable before Gable was; he met with presidents and was renowned as the greatest athlete of his time. He was an Iowa farm boy who became known around the world, and in time he became the first part of the state's wrestling history. The sport grew and thrived as something of a calling card, and Gotch had significantly to do with that. Especially, though, the sport succeeded in the small towns, in the way that schoolboy football did in Texas and basketball in Indiana. It wasn't that nobody else did it; it was that Iowans decided to adopt it. They gave wrestling a place of importance that it would not be granted in very many parts of the United States, and in turn, Iowa became known as a place that not only loved the sport but produced its finest competitors. Gable's wildly successful career at Iowa State in the 1970s sealed that idea, and when he became coach at cross-state rival Iowa University and turned that program into the most astonishing winner in the history of the sport, the state's reputation was sealed.

Now wrestling's place in Iowa has come to the point that Jay Borschel can matter in ways he sometimes finds difficult to fathom. They've been conducting the State Tournament as an officially sanctioned event for 80 years, and of the tens of thousands of wrestlers ground through that mill, exactly fourteen have ever come to the brink of greatness at which Jay now finds himself. So yes, they'll talk about him; and he will have to decide for himself how much of what they say matters.

It is difficult to be sure that Jay even believes most of what he says, because he doesn't make it a practice to stay serious for more than thirty seconds at a time. His response to the media and public attention is either to seize on the few negatives thrown his way—it's too much weight to cover in one career; there's somebody out there waiting for him with a surprise performance in Des Moines—or to dismiss them completely, usually with something like a wink. Wrestling is everything, yet Jay remains grounded in reality: When he takes me one night to watch the sold-out, top-ranked Linn-Mar boys' basketball team and its heavily recruited guard, Jason Bohannon, Jay waits until we enter the gymnasium and then deadpans, "I thought you might want to see what it looks like when it has people in it." When someone mentions that his girlfriend, Jillian, a cheerleader, had asked specifically not to be assigned to the Lions' wrestling team at the start of the winter season, he replies dryly, "Her and everybody else on the squad."

But, of course, that's fine. It has to be. If wrestlers are going to live by an outsider's code, they have to accept and even embrace that status. Streicher makes sure they feed on it, that they use it as fuel. Streicher has got the standing for it: A two-time state champion who went on to wrestle for Gable at Iowa, Streicher won't hesitate to use "unappreciated" as a rallying cry. As he sees it, it's good for the soul.

It is what makes wrestlers better: They do this work and pound their bodies until they scream, and sweat out boxes worth of salt; they push their muscles somewhere beyond whatever they may have imagined as the snapping point. And they do all of this, or at least most of it, absent the expectation that anyone in particular will applaud or even really notice. So few people outside the fraternity see the nights the wrestler spends in voluntary hunger, unwilling to risk eating a decent meal. No one sees the workouts to which there is no fair comparison at the high school level. (Wrestlers tend to believe that only swimmers have the slightest idea of the kind of physical sacrifice they make for their sport—and even then, swimmers generally don't go home and turn away from the dinner table in order to cut down another three-quarters of a pound.) No one sees any of that because wrestling is a gladiatorial spectacle, and even though most people in Iowa do understand how it happens, there isn't anyone clamoring for a close-up look. Wrestlers spend their hungry, thirsty, angry nights alone. They crawl into the corners of their beds, balled up and waiting for morning to come so they can work out again and then, finally, allow themselves a little food. They suffer their defeats in full public view, with no one to help, no one to take away the shame of giving up points from their teams; and when they do win, their victories will be the most short-lived things in the world, because tomorrow begins another week, and another week brings hunger and pain and sweat and uncertainty. And no one understands that more intimately than their brothers on the team. How could anyone, really? It's the most exclusive club in the sports world. And that, to Streicher, is what makes it sacred.

It is Doug's job to see that his young charges understand they are doing God's work, or at least the work of the patron saint of anonymous labor. The slogans and sayings taped and pinned to his walls at Linn-Mar make that plain. On one wall rests a long ode to the loneliness of the wrestler, this man among children. Here, inside the room, reside martyrs to the cause of superior conditioning, people who will work harder for it and want it more badly than anyone on the planet. And Jay believes in that ethos straight down the line. He welcomes the world's indifference. He will make them notice. In the end, they'll have no choice but to acknowledge what he has accomplished.

Jay doesn't feel like messing around, but maybe that's because it is already February 3 and the calendar is moving so rapidly toward Des

Moines—exactly twenty days, now, before Jay's anticipated first
match at State. Maybe it's because he hasn't had enough matches
yet to feel fully comfortable in what he's trying to do, what he is
going for. Or maybe, judging by his sidelong glances toward the
bleachers at Iowa City High School, it is because he knows Gable
is sitting over there to watch.

Gable's presence at the school isn't necessarily a shocking thing.
City High sits just down the road from the university itself. This is
Gable's school, more or less. It's the place where the legend is most apt
to wander through, in part because one of his daughters attends, in
part because it isn't much more than a few blocks from his home, and
in part because City High, under coach Brad Smith, has consistently
put together a competitive—at times excellent—team.

Jay doesn't care why Gable is here, only that he is. The truth is,
Jay doesn't have the slightest idea of Gable's opinion of him. Gable
must know who he is, because everybody in Iowa wrestling knows
who Jay is. Gable undoubtedly knows Jay won't be taking classes in
Iowa City this fall, because that's Gable's job, to know that sort of
thing. But Jay wouldn't miss this opportunity to show Gable what the
University of Iowa is going to be missing. He will, tonight, face City
High's Josh Keller, and this match will be over before it begins.

Jay attacks first, spearing one of his opponent's legs almost immediately after the whistle; Keller, who is no bag of rocks, is trying
to scramble away from a lockdown almost before anyone realizes the
two seniors have begun the first period. It is Senior Night for Iowa
City at the gym, which makes it officially a bad time for Keller to lose.
He's the 171-pounder for his team, so he's the one who has to be out
there. The other guy on the mat right now has three state titles and
still manages to wear a chip on the shoulder. Josh can do the math.

Once he goes into match mode, Jay never looks anywhere
near the place where Gable sits, because he would never do that.
It is disrespectful, for one thing. Besides, he knows that Gable,
along with everyone else inside the City High gymnasium, will

be looking his way, just as they look at his longtime friend, City's Kyle Anson, in the 125-pound match. Kyle is another of those wrestlers with greatness attached to his resume, another one whom the people watch because they already know they will be following him again in Des Moines a few weeks hence. Kyle is a wonderful wrestler, all guts and heart, technically just so sound. He won't be attending the University of Iowa, either.

By the time Jay drives Josh Keller hard to the mat early in the first period, the mystery has been taken out of the match. Jay takes Josh down again several seconds later, then uses his arms to lever Keller onto his back. Jay relies upon his legs, which have become his most powerful attribute, to do the heavy work, slowly inching his opponent into position to expose Keller's shoulders to the mat and then plant them there. The strength in Jay's arms prevents Keller from squirming free. The pin, when it comes, is almost a relief after watching Josh struggle to gain a toehold or find some daylight. It is Jay's gift as a wrestler: He has become a master of anticipation and adjustment. He makes the little moves, almost imperceptible, that expose his opponent. He can get himself out of a jam with what appears to be the slightest realignment of his knees, or the direction a foot is pointing. Against Keller, he has sprung back and forth around his opponent's hunched-down body on the mat, looking for that small opening, and finally has found it: a knee plunged into Josh's flank, which forces open just enough room for Jay to thrust his right arm under the left arm of Keller. It is this move that eventually forces Josh onto his back and out of the match.

"Iowa could have had that," Jay says later. "It's the only place I ever thought about going."

It only makes him one of the thousands.

The one sure thing, all the way through the journey, was that the Iowa campus was the final destination. Jay knew that from the start, and so did Dan, and so did Mitch Mueller and Kyle Anson and Ryan Morningstar and Joey Slaton, and their parents, and most of their friends, and their coaches and—pretty much straight down the line—anyone who knew the first thing about them. They were kids and they were going to achieve greatness; and in time it would be the University of Iowa that came for them. They would go in together, this collective of talent, all of them pushing each other to greater heights. They would go to Iowa City to honor the legend of Gable, to crown champions and dream Olympic dreams; and they would do it as a group, because there was nowhere else in the world that an Iowa wrestler would go.

Pablo Ubasa knew it. Nearly a decade earlier, when the boys were just starting out, Ubasa had been just barely in the process of putting together his Hawkeye Kids Wrestling Club, a thing created in the shadow of Gable's NCAA program specifically to feed the hopes of fledgling stars, when he received a call from Bill Anson. Bill wanted his fifth-grade son Kyle to come learn a few things. Soon, Pablo's club was filled with future stars: Jay Borschel and Dan LeClere, Mitch Mueller and Ryan Morningstar, Joey Slaton, T. J. Sebolt and Chad Beatty. It wasn't long before Pablo took Jim Borschel to one side and said, "You're going to pay me back one of these days"—in victories, he meant, and of course he was right. He just never counted on the fallout.

From the beginning, these wrestlers were all going to the University of Iowa to make their dreams come true. They talked about it. It was almost assumed. They were going to where Dan Gable was.

Only that's not Gable who sits there anymore. And they're not going.

By the time that Jay, Dan and Joey used the same press conference in the fall of 2004 to announce they were leaving their native state for

Virginia Tech University, everybody understood that the shit had hit the fan completely. Gable, long the face of the Iowa program, was no longer the coach, having drifted into a weird netherworld as an assistant athletic director and sort of all-around crisis manager for the sport. In his place was Jim Zalesky, one of the toughest wrestlers ever to come slamming through Gable's program, a coach already in his eighth year—was this even possible?—as Gable's replacement, if not precisely his heir. Tom Brands, the man who had lost out to Zalesky in the race to succeed Gable, had bolted for Virginia Tech and then swooped back in and, in a stunning development, taken these great Iowa high school wrestlers with him. Gable, whose mere presence for years seemed to magnetize the young talent in his home state, now spent huge chunks of his time traveling to other places, where wrestling was endangered, and stumping for the sport's survival. And despite the slowly gaining sense that things weren't right with Zalesky's program in Iowa City, Gable, the man who cast a shadow so long that full generations of boys and men might find themselves under it, could only do so much. He had his hands full with other trauma. Wrestling was bleeding all over.

Despite a remarkably rich recent history, with Iowa State (when Gable wrestled there) and Iowa (once he became coach) joining powerhouses like Oklahoma State and Oklahoma to create great rivalries and perennial world-championship possibilities, the sport has been decimated at the NCAA level. This is particularly true in Division I, where wrestling has become a fashionable target for athletic departments looking to either cut costs or yank themselves into the gender compliance mandated by Title IX, the federal law that requires equal athletic opportunity for men and women at the collegiate level. Generally speaking, only a fool would fail to link the two goals, and very few sports offer such a tempting two-birds-with-one-stone effect. Over time, wrestling has become an almost irresistible cut: a money-loser with, usually, nothing approaching female equivalency. A university administrator could close out the wrestling program and proclaim himself a holy man. In staggering numbers, that is exactly what university presidents and athletic directors have done.

From a high-water mark of 375 wrestling programs in 1980, the NCAA's total by the turn of the century had dropped to 238, and it continues to decline. At the scholarship level of Division I, the news is bleaker still: By 2004, according to several estimates, the number of D-I schools offering wrestling as an NCAA program had been cut nearly in half, to fewer than 90. One by one, wrestling coaches have found themselves dragged under water by the circumstances surrounding the modern large-scale athletic program, with football sucking up vast amounts of money and resources (though by most accounts the majority of NCAA football programs in the country actively lose money) and the rest of the department having to fall in line—or by the wayside—in order to compensate.

In short, wrestling is under siege. And as it typically has done over the past few decades, the wrestling community looks to Dan Gable to defend it, a charge that not even Gable, the most famous and beloved wrestler in modern American history, can meet. Still, he tries, which has the deleterious effect of taking him ever farther away from the University of Iowa program that he essentially molded himself. His cherished Hawkeyes, under his handpicked successor, are hemorrhaging talent, losing Iowans to places those wrestlers never even contemplated while growing up. Gable can't seem to do a thing about that, either. Nobody trains you for this kind of stuff on the mat.

Listening to people talk about Gable and quote Gable and post his say-ings on their walls and treat his words as scripture, one finds it amazing that he can walk into a room without instantly drawing the air out of it. In fact, here on a school night, the man can enter the City High gymnasium and not even be recognized—that, or they're so used to seeing him around that he no longer is capable of making a dramatic entrance. Either way, he just sort of slips in one of the side doors around the time the varsity match is ready to begin, this slow-moving man on crutches, wearing a yellow, long-sleeved Iowa Hawkeyes T-shirt, sweat pants, boot-slippers and a white-lined winter cap with earflaps that button up on two sides. He wears glasses, as he has worn for years. On the top of his head, the hair has been reduced to a fading wisp. He moves purposefully but carefully, so as not to aggravate a left hip that has recently undergone its second replacement surgery. The right hip is up next, and after that Gable is hoping nothing else falls off or withers away from a body that he for years employed as, essentially, the subject of an ongoing experiment with the outer limits of self-inflicted physical torment.

He moves over to the first row of bleachers, well off the far side of the mat. He has a vantage point, but not at center. His youngest girl is a statistician for the wrestling team, and his wife is out of town, so Gable basically finds himself killing time, watching a little wrestling, unapproached, unbothered. Past him, students and varsity athletes scurry back and forth, oblivious to his presence. Gable seems smaller now than ever could have been possible, considering the height and the breadth of his achievements. It is incongruous, putting this physical being together with those grand things accomplished. But, of course, no one in sports is a giant forever.

In work, Gable was always something larger than his actual size—and that may be the way to describe the best of wrestling, really. The best wrestler, once upon the mat, can become something bigger and more special than he is in any other walk of his life. The thing about wrestling that constantly surprises, no matter how much or how long you hang around the sport, is that most of the people at its highest levels would never look imposing were you to see them in jeans and a sweatshirt, toting books across campus. They are mortal young men until they wrestle, and then they are gods, small gods of surprise and tumult.

With Gable, the opposite is true. Gable is now the myth who only becomes human when seen in person, and in person he is diminished. There is no elegant way to put it: The man is beat up. Oh, that's still Gable in there. The passion in his voice when he speaks is as true as it ever was. The mind is sharp, questioning. He spends a tremendous amount of his time doing, not watching. When they talk about Gable, as they almost always do around Iowa, they understand that they are speaking of a man who has lived his entire life going forward.

But even Dan Gable can only go so hard for so long; and now, here in the early freeze of 2005, you can see the payback. Gable used to blow into a room with the same sense of urgency that he did everything in his life. He is the guy who, as a college student, ran across campus at Iowa State University not for the exercise (though he didn't mind that) but because walking took too long. Now he comes into the Iowa City High athletic building on those crutches, taking his time along frozen sidewalks; he peers through the windows into the gymnasium, sees the crowd on one side behind the scorer's table, and disappears around to the other side, the far side, a less crowded area where he can move deliberately without holding anybody up or getting trampled.

He is living these days inside a body that he has routinely brutalized for years and that now has had enough, and has decided to kick *his* ass for a while. He is an uncomplaining mass of ache. Gable has endured tremendous pain over the years from recurring knee ailments that he didn't want to treat surgically while competing, from deteriorating hips that required replacing while he was still actively coaching the Hawkeyes, and now from this second round of replacements on those hips. He has undergone eighteen operations of various size and scope. He doesn't want to go through surgery anymore because, he says, he doesn't react well to it, nor to the medications that usually accompany a procedure.

"I've wrestled a lot of years" is how Gable explains his current battered state. "I wrestled competitions, and then I wrestled when I coached, because that was the way I wanted to coach, by wrestling. Even the past several years I've been out there on the mat. It's really only been the past few months that I haven't wrestled." He pauses for a short second, as if to double-check and make sure the school principal isn't sitting a row behind him. "Well, I've wrestled a couple of times," he adds, "but not as much." With two hip replacements, it strikes one as a reasonable enough compromise.

Gable created the template for an approach to successful wrestling that is as daunting as it has been successful. Even his admiring contemporaries, back when he was going through high school undefeated and through college with a single loss, found his ways borderline crazy—the three and four workout sessions per day, driving home from long runs with the windows rolled up and the car heater at full blast, losing something like sixty pounds per week (the same eight or ten pounds a day, every day) by the sheer volume and repetition of his conditioning and strength sessions. Even now, sitting here in the gym, body and legs angled in such a way as to relieve the postsurgical pressure on his hip, Gable radiates energy. He speaks quickly and definitively about everything connected with the sport, from its popularity in Iowa through to its tenuous status on college campuses—and as he speaks, there is never a question of authority or validity.

From his roots in Waterloo, Gable became the towering figure of the pursuit, and in so doing, he changed wrestling in his home state forever. It went from a parochial interest to a full-blown mania, and the fact that Gable wasn't the first great wrestler Iowa had ever produced became largely irrelevant over time. He was the name. He was the brand. Wrestling was Gable; ergo, wrestling was Iowa. It will forever be impossible to overstate his influence; even as Gable lives through his own bizarre reality on that front, he cannot—and won't—deny the essential truth of that. What Gable says, goes.

"If you go back over the last one hundred years, there are two things about Iowa that everybody's going to know," Gable says. "The first is that it's an agricultural state, with the crops and the corn production. Everyone knows about the farms. Iowa feeds the world. People everywhere have heard of Iowa for that. And the other thing that people know about Iowa—and maybe not the masses, but in so many different corners of the world—is the wrestling. Not so much the local wrestling, but the Olympic-level, world-class wrestling, on that level. The gold-medal winners and all that. In places where they wrestle, places like Mongolia and Uzbekistan, they have heard of Iowa for that one thing alone. It's kind of unique. And it's because we've been good at it for a hundred years."

It is also because Gable is an Iowan. Anybody who knows anything about wrestling, and a whole host of people who know almost nothing about it, can summon up that last name—Gable—if nothing else. It has to do with the Olympics, certainly, and his unparalleled work at the 1972 Munich Games, taking the gold medal without losing a match. It has even more to do with his standing as perhaps the greatest wrestling coach ever. Put that together with his globetrotting work in stumping for the sport—for the relevance, that is, of a lonely, time-consuming and long-term-reward endeavor in an age of quick-fix fun—and the shadow is cast both long and wide. Cael Sanderson, who followed Gable's footsteps in attending Iowa State University to wrestle, actually went undefeated through college, and became an Olympic and world champion. He still barely makes a dent in the cast-iron armor of the Gable legend.

Gable himself appears to move easily through his own notoriety. He shows up all over the place, conducts clinics, makes dinner speeches, holds motivational seminars, acts as a consultant, appears at fund-raisers. He is constantly in the public eye and well aware, even hyper-aware, of his legacy. When I mention how hard it must be for Jim Zalesky to have followed him at Iowa, and how even now people look upon him as the coach and indeed still address him as "Coach Gable," Gable immediately replies, "Well, when you won 21 Big Ten titles in 21 years, and 15 national titles, and were close for just about every one of the others . . ." In other words, he hasn't forgotten about his own record—and given that record, who is to be surprised that it is hard for Zalesky to follow the Gable legend? Indeed, there are some close to Gable who aren't even sure he particularly wants Zalesky to succeed, even though it is impossible to conceive of anyone ever cutting into the Gable record. But one thing is unquestioned: Iowa wrestling is in a full upheaval. Dan Gable may not be able to do anything about that.

It has been said that this is one of the great senior classes of wrestlers in Iowa high school history. It may ultimately prove to be the greatest class ever, in terms of awards, trophies and championships collected. How many members of this class are committed to the storied program that Gable built? "Iowa only got one of those guys," Gable replies immediately. "Only one of the major ones. We've got Morningstar coming to Iowa, and there's [Mitch] Mueller going to Iowa State, and this one, Kyle Anson, he's going up to Northern Iowa. And then those other three"—Jay and Dan, plus Joey Slaton—"went out to Brands."

And about that? "It's the coach's decision," Gable says after a momentary hesitation. "That is really for the coach to decide, and I try to stay away from that as far as I can."

When it comes time to discuss the bleeding of Iowa talent out to programs that are not his, Jim Zalesky will at first, and very politely, wonder out loud how good that talent really is. He will compliment Jay and Dan while explaining that there is a huge difference between high school success and collegiate, Olympic, world-class success. There are lots of wonderful high school athletes, in all sports, who discover only after the fact that their finest moments have already passed, and the trick for any good college coach is to get it right more often than not when betting on the ones who have greatness ahead. "I think it's a good group—for Iowa," Zalesky says of the seniors. "But you aren't going to know how good they are until four, five years down the road in college. The big thing in college is, you've still got to have the hunger. You've still got to have the goals. Sometimes high school kids that are real successful, when they get to college, they get more pressure on 'em because they've been so successful, and sometimes they don't have the same desire as maybe a guy who was only a one- or two-time state champion but still wants to prove himself, that hasn't won all the national awards and everything."

Zalesky sounds perfectly sincere, yet this is almost incomprehensible as a rationale. Jay Borschel, Dan LeClere and Joey Slaton are three of the winningest wrestlers in the history of the state. And while high school success alone is no guarantee of great college careers, what barometer would strike Zalesky as more reliable? When Tom Brands and his assistant coaches got ready to build the program at Virginia Tech, they targeted five wrestlers in Iowa: Jay, Dan, Joey, Mitch Mueller and Ryan Morningstar. "Not because they're from Iowa, but because they're the best kids in the country," Brands says. "They may not be ranked No. 1 in the nation in their weight class, but they've got the work ethic and the attitude and the roots. I knew that they were a fit."

Brands never wavered in his pursuit of those five. He lost Mueller quickly, when Mitch informed him that he wanted to stay close to home, but continued to recruit Morningstar to the bitter end even after it became apparent that Iowa was Ryan's choice and that Ryan's father, Scott, was brokering a scholarship with Zalesky. Every coaching instinct told Brands that he could contend on a national scale, produce NCAA All-Americans, with this group. What did he see that Jim Zalesky didn't? What, after all, could be more important to a program like Zalesky's than to keep together the homegrown kids, the ones who would bring their own rooting sections as they carried on the traditions of wrestling at Iowa?

And also: What could be worse than watching them go?

Gable understands what Zalesky has to deal with, including the fact that there isn't always a place, either in terms of opportunity or scholarship money, for every wrestler whom a coach would like to consider. Still, when asked about the net effect of having Iowa wrestlers leave Iowa to attend college, Gable replies simply, "It hurts," and for the first time in the conversation he doesn't seem to have anything to add. It's tempting to conclude that Gable is biting his tongue, trying not to snap back on Zalesky, his own assistant and basically the man Gable chose—over Brands—to carry on the program when he stepped down.

The book on the recruiting situation, from those outside the program, is that Zalesky is under such constant pressure to win—and win now—that he could not afford to wait for this particular crop. He had to harvest early, a year or two before the super-seniors were to come out. And so he went and spent a major portion of his available scholarship money on "imported" talent, freshmen like Charlie Falck (born in Iowa, but attended high school in Minnesota), Mark Perry (New Jersey) and Alex Tsirtsis (Indiana). When it came around to the fall of 2004 and the heavy recruiting period, Zalesky already had many of his weight classes filled with wrestlers who, while indisputably of high caliber, might not ultimately prove out as capably on the NCAA level as some of the Iowa-grown kids. The coach was almost out of scholarship money and guaranteed slots. His options were shrinking by the day.

It also is worth acknowledging that Jim Zalesky is in the most impossible coaching situation in the history of impossible coaching situations, taking over from a man whose achievements so tower above both the school and the sport as to put just about everything around them into eclipse. Gable's departure as coach in the late 1990s shook the state and the program's most ardent followers to their foundations. He had given Iowa something to be proud of beyond record corn crops and the world's greatest cereal manufacturing plant, and the reward for that was godhead status.

Some coaches would've been sharp enough operators to have passed up the job, banking on the age-old sports adage that it's always better to be the guy who comes *after* the guy who follows the legend. But Zalesky and Brands had spent most of 1997, Gable's last year as coach, in an unspoken but widely acknowledged competition to be the one tapped by Gable to continue his work. There were hints that it would be Zalesky, as Gable turned to his top assistant several times over the course of the 1996–97 season to take over, especially when Gable had to undergo the first of his hip surgeries. Brands had Gable's fire but not necessarily his finesse; he could exhort with the best of them, but one of Gable's great and underappreciated gifts was his ability to inspire and challenge his wrestlers without having them hate his guts. Brands was as explosive as Zalesky could be aloof, but Zalesky, cool sometimes to the point of appearing devoid of charisma, demonstrated tremendous grace under pressure. Ultimately, the job was his. Brands reluctantly accepted his consolation prize: Top assistant to Zalesky, and chief recruiter.

By the winter of 2005, Zalesky's head-coaching career included three NCAA and three Big Ten team titles and a whole host of individual conference and national champion wrestlers, and it was nowhere near enough. The Hawks had not won a national crown in five years, and the suspicion was beginning to creep in that Zalesky had done his best work in the first three seasons of his career, 1998, 1999 and 2000, when he basically was coaching athletes chosen and recruited by Gable to fit Gable's system. On his own, Zalesky, with Brands out front on recruiting, getting people fired up to join the Hawkeyes, had signed some tremendous wrestlers but hadn't been able to put together a team capable of winning it all—and second-place finishes at the NCAAs, no matter how spectacularly they were achieved nor from what difficulties forged, no longer were acceptable at Iowa. Gable had set the bar that high. Jim Zalesky needed to start winning it all again.

All of which makes it such a puzzle that the fall of 2004 did not become one of the great talent hauls in University of Iowa wrestling history. Here was this senior class, so loaded with elite Division I potential, and every one of the kids had grown up thinking that someday, maybe, if they hit the weights and ran wind sprints until they puked, if they wrestled so hard and so long that they (like the great Gable was said so often to have done) might have to drag themselves by their arms across the wrestling room at the end of practice—if they did all that, then maybe they would one day find themselves in the yellow-and-black of Iowa.

So Zalesky had that going for him, the way he did every year at recruiting time when it came down to the kids from the home state. But this year was different. Zalesky was the same competent coach he had always been, but he no longer had Brands in his corner. Brands had finally followed his ambition and secured a job trying to turn Virginia Tech's straggling program into a national power. He was pure energy and desire, and he electrified high school kids with his pitch. After Tom Brands came to people's houses for a visit, half the *parents* were ready to sign up for six a.m. workouts. He communicated his passion for the sport with sincerity; he could actually make you understand that it was a life-and-death proposition to him, no matter how ridiculous that seems when put down on paper. With his enthusiasm and his clearly defined direction, he had Jay hooked early on. He had such an admirer in Dan that the day Brands announced he was leaving for Virginia Tech, Dan remembers thinking to himself, "Iowa may not happen."

What Dan was beginning to realize (and Jay was to discover as well) was that his interest in Iowa had had significantly to do with Brands, whom both boys saw as the next best thing to wrestling for Gable. When Dan watched the Hawkeyes in action, he was always struck by the way that Brands did most of the coaching, and almost all of the yelling. "Zalesky looked more like an organizer than the coach—he kind of stood off to the side," Dan says. "It was like he was running the business. Brands is just totally different. I had to think about it, and I thought that Brands was the coach who could help me get to the next level, make me better. If Brands was still at Iowa, I'd be at Iowa."

Even if there had been no scholarship money to give?

"If Brands was at Iowa," Dan repeats, "I'd be there."

So Brands was going to make that much difference to the LeCleres and the Borschels of the world, and Zalesky had to find a way to bridge that gap. He had assets, the greatest of which was the fact that his school was still the object of the boys' wrestling dreams. The Hawkeye wrestling room was still the place where Gable might at any time wander through, stopping to help a wrestler with his positioning or tell a freshman about something he'd seen on tape that might reveal an area to be strengthened. It was a place rich enough in its history and strong enough in its current incarnation to attract the high-profile likes of Falck and Tsirtsis and heavyweight Matt Fields, the former state champion from North Cedar High. It was the ultimate home-field advantage. But it alone wasn't enough.

It was going to be up to Zalesky to make the seniors understand how much he wanted them in Iowa City, how huge a mistake they'd be making by even considering someplace else. He was going to have to overcome his own natural personality, the distance that he tended to put between himself and the parents and athletes whom he met. And, of course, the whole world of wrestlers is not created equal: Zalesky was going to have to decide how many of the seniors he really cared about going after.

The answer: Almost none, until it was too late.

While Brands did everything but burrow a tunnel between Blacksburg, Virginia, and the homes of the coveted seniors of eastern Iowa, Jim Zalesky went the other way. He played coy. He may actually have been as indifferent as he appeared. He made a visit to the Borschels' home and had dinner, yet it was Jay and his parents who found themselves constantly having to restart the conversation. "We couldn't get him to talk," Jim Borschel says. Zalesky hosted Dan at Iowa City on an official NCAA visit, but because Dan's parents were not in attendance, he couldn't talk about scholarship money. "So he told me he'd call our house in a couple days and tell my dad the whole financial deal," Dan says. "He didn't call again for weeks, and Brands was after us constantly." This was the same Dan LeClere who had openly stated in the newspapers the year before that Iowa was the place he wanted to be. He had played his hand. Now, it seemed, Zalesky was revealing cards of his own.

Brands, in the meantime, launched a power play. Believing that his Iowa recruits would have a hard time contemplating life so far from home, he persuaded Jay, Dan and Joey to visit the Blacksburg campus together, on the same weekend. It was the Virginia trip that sealed the deal. Brands radiated enthusiasm and promise. Brands already had scored a huge coup, pulling down perhaps the most coveted recruit in the nation, a Michigan highschooler named Brent Metcalf. This group, this incoming squad, was going to be remembered forever as having put Virginia Tech on the map as a wrestling power. They would be remembered here. Just listen to Brands. It was a done deal.

Even after seeing the comparatively meager workout facilities, even after being reminded that there is no crowd for wrestling quite like an Iowa crowd, Jay was so convinced of what he wanted to do that he verbally committed to Brands on the spot. Brands, along with Jim and Carol, encouraged Jay to take a few days and think it over; but there was no need. Jay had found the coach who would believe in him enough to want to make him a champion, and who would challenge him enough to help him get there. There was no point in carrying on a charade for public-relations purposes. Zalesky had brought nothing to the table. He hinted at no real enthusiasm. He looked like a man who needed to be somewhere else. As much as Jay thrived on doubt, he didn't want it coming from his own coach.

In the end, Jay didn't even make an official visit to the Iowa campus where he had grown up as a wrestling entity. Joey Slaton, the same. Kyle Anson and Mitch Mueller both felt they received barely a glance from Zalesky, though they were attending high schools a short distance from the Iowa campus in Iowa City. Mueller wound up going to Iowa State, while Anson committed to Northern Iowa and coach Brad Penrith, another Gable acolyte. The LeCleres realized early on that because Zalesky already had locked up so many of the spots, there really wasn't going to be much room for Dan to go in and make an impact.

Zalesky, consumed with the real-time pressure of his job at Iowa, had gambled his scholarship money on the athletes already in uniform and then spent the 2004–05 season using many of those wrestlers far sooner, and to far greater reliance, than Iowa traditionally did with its incoming freshmen, many of whom were "redshirted" that first year, meaning they would practice but not compete in dual matches, thus preserving all four years of their NCAA eligibility. And the fissures in the program with regard to the local talent had slowly become more evident, highlighted, perhaps, by the decision of Mack Reiter two years earlier to bypass the Hawkeyes and Zalesky in favor of the University of Minnesota, a four-time state champion blowing out of Iowa completely. Two years later, Reiter, after sitting out a redshirt season, was on his way to being named the Big Ten Conference's Freshman of the Year. Meanwhile, several publications had listed Iowa State University's recruiting class as the strongest in the nation, with Tom Brand and his ground-floor project at Virginia Tech ranked second. Iowa? Somewhere around 10th in the country. Even allowing for the vagaries of such a ranking system, it was looking ugly.

Borschel. LeClere. Anson. Mueller. Slaton. Morningstar. Six utterly superior high school seniors, in the most wrestling-crazy state of them all, with built-in fan bases and followings that would accompany them throughout their college careers at Iowa. Three went to Tom Brands and the NCAA wrestling equivalent of a start-up company at Virginia Tech. Only one, Ryan Morningstar, was bound for Iowa. Morningstar was undeniably a great talent, and Zalesky later added Chad Beatty, a strong upper-weight wrestler from Class 1A Wilton. Yet the unshakable feeling in the eastern half of the state was that Zalesky had just blown the greatest opportunity of his coaching career to lock down home-grown, conversation-stimulating, fan-invigorating talent for years to come.

To Zalesky, this represented only the latest in a series of difficulties that trace, however ironically, to Gable's massive success. Gable didn't simply produce winners; he produced future coaches. Those coaches have now begun to fan out and make their influence felt in places other than Iowa City; it was a former Gable assistant, J. Robinson, who scored a major coup by bringing Mack Reiter to Robinson's program at the University of Minnesota. "There's probably ten, eleven head coaches that have Iowa connections, and there's a lot of assistants out there, too," Zalesky says. "That just makes it tougher sometimes to get the job done. It's a bunch of [Gable's] guys who have been through this program and know what we do, and know what it takes to win."

But Zalesky sees other factors behind the mass defection. He sees young athletes who cannot look past today, who cannot look past guaranteed scholarship money at whatever school happens to be offering it or who can't abide the idea of not having a varsity position waiting for them when they arrive. He sees high school seniors, like Jay and Dan, who spent so much of their waking lives hanging around the Iowa program that there is no longer anything exciting about the notion of going to college there. He is slightly dismayed at the tunnel vision of some of the local high school wrestlers who consider his program only, and would leave the state before wrestling for, say, Iowa State University or the University of Northern Iowa.

And it goes beyond that for Zalesky, himself a former Iowa high school star alongside his talented brother Lennie, who went on to become the head coach at the University of California at Davis. What Jim Zalesky sees, when he looks at the landscape of Iowa wrestling, with its history and its traditions and its astonishing unspoken pressures, is a generation of kids who, in the end, might just want to get the hell out of the state to get some peace and quiet.

"Especially with this group," Zalesky says, sitting behind his desk in the wrestling office at Carver-Hawkeye Arena. "The parents were so involved, you know, the dads and the parents. And a lot of times I wonder: Are these kids just wanting to get away from their dads, too? You know? 'Cause the dads are always on 'em, telling 'em what to do, and to me that could get old. My dad never said a word to us. He never said a word edgewise. He was in the stands cheering for us, but he never told us when to work out, or go get your workout in, or do this or do that, or watch your diet, or anything else. It was all on your own: You want to do it, fine, I'll support you, but you're doing it. Anymore, you see so many parents involved. And that's where recruiting gets tough, and some of this stuff I think gets a lot tougher than it used to be."

When Zalesky's take on what has transpired is relayed to Jay, he appears momentarily to be at a loss for words—but he finds them. "He never gave me any reason to come," Jay finally replies. "He came to our house, and there was just . . . nothing. He never made me feel like he wanted me to be there." Likewise, Dan is adamant that the only place he ever dreamed about attending was Iowa, but Zalesky never made him feel there was a place for him in the wrestling room. It was the same for all the boys, for Joey and Mitch and Ryan and Kyle. They all wanted the dream of competing for Gable at Iowa, and after they saw Gable go away they found a suitable replacement in Tom Brands; and then Brands left, too, and suddenly they were facing the reality that the Iowa program they'd wanted all their lives was not, strictly speaking, the one placed before them now.

Dan Gable listens to the recent history, and he takes in the news coolly. Gable knows it was a swing and a miss for Zalesky, but he clearly feels constrained in what he can say. Still, Gable won't skirt the issue, nor will he excuse Zalesky for his role in it. When it is suggested that one of the obvious problems this year was the lack of scholarship money to give to people like Jay and Dan, Gable agrees, but then adds, "If you're running low on money, you've got to make wrestlers feel wanted in other ways. There are other reasons to wrestle at Iowa besides money." (True enough: Both Jay and Dan, as well as their parents, say they never would have let money be the issue if either wrestler had wanted to go to work for Zalesky.)

How about the notion that there were too many wrestlers already in the Iowa program at certain weights? "Oh, sure," Gable says. "But when you've got good prospects . . . I sometimes had three and four kids coming in at about the same weight, but then we'd spread them out after they got to college. There's a process there. Where you're wrestling in high school, weight-wise, isn't necessarily where you're going to wrestle in college. I never minded having a bunch of guys in the same general weight area—something always seemed to work out."

Gable reflects for a moment. "I will bet you that those guys all wanted to go to Iowa," he says. He may not know how right he really is.

"I blame Iowa," Pablo Ubasa says of the current mess—sincerely, not bitterly. Ubasa, a former Iowa walk-on, obviously loves the program, and he thinks of Gable as a surrogate father. These seniors, in turn, are his kids, the first group of wrestlers Pablo ever had, when he was beginning his own fledgling coaching career. He envisioned watching them take their skills to the NCAA level right in front of the home folks. Even if it was over-reaching to think there could be a place on the Hawkeyes' roster for every member of this super-senior group, Ubasa didn't mind daydreaming. After all, it wasn't merely what he wanted for the wrestlers; it was, uniformly, what they wanted for themselves. They worked through the years with that goal in mind, and as they got better and better the dream became just a little more vivid. When they hit high school, it became obvious that this was no ordinary class of wrestlers, not some bizarre geographical fluke. Iowa's tradition-bound, time-honored system of putting little wrestlers into the long pipeline had produced, this time, a staggering collection of talent all within a 70-mile radius—and all right under the nose of the University of Iowa's wrestling program.

"They saw these guys coming up through the ranks," Pablo says. "You could see them coming for years. But then when they got to senior year there's no room for them. I mean, Iowa has to do what it has to do. I understand all of that. But I know these guys all wanted to be there."

Under Gable, Pablo never got beyond second string as a

wrestler, but his love of the sport was obvious to the coach, and it was no surprise when Ubasa formed the Little Hawks Wrestling Team in Iowa City. In fact, Gable not only encouraged Ubasa, who still stops by the coach's household on a drop-in-anytime basis, but Gable arranged for Ubasa's fledgling outfit to conduct its workouts at Carver-Hawkeye Arena, a practice that continues today. Talk about your dream scenarios: Pablo could take his little wrestlers out to the big floor and let them think their thoughts, walking around in their size extra-small yellow-and-black Hawk-eyes T-shirts. It was a dream made concrete by the two decades of winning under Gable, years in which Iowa was reimagined as a household word connected with the sport—the generic, default expression of wrestling. And all of that is fascinating not in the least because it is the other large-scale state school, Iowa State University, that brought forth the two best collegiate wrestlers of all time, Gable and Sanderson. Yet all of Iowa State's success in those years cannot overpower the history; Gable's relocating to Iowa City to coach, and dominate with his teams, swung the balance to the Hawkeyes seemingly forever. Even this past fall, when Dan LeClere began to see very clearly that his lifelong dream of wrestling for Iowa was dissolving before him, he couldn't bring himself to consider Iowa State, not even with the great success the program has enjoyed under head coach Bobby Douglas. Dan was raised to believe that college wrestling meant the University of Iowa. In the end, he just couldn't shake that notion, not even in order to remain in the state.

Not so for Gable, of course, but that was then. After Gable sliced through high school at Waterloo West, he took off for Ames and Iowa State. It's part of the reason that Gable's emotional reach in the state extends so wide and so deep; he brought global acclaim to both of Iowa's largest universities, first starring as a two-time national champion wrestler and Olympic gold medal-ist at Iowa State and then coaching the University of Iowa to its greatest heights ever. That is one hell of a neat trick, which may explain why nobody else has ever done it.

Gable wrestled to an undefeated high school record and three state titles. He blasted through college undefeated, all the way up to the final match of his NCAA career. And then Gable suffered one of the greatest upsets of all time.

It may be the most notorious defeat in the history of Iowa, because Dan Gable didn't lose. He went 181-0 through high school and nearly four full years of college, up to the 1970 NCAA championship match at 142 pounds. There couldn't have been a worse experience for a wrestler in the United States during that time than seeing Gable's name on his side of the bracket. It was like being a .240 left-handed hitter, glancing at the day's pitching probables and seeing KOUFAX written on the other lineup card. People were beaten by Gable before they ever got on the mat, the way kids in high school now were beaten before they stepped in with Dan or Jay. People had been losing to him for so many years that it was considered a victory by most opponents to simply stay in the match for a while, not to get pinned in the first period or lose by more than a dozen or so points. Anything you got against Gable was the greatest achievement, because Dan Gable was the best in the world. He was going to become the first wrestler in recorded U.S. history to go all the way through high school and college without a defeat. One hundred eighty-one and zero.

The single most amazing thing about Gable is that he became larger in defeat than most people do in a lifetime of victories. By the relatively simple act of losing the final wrestling match of his college career, Gable now appears, however unwillingly, to have conferred some sort of greater wisdom upon generations of Iowa wrestlers. He made people in the sport understand that no one is ever safe—that even with maximum work, superior conditioning and brilliant technique, there is no such thing as a sure thing. Gable had everything on his side in his final NCAA match except the wrestler at the other edge of the mat, a man named Larry Owings, one of the only men in Gable's final years who even dared to believe he could beat Gable. Owings's 13–11 victory was stunning on every front, but perhaps most of all for the fact that, down near the finish, Gable appeared not to understand he was trailing. He didn't recognize that Owings's final takedown had earned him extra "predicament" points for driving Gable's shoulders close to the mat, putting Gable in the predicament of being perilously close to a pin. It wasn't until only 17 seconds remained that the value of those points became clear for Iowa to see. They're still getting over the shock.

People now train their guts out, like Dan Gable did, in the hope of someday being great wrestlers—and yet they seem to know that, like Gable did, they can suffer defeat despite having given themselves every possible chance to win. It's not really so purely fatalistic a thought, of course; for people like Jay and Dan, even a close match is taken as a loss—they're that serious. But one of the most memorable lessons of Gable, incongruous as it sounds when placed in the context of his entire glorious career, is that even winners lose.

Stranger still, perhaps, Jay will probably wrestle longer than did his idol. Gable retired from the sport at age 23, a time when he easily could have spent another half-dozen years or more in international competitions and likely dominating those competitions.

For years, Gable's mother, Kate, had found herself almost physically unable to watch her son compete, and that is saying something. She was a woman tough enough to have pulled herself and her family through any number of difficult situations. She had somehow survived the unfathomable discovery, just after Dan's sophomore year in high school, that the Gables' daughter, Diane, had been raped, murdered and mutilated by a neighbor boy while the rest of the family was on a fishing trip. (It remains a chapter in Dan's life that he rarely discusses, although by now it is a well-known and oft-recited fact that it was Dan who insisted the Gables not sell the house in Waterloo, in which his older sister was killed.)

Kate was every bit as hard-willed as one would expect a parent of Dan Gable to be. In fact, she was the one who drove to Ames about a week after Gable's shocking defeat by Larry Owings, got in her son's face and told him that his time of self-pity was over, that it was time to get back after it. Eventually, though, even Kate finally had enough.

"It was so hard on her," Gable says now, sitting in the friendly warm City High gym, the sounds of wrestling surrounding him. "She'd go stand outside the room when I wrestled, just go out there in the foyer. She'd come back to the door every now and then to look through the glass, but she couldn't stay in the gym."

Gable pauses. "This sport, it's a heart-wrenching sport," he finally says. "I'll be at the State Tournament this month, and I will guarantee you that I'll choke up. I'll feel so good for the guy who is winning the championship—he's earned it, it's finally there. But then you look over at the wrestler he just beat to win it, and that guy is crushed. And I just choke up for that guy. It's personal."

The perspective is so clear. Iowa has been touched by the single sport, which rooted itself in so many family histories, defined so many towns. "It was these strong boys coming off the farms and into the wrestling rooms," Gable says, "although, when I was coaching, I had great wrestlers who came from all over—it wasn't just farmers. But no matter who it is, it's a personal sport. This is beyond playing a game with a ball. There are no teammates to help you when you're on the mat. It's physical. It's close. It's independence. And if that's your flesh and blood out there, it can get real . . ." Gable trails off. "It can hurt a lot," he finishes.

It finally hurt his mom too much, as the sport filled up Gable's heart and broke down his body. It charged a toll. At the time of his "retirement," Dan appeared to go out on top. He had not let the NCAA defeat define him; he had become an Olympic champion, a world champion, the most acclaimed athlete of his time. Kate Gable probably never dreamed that Dan would go on wrestling even as a coach, that he would continue working out and pushing himself to absurd limits and then beyond—that he would retire as an officially sanctioned wrestler, but never as a competitive one. She probably didn't guess at the time that he would ultimately suit up and take the mat against entire legions of elite wrestlers to come, coaching them in the process of pounding himself physically, hurling himself at them like waves against the breakers.

All that Kate knew, at the time, was that she was tired of going out in the hallway. And that really is why the great Gable walked away—which, not to put too fine a point on it, he is not actually able to do at this moment. No, at this moment the crutches will have to suffice, and after his left hip gets to feeling better, they'll take him in for his nineteenth surgery, and at some point one assumes that Gable will hit the road again, making what amounts to a modern-day whistle-stop tour on behalf of wrestling, trying to prop up the sport on the college campuses where it lies dying under layers of bureaucracy and paperwork, trying to keep it alive in the minds and budgets of cost-conscious athletic directors and lawsuit-timid university presidents. He will travel the continent and beyond, from country to country. He won't stop. He may never stop.

Inside the Iowa City High School gym, the dual match is over. City High has easily beaten Doug Streicher's Linn-Mar team, which looks like it is one solid year away from being competitive with the elites, with promising kids who still need to figure out how it's done at the highest levels. Jay has won in his usual overwhelming manner, as has Kyle Anson for City High, which means the people who came to watch these two stars have gotten their money's worth. Dan Gable sees Jay and Kyle for what they are: two terrific young wrestlers who no longer have Iowa in their futures. There was a time when he would have had more to say about that.

Instead, this time, he gets up to go. He proceeds cautiously but with no hesitation. "I think I still have a lot of getting around left," Gable says simply, and he smiles and pulls on his fur-lined cap, and he gets ready to hobble out into the cold. Moving forward again.

CHAPTER 9

Same Team

If Jay has no doubts about his decision to forgo college in Iowa, he also harbors few illusions about the fallout. "They probably think we're traitors," he says calmly, sitting on the bed in his room, fiddling with his guitar. "I figured that."

He figures it, perhaps, because he has already long anticipated it, because it is how Jay processes things lately, through an outsider's eye. At the far edge of his high school career he has slowly begun pulling away. He keeps his cadre of friends at a purposely small level; when I ask him with whom he stays in touch, he thinks for a minute and then says, "I call Mitch or Kyle sometimes." Otherwise, goes to practice, hangs out with Jillian, gets something to eat, and hits the health club for a nighttime session with the weights. School itself has become almost an afterthought; Jay is breezing through his senior classes with minimal effort. He can't tell if he is being rewarded for years of fairly decent work in the classroom or if his senior courses are just too easy. Either way, he is investing little time there. "Conserving," he says with a smile. He will use any leftover energy, after all. He is insulating, getting himself inside a protective cover as he hunkers down to focus on the only thing that is currently before him, this sports thing, his definition of himself. Winning can be as lonely as anything else. Jay wants to get on with it.

Of course, there is no real "they" out there. Iowa may have been collectively taken aback at the sight of three top wrestlers all heading off to Virginia Tech together, and there certainly were those who immediately set about explaining why Jim Zalesky didn't actually need those three in his program. There were some who questioned the wisdom of Jay in choosing to leave the state for college when he just as easily could have found a way to stay home. But, anecdotally at least, those people constitute a minority. The mass of wrestling fans in Iowa will be rooting for Jay and Dan to become four-timers at State three weeks from now, because the majority of wrestling fans in Iowa truly love the sport. And because it is theirs.

The Mississippi Valley Conference tournament, held in Dubuque the first week in February, is technically the beginning of the run-up to the State Tournament. In reality, it is nothing so much as a reunion. Because of their teams' affiliations with the conference, Jay's closest friends are here: Kyle Anson, Mitch Mueller, Joey Slaton. It's a celebration of some of the finest wrestling around, one they all have come to look forward to. It is a great time. Assuming, of course, that nobody screws up.

For four years they've been coming together at this time, the one time of year when the families know they'll see each other all at once. A while back, Jim and Carol Borschel and the other parents managed to sit down for a pre-tournament breakfast together, and they've been coming together ever since, trading stories about the year and catching up with the people who have been their running partners throughout this entire thing. It is the breakfast that cements the relationship for another year, a year of phone calls and cross-checking on rumors and asking questions of one another and spilling the bad news, such as the time in the boys' sophomore seasons when Jim had to call Bill Anson and tell him sadly, "It looks like it's going to be 125."

Jim meant 125 pounds, and what that signified, in all likelihood, was the sharp end of the stick for one boy or another. As freshmen, Jay had won his state title at 103 pounds, Kyle at 119. Now both boys were slotted in at 125, the product of their growth, their coaches' decisions and their teams' needs. Since both of them competed in Class 3A, something had to give. You can only do so much to get around the realities of the sport you're in.

This was exactly the situation that the families had tried to avoid—and had done a remarkable job of avoiding, for so long. As the boys grew through Pablo Ubasa's club years, they began to deliberately fan out, wrestling away from each other, each hoping to become a state champion in his own right, each knowing that his fiercest possible competition for a crown might well come from within his closed little circle of friends. Jay's only high school defeat, as a ninth-grader, had come at the hands of Joey Slaton, right here at the conference tournament, in the finals, in front of God and everybody else. But Jay avenged the defeat on the biggest stage, pinning Joey in the 103-pound finals at the State Tournament, winning that first title while denying Joey his. It was both a wonderful moment and a wrenching one. It was impossible not to want to win—these were wrestlers, not trainers—but Jim Borschel hoped never to see it again. In a national competition, sure; that was unavoidable sometimes. But not here in Iowa. Not with one of the good guys having to take the body blow.

Jim didn't get his wish. It was 125 pounds for both Jay and Kyle in their sophomore years, and the season played out with a sort of inevitability about it. The two wrestlers clearly were at the top of the talent pile; it was a sure track to a confrontation. Jay won that confrontation at the conference and district tournaments, and then, at State, the draw put Jay and Kyle on the same side of the bracket, meaning they would meet in the semifinals. When Jay won that match as well, on the way to his second championship, it marked the death of the dream for his friend. Had he not run into Jay in 2003, Kyle might well have been going for four-timer history himself in the winter of 2005.

Informed by that experience, Pablo Ubasa's little crew began branching out in earnest. Jay shot up to 152 pounds for his junior year. Mitch Mueller went to 135 pounds, Joey Slaton to 119. Kyle stayed at 125. Dan LeClere and Ryan Morningstar, wrestling in Class 1A, were two weight-classes apart. They all had finally figured out how to go around each other completely. Now all they needed to do was make that strategy pay off—and, in their junior years, in one glorious week at the Barn, they did. Everybody won; it was state titles across the board. It had all worked out. Once.

On this day in Dubuque, it is time to come together once more, to see if everybody can somehow make it all work again. And though Carol Borschel good-naturedly covers her ears and begins singing in an attempt to avoid the breakfast-table conversation, the truth is that this is the last meal, the last get-together before the last State Tournament. The families, individually and as a group of friends, struggle to accept that reality. As Bill Anson puts it, "Our kids have spent more years wrestling on their own than with teams," and what he means is that the families have spent so many summers traveling around in their minivans and their SUVs, finding freestyle tournaments in Oklahoma and camps in Minnesota and nationals in North Dakota and everything else, that to come to the end of the line now seems almost incomprehensible. They have forged their friendship not just in the wrestling room at Pablo's club, but out on the road, in family restaurants and no-frills motels. The boys have become young men out there, learning how to win and, occasionally, to lose; and now the older men and their wives sit around a table in a restaurant, perhaps a mile from the site of the final conference championship, vaguely shocked at the passage of time and the realization that, after all this, it hasn't quite worked out as planned. Certainly it has not worked out as they might have dreamed it. None of their sons, after all, will be wrestling for the University of Iowa, the way it always seemed that it would happen in the days of those Little Hawkeyes.

"Weird how it wound up going," says Jim, and the others around the table nod thoughtfully. It isn't just the kids who dream.

When the families arrive at the gymnasium, they part quickly, the way they always do, and head for their respective cheering sections to see if they can bring home a winner. Down on the floor, their boys have long since been with their teams, getting loose for a full day of work. It will be three or four or five matches, depending upon how things go. The smart money says three.

Jay is now in his zone. It is his time of year. All anyone can do, from here on in, is wrestle against him, and that is all he wants. Just off the mats at Hempstead High, he appears utterly relaxed, now clowning with his teammates in the bleachers, now putting in the earbuds of his MP3 player to listen to music, waiting for the opening bracket of the 171-pound class to finally come around. He gets to go to work today. At this point, that is all he asks. Jay has been here before. Nobody has to tell him how to deal.

When the time for his first match comes, Jay is ready, bouncing back and forth on the balls of his feet, his calf muscles flexing with each movement, upper body loose, arms already well into rehearsals of his moves. Jay switches from court jester to mat dominator with a speed that even his super-senior buddies find severe; you could get whiplash watching him morph from the guy with the tattered T-shirt and the squirt-bottle of water into the three-time state champ who is chasing his Iowa immortality. He is on the mat for barely 30 seconds before pinning his first opponent, a complete testament to the kind of day it is going to be for Jay. The early rounds aren't always pretty for a top seed, anyway, wrestling against kids who haven't yet arrived in terms of match readiness, but Jay is especially focused here. He has his friends here today, his wrestling peers. These are the people for whom he had better bring out his best game to show off. Jay wouldn't have it any other way.

Up on the catwalk above the action, Kevin McCauley smiles and shakes his head in light wonder. This is what McCauley stayed around for as a coach, to see days like these, with Jay on the floor tearing a tournament bracket inside out and all the people on hand to witness just how magnificent a wrestler he can be. Jay is so quick for his size and almost impossible to turn over, and yet he prefers an offensive match. He likes to attack, not to stand still. He loves the action of wrestling, not the nuance—but he gets them both, understands them almost instinctively. And Kevin, one of the people who helped develop that instinct in Jay, has stayed around to see the best of it.

As a coach, McCauley had one foot out the door at the end of last season. A former Linn-Mar wrestler himself, Kevin looked up one day and realized that, nearing age 40, he had spent more than a dozen years shaping and caring for other people's kids in the wrestling room—that in addition to his duties for the school district, working with at-risk students. Now, with two young children and a third on the way, Kevin's own family needed his attention. His wife was a nurse, and she had discovered that she could receive full-time pay and benefits by working two full-shift details at the hospital through the weekends, essentially cramming a week's work into two long days. Wrestling, of course, happens on weekends. Kevin had to make a call. He decided that it was time for him to be home on Saturdays and Sundays so that his wife could effectively be with their children the other five days of the week. But his wife wouldn't agree.

"She told me to wait one more year," Kevin says. "She told me to stay on for Jay's senior year. I mean, it's a once-in-a-lifetime thing for me, a four-time state champion from your own school. She said, 'Stay with Jay through this.'"

It had worked for Jay in the past, to be surrounded by the same group of coaches each day, to go to Des Moines each February with the same supporting cast. He even insisted on the same pre-match warm-up for the championships, and Kevin was a part of that warm-up—part of the whole week, really. It was as if Kevin needed to be around in order for Jay to succeed, and Kevin's wife understood that. McCauley himself didn't need the motivation. He could put off the end of his coaching life for one more year if it meant seeing how this thing played out.

Now, looking down from the catwalk, watching Jay take apart his first victim of the day, Kevin sees a young wrestler who has come remarkably close to realizing every last bit of his potential on the high school stage. This next act may well be Linn-Mar's finest as a wrestling program. "She was right," Kevin suddenly says. "It was worth staying."

Just down the way, Jim Borschel leans against the wall, watching the first match play itself out. Carol logs her usual miles, flitting back and forth, seemingly putting herself through her son's moves as he executes them down on the mat in real time. It isn't merely blowing off steam; this is how Carol works her way through every one of the Linn-Mar wrestlers' matches. What Carol doesn't yet know, not that it would matter too terribly, is that this isn't going to be one of those nervous kinds of days, at least not where Jay is concerned. Jay has spent a winter watching teams run away from him, but the beauty of the tournaments is that there really is no place to run. He finally has the wrestling world right where he wants it.

In the conference semifinal, Jay draws Dan Chmelar from Hempstead, the one whose coach wisely but anticlimactically moved him away from Jay during the teams' dual meet a few weeks ago in this gym. "Jay didn't forget that," Jim says; and now, with a conference's worth of fans looking on, the opportunity is there to do something about it.

When the referee fires a shrill blast through his whistle to begin the match, Jay closes on Chmelar immediately. There is no hesitation. There is no question about choosing a proper angle. Jay is on the Hempstead wrestler almost before the ref can get out of the way. He comes in furiously, attacking in one fluid motion, from one side of the center circle to suddenly having two hands on his opponent and taking him down. It takes maybe four seconds from whistle to takedown. This is a professional hit.

Jay doesn't just want to beat Chmelar; he wants to send a message. He actually has nothing against the boy he is wrestling; it's the coach he's trying to communicate with by pummeling the kid on the mat. Three times, Jay takes down Chmelar and thrashes him around, only to allow him eventually to come back to his feet so that Jay can do it again. It becomes evident in the first minute of the match that Jay can probably record a pin if he wants to, but this is different. He is operating on another level entirely. This is a statement.

Again Chmelar gets to his feet, and again Jay savages him to the mat with a combination of attacks. He meets Chmelar chest-to-chest and throws him down using only his upper body. He dives low to spear one of Chmelar's legs at about the shin, then jacks the wrestler up onto one foot and shoulder-drives him face-down. Jay doesn't quit until midway through the second period, by which time he has piled up a 19–3 lead and the official stops the match on a technical fall.

Dan LeClere *(front)* prepares to break his opponent's hand-lock and stand up for a one-point escape, a routine that shockingly failed him in the semifinals of the 2005 state championships. *(Courtesy of The Predicament)*

The pressure to win four state titles is clear: Anything short of four-timer status, and Jay *(left)* and Dan will be remembered as merely very good wrestlers, of which Iowa has produced thousands. *(Courtesy of The Predicament)*

Jay Borschel's success as a wrestler lay significantly in the fact that he was rarely out of position. He's actually in control here, using his arms to pull his opponent up by the legs and expose his shoulders to the mat.

All photographs courtesy of the author unless noted otherwise.

Carol, Jay, Jim and
Hannah Borschel
on graduation
day. Jay's decision
to leave Iowa to
attend college
sparked its share
of controversy.
*(Courtesy of the
Borschel family)*

Jay Borschel *(top wrestler)* begins
the process of wrenching his
opponent's arms behind his
back—the "chicken wing"
maneuver. *(Courtesy of The
Predicament)*

Jay's interest in the media
lay mostly in what they
would say or write about
him that he could use as
motivational fuel. Here
he is interviewed after
a tournament his senior
year. *(Courtesy of the
Borschel family)*

Dan and his girlfriend, Leah. Dan's decision to attend Virginia Tech meant a temporary separation for the couple before he returned to Iowa in the fall of 2006.

When Dan isn't wrestling, the fiercely competitive relationship between Dan and his father, Doug, dissolves as they bond to coach younger brother Nick, who also has state-title hopes.

Particularly in weekend tournaments and duals, Dan *(left)* wastes little time and energy on the mat—he goes for the pin as soon as he can possibly get it. *(Courtesy of The Predicament)*

The LeClere family farm, winter 2005. "Look, nobody farms for fun," Doug LeClere says; the value is in the land, not in any single crop.

Nick LeClere *(wrestling on top)* uses a near-fall to pile up points and keep himself alive at the 2005 state championships after a season of injury and illness.

Mike, Nick, Chris, Dan, Mary and Doug LeClere in the gymnasium at North-Linn High School, where every male in the family has wrestled at some time or another.

Dan Gable, the benchmark for greatness in the sport in Iowa, was among those disturbed by the fact that three of the state's top high-schoolers chose Virginia Tech for college. Here he levers his Greek opponent, Stephanos Ioannidis, to canvas during their 150-pound wrestling bout in the 1972 Olympics. Gable eventually won the gold medal in the lightweight (150 pound) class. *(AP Photo)*

North-Linn Assistant Coach Larry Henderson *(seated at left)* and Head Coach Brad Bridgewater watch Dan intently from the side of the mat at the 2005 state championships.

Tom Brands *(third from left)* did everything but burrow a tunnel from Blacksburg, Virginia, to the homes of Dan, Jay and Joey Slaton during the recruiting process.

Motto adorning the wall in the Linn-Mar wrestling room, a program run by Dan Gable acolyte Doug Streicher.

Don't worry over what other people are thinking about you. They're too busy worrying over what you are thinking about them.

Alongside the words of doubt that Jay liked to tape to the walls of his bedroom for motivation, he also included this nugget from Tom Brands.

The North-Linn wrestling room, a 26-by-46 converted garage, used to house the school's shop classes.

For most of four decades, the only way to see the state wrestling tournament was inside the creaky old building affectionately known as the Barn.

Finals night, the only night of the session for which reserved tickets are required, routinely sells out months in advance.

Eleven thousand people fill the arena, in groups of 100 or 200 from every small town that sent one of the 632 wrestlers that made State. The tournament is easily the largest of its kind in the United States.

Jay looks to the rafters of the Barn during the 2005 state championships, where his family has watched what may be the final match of his high school career. *(Courtesy of The Predicament)*

Dan carried the weight of representing both his community and his wrestling family into the final match of his high school career. Here he celebrates his win on the shoulders of Coach Brad Bridgewater with his father, Doug, ready to congratulate his son. *(Courtesy of The Predicament)*

Upstairs, Jim watches the match dispassionately, more interested in how Jay is wrestling than in settling any scores. "You kind of saw that one coming," Jim says. In the end, he was right in what he'd shouted at Hass back in January: You can't hide from Jay forever.

It is that kind of a day, straight down the line. Kyle blows through his opposition and into the finals at 125, and there he pins his opponent—another conference crown for him, and this one with an exclamation point. In the finals at 130 pounds, Joey Slaton pushes his season record to 33-0 with a technical fall over the fourth-ranked wrestler in the state at his weight class, and it is a thorough and proficient sort of dismantling of a quality opponent. At 135, Mitch Mueller scraps his way past Zach McKray, his longtime nemesis, a wonderful wrestler from his crosstown rival school in Iowa City. For two years, Mitch and Zach, two of the top athletes in their class, have been engaging in great battles on the mat, and this one is no exception. It ends 6–4 in Mitch's favor, and it's easily the most electrifying match of the day. Virtually everyone assumes that it is a preview of the finals to occur again at the district competition—and, later on, in the Barn itself.

Later, Jay's 18–3 drubbing of Robbie Kramer, the No. 3–ranked wrestler in the state at 171 pounds, underscores the gap between Jay and the field of competitors trying to overtake him. Though Kramer is obviously a solid wrestler, Jay takes him down repeatedly and pushes him around on the mat; it is all Kramer can do to avoid being pinned. "He's on a mission," Jim says, a touch of admiration in his voice. God, how Jim loves to watch Jay do his thing.

After the final presentations, the boys all stand out on the mat together, their parents off nearby. There is still time for a few more photographs, for the albums. Jay and Kyle will stand together for one shot, their reward for having been named the most valuable wrestlers of the tournament. Not far away, Doug Streicher has room for a few smiles himself: While Jay was pounding his way through his bracket, Streicher has seen progress elsewhere as well. At 103 pounds, Matt McDonough has had a great day, winning his way to the finals before being cut down by the top-ranked wrestler in the state. At the far end of a long season of work, Matty suddenly looks like a wrestler worthy of consideration for the Barn.

But that is yet to come. Here in the middle of the mat, it is the seniors, together again, smiling one more time, already looking forward to their final charge at those state championships. There is Jay, and Mitch, and Kyle, and Joey. The weights have been spaced; the competition has been thinned. They are four returning state champions, and the chance is there to go out on a glorious note. It all sets up so perfectly. It seems strange that, in the end, one of them will leave Des Moines in tatters.

CHAPTER 10

The Youth Movement

They start them young.

Young and stupid, preferably, or at least young and as empty-headed as possible. The point, either way, is for them to receive the information that may someday lead to their knowing what to do at championship time. They start kids wrestling as soon as they safely can be tossed onto a mat, and they set them in competitions at around age 5. You can be a kindergartner on the weekdays and a wrestling maniac on the weekends, and, in fact, that's pretty much the preferred option. It certainly worked for Dan and Jay.

Perhaps it also will work for one of the hundreds of kids scattered about the North-Linn gymnasium on a Sunday morning, surrounded by hundreds of parents, each slightly more out of control than the last.

With the addition of the middle school at North-Linn a few years back, it is now possible for the students of the area to drive to the same address for six years before heading off to college, which, the statistics suggest, is exactly what they'll do. In the early years of the new millennium, Iowa's reported literacy rate of 99 percent was the highest in the nation, and its 85 percent high school graduation rate was far above the national average of 71 percent. Iowa led the nation in the per-capita obtaining of college undergraduate degrees, and it was said to be the No. 2 book-reading state in the union. The kids show up for school and actually learn something, and they have the diplomas to show for it.

Today, Sunday, driving along the snow-blanketed roads that lead to Troy Mills and eventually over to the high school, it is a jolt to come upon a North-Linn parking lot that is absolutely packed, to the point of cars hanging off its edges and parked at all sorts of squeeze-in angles. This is the day of the Little Lynx tournament, a chance for kids from kindergarten through eighth grade to come find competition against like-minded wrestlers. These are the ones who'd rather be inside sweating and grunting than outside in the snow—or, at the very least, the children of parents who feel that way.

Inside the North-Linn gymnasium, the world is a blur of color and action and—to put it plainly—the piercing shrieks of the wrestling moms and dads. They say that you haven't experienced the mania of wrestling until you have seen its littlest practitioners in action, but it's their parents who put on the real show. There is probably a doctoral thesis in practical psychology to be written about the gyrations and dramatics of the parents, some of whom have come to the conclusion that their 5-year-olds are on track for college scholarships despite their never having wrestled competitively before. They dream of kids who are young and know a few moves but who will become, in time, quicker, stronger, more tolerant of pain. They will become technicians of the sport. They will see two moves ahead of their opponents, like a great shortstop anticipating where a ground ball is likely to be placed by a particular hitter.

The parents see these little tykes in the gym on Sunday and

they do not see children wrestling on a mat. They see, many of them, a future.

In Iowa, the kids' clubs provide the foundation for almost every top-level wrestler at every class of high school competition. They get the boys early and teach them right, a formula that would come as no surprise to anyone who has ever run a Little League baseball team or a CYO basketball league. Sports are about traditions handed down and coaching secrets passed along early, and it happens that in Iowa, wrestling matters exactly enough for it to be treated with the same care and ultimate respect as the major sports might be anywhere else. The kids clubs are no joke. They are the seeds of serious sport, and they will someday sprout champions.

The gym is overflowing with wrestlers and coaches and families, the older athletes working not only on behalf of their schools but as a sort of living example of what the young wrestlers might aspire to. Dan is at the scorers' tables, a volunteer along with most of his teammates in Brad Bridgewater's army of free labor (this is a moneymaker for the wrestling program, after all). Dan sits in a gray long-sleeve T-shirt with crimson lettering on the back—Virginia Tech colors, basically—that declares, HARD WORK SOLVES EVERYTHING. It is a slogan often attributed to Dan Gable, though there is no record of Gable actually having said it. But Gable did once remark, "After wrestling, everything else in life is easy," which is a slogan you'll find tacked into the cinder-block wall of Doug Streicher's office at Linn-Mar High. And Gable did mean that. It has been noted, repeatedly, that the day after he won his gold medal at the Munich Olympics in 1972, he ran four miles. Maybe the T-shirt is right.

The North-Linn gym is just ablaze with activity. It is a four-ring circus of little scramblers and more accomplished eighth-graders taking their turns, the mats stretched from wall to wall across the basket-ball court. Doug stands in the midst of things, helping to run the tournament. Every so often he excuses himself from behind an official's table to jog out to the mat and instruct one of the Little Lynx wrestlers on a particular move.

For Doug, this is the only place to be today. Dan and his team-mates have a rare idle Sunday, specifically so they can make this tournament go off smoothly, but Doug would be here regardless. He may well keep on showing up here for years after all his boys are done wrestling at North-Linn. The reason is simple: Doug's history is pretty much the history of wrestling at the school.

He grew up on the farm in Coggon, attended high school here. He will live his days here, and he will die here. He wrestled on the high school team and reached the State Tournament in 1978, a year when North-Linn sent six wrestlers to Des Moines. It was a huge breakthrough for the program, a watershed event still often mentioned among the wrestling faithful. When Doug got to Des Moines that February, he felt that he had truly ac-complished something—and considering the odds against reach-ing the tourney, he had. But it was when he saw the wrestlers that went on to become champions, saw the dedication and the heart and drive—and, of course, the jubilation in victory when it came—that he decided his kids should someday be able to expe-rience that for themselves.

And so he is driven now, driven as the father of wrestlers in a way that his colleague, assistant coach Larry Henderson, says Doug never was as a wrestler himself. Oh, he worked hard; no-body reaches the State Tournament in Iowa without working his ass off most of the time, almost every day of the week, for months on end. But that intensity of effort was nothing compared with the white-hot approach to wrestling that Doug takes now. He is completely focused on the goal for his sons, and for North-Linn's other wrestlers. He wants it for his family and for the team. He wants it for the town. He ought to feel right at home in this gym, on this day, around these little kids with the big parents and their bigger dreams. He is one of them.

Near the end of the morning session, the noise inside the building suddenly recedes. Near the middle of the mats, the action has stopped. As people mill around, a wrestler lies on the mat, unmoving. "Let's give them some room, folks," intones a voice through the public-address system.

To spend even a few minutes around wrestling is to understand one of its immutable laws: People get hurt. This isn't by accident; it's by design. A wrestler's job is to inflict immense amounts of pain and suffering on his opponent, often by means that look outright cruel but in fact are the products of months of hard labor spent in perfecting the technical aspects of the sport. Wrestling is about power and leverage, and it is very clean in its consistent reward of the person who uses both to his greatest advantage. To quote from the book *Coaching Wrestling Successfully*, "A clean, hard-fought wrestling match is the most honest of athletic contests. There are no technological interventions, no teammates to blame, no panel of judges to bias the score. In wrestling, you compete or you quit. No alibis. I like that." Dan Gable wrote that. And the unspoken addendum is this: If you should quit, be it mentally or physically, and you are still at some indeterminate midpoint of an actual match, then you stand roughly a 99 percent chance of getting hurt.

Then again, you can also get hurt because you landed wrong, or because the other guy put you in an arm-bar or a chicken-wing, one of the holds designed to apply pain, or because your shoulder got wrenched over the wrong way, or your knee got yanked in one direction while the rest of you was headed in another, or, hell, pretty much anything. Injuries come even to the most prepared wrestler, which makes it all the more noteworthy that so many of the great super-seniors of 2005—Jay, Dan, Joey and the rest—have gone through entire careers without significant physical setbacks. The odds would have suggested otherwise.

On this day, the wrestler is prone, face-up on the mat, his match in a timeout. Those who are following the action wait expectantly for things to resume. That's the norm with injured wrestlers, especially in mid-match: head off to the side, grab some quick treatment (a wad of tissue stuffed up the nose, a bandage wrapped around the scrape), and continue with enthusiasm. Only this time the boy doesn't get up. The people attending to him are afraid to move him too vigorously, and after a few moments it becomes apparent that somebody has gone to call the paramedics. Not long after, an ambulance pulls up outside, and two men walk inside, pushing a gurney. Moving carefully, they slip a brace around the boy's neck, and then place him on the gurney to wheel him out.

The spectators make room at the doors for the boy to be removed; otherwise, things continue apace. As the boy had been attended to, wrestlers on three other mats had kept up their matches, finishing the day's early-session schedule. The tournament won't stop for injury.

"That's the first time I've seen someone taken out to an ambulance during a wrestling tournament," says a woman standing against one of the painted cinder-block walls of the gymnasium. Blond and youngish, she has driven her two grade-school sons from the town of Solon, perhaps an hour away, to get them some tournament experience.

She thinks for a moment. "Oh," she adds. "Except for last week."

Last week, the woman was working the concession stand at Solon's own weekend tournament when a young boy, an eighth-grader, maybe, came out of the gymnasium toward the hallway. Fresh off a frustrating defeat, he had stalked away from the mat and headed for the exits, trying to find an outlet for his rage. The gymnasium door had a window of thin rectangular placements of wired glass, through which generations of rubberneckers have peered in an effort to find out who was winning the basketball game inside. For the enraged wrestler, it would do as a target.

His punch packed some power. The force of the blow smashed his hand through the window of the door, sent glass spilling to the ground. Slowly, suddenly calmer, the boy pulled away a bloody arm with glass shards stuck into it at various angles. The entire transaction took maybe three seconds.

"And it was a freezing day, and so now they have to wheel him out to the ambulance like this," says the woman, holding her arm in an L-shape, her fist pointed toward the gymnasium's ceiling lights. "He's like that, all cut up, headed into the freezing air. And he can't wrestle no more. His season's over right then and there."

She smiles thinly. "I'll bet his parents were wild about that. So, anyway, I guess it's been two weeks in a row, now."

The wrestling room is not a place for the meek. For those who happen to be a tad queasy of stomach, the choices are pretty much limited to the following: (1) get over it; or (2) get out. There are mothers by the dozens in the stands on this day at North-Linn, but they're not like other mothers. Whether they wear it anywhere else in their lives, upon entering this place they don a mask of toughness that will enable them to get through a day of competition that, while it doesn't always deliver something horrifying or graphic, holds out at least the promise of such dark wonders with astonishing regularity. And the mothers—the parents, that is—understand about wrestling. There isn't a mother of a wrestler who is going to confuse a weekend tournament with summer camp at Boys State. The parents know the score. But they were also raised with wrestling if they're from Iowa, or at least raised with the recognition that wrestling matters and will be accepted, glory and gore alike.

When I told Jeff Nelson, the father of Linn-Mar wrestler Jason Nelson, that I was headed off to the Little Lynx tourney at North-Linn, he smiled and nodded knowingly. "Talk to me when you get back," he said. "I'll be interested to hear how you think it went."

As it happens, Jeff knows exactly how it will go. Years of working the junior programs (at Linn-Mar, it's the Little Lions Club) have honed his understanding of the parent-fan to a fine edge. Nelson has seen the best and the worst of it; his view is that it gets grimier as you go down the age brackets to the wee ones. "They're just new to the whole thing," Jeff says, "and they can't figure out how to handle it. You'll see all sorts of things at the tournaments that you almost never see as the kids get older— parents fighting and all that. Wait till you see ours." The Little Lion tournament, he means, referring to a massive wrestler hoe-down the day before Valentine's Day.

On this day at North-Linn, things are proceeding routinely, which is to say the place is all but on fire. Parents, who technically can be classified as "coaches" and thus allowed match access in these kinds of nonteam settings, pack themselves down around the four mats. They crowd into corners and the spaces by the far walls of the gym in order to close a few more feet of distance between themselves and the wrestlers on the mat at whom they are screeching their ever-changing sets of instructions. "I never actually hear any of that when I'm wrestling," Dan says, but of course he has trained himself to filter out most of the noise and words during a match. At the younger ages, the kids hear everything. They just can't help it.

At the north end of the gym, on the farthest mat, two wrestlers are finishing a match that had started even, but now is beginning to spiral out of control. One youngster has established his dominance and is asserting it. The other kid is . . . well, he's 5 years old, is what he is. He wrestles the way you'd expect a 5-year-old to wrestle, awkwardly and with nine parts effort to one part technique. Today, he has drawn an opponent who clearly understands a ton about wrestling for his age, and who is applying the kinds of arm-bars and leg holds that kids in the second and third grade are normally just beginning to learn.

Result: The less accomplished boy is getting goat-roped right out there in the middle of the mat. It happens at every level of wrestling, up to and including those titans of the college sport and beyond. People have gone all the way to the Olympics and then gotten smashed flat. It fails to qualify as breaking news.

As the kid soldiers on, struggling against a clearly superior opponent, his mother is sprawled on all fours near the edge of the mat, pounding fists into the foam rubber and demanding a better performance. What begins as basic encouragement soon dissolves into a rant. "You do this now, Jed!" comes the scream across the room. "You break him down right now! You DO it right now!" At one point, the boy glances over into his corner, as if to try to quell the verbal riot, but her screams just keep coming. In fact, as the match wears on, and it becomes increasingly apparent that this little kid is going to lose his little-kid match to the other little kid, it is the mother who flames out of control, the invective coming hotter and harder with the passing of the seconds—and finally it is the boy himself who decides enough is enough.

Still in the throes of the match, he suddenly grabs one knee with both hands and begins shouting, and the referee quickly calls an injury timeout in order to give the boy a moment to figure out whether or not he can continue.

The little fellow wants off the mat, and so should anybody watching the thing. Even understanding the basics of wrestling, there is nothing remotely fun about seeing a kindergartner get whipped by some other kindergartner. It's sort of like watching the class bully push somebody around for a while, then walk off with all the juice boxes and the lunch money. But the sight of this 5-year-old out there, grabbing his knee and hollering, sends his mother into another orbit entirely. Facial expressions change. Veins bulge. In the same instant that the boy goes down with his injury, her shrieking reaches a level that wouldn't normally seem possible in public company.

"Get up!" she bellows. "You get up right now! You shake it off and you get back in there right now!"

The boy begins to cry, lightly at first and then in great heaving sobs. His shoulders shake from the effort. But his mother makes no move to come across the mat and console him. Instead, this parent waits with clenched teeth for the boy to do as he was told.

"Get . . . up . . . NOW," she yells to the boy—a threat as much as an instruction. It seems as though there ought to be some unbearable tension in the air; it's almost like a family drama being played out in public. Instead, the mood around the mat is mostly nonchalant. As the shouts and the volume increase, the other parents gathered in the gymnasium do not so much as raise an eyebrow. Clearly, they are veterans of the youth wrestling scene.

"Well, you gotta toughen them up," says the man next to me. "They might as well learn it now if they're going to stay in the sport. You don't just quit because something's bothering you. You gotta work it out for yourself."

In fact, this boy has worked it out for himself: No way is he going back out there to get ground into a pulp. He signals the referee that he cannot continue, and, mercifully, the match is called due to injury default. The other little boy, the one with the advanced skills, has his arms raised in victory and then walks quietly off the mat. The other child, the one who could not continue, seems to sense that relief has come, and although he is still crying, he can't wait to run back to his corner for some consolation.

He doesn't get far. As he approaches her, his mother throws him a disgusted look. He continues to approach her, crying. She turns on her heels and leaves before he can catch up.

About ten minutes after this surreal scene plays out, I come back into the noisy gymnasium at North-Linn from having been in the locker room, and I scan the bleachers for the boy. He isn't in the place where he had been before, the place where he sat crying after trying to follow his mother into the stands, but after a minute or two I locate him.

Two rows down. Sprawled across his mother's lap. Laughing and giggling as she tickles his stomach and rubs his head while she speaks pleasantly with the people around her, reaching into her cooler to give her son a drink and a snack—so he can be ready for his next match.

It is a day full of rangy brunettes and bottle blondes, and dads in overalls, and dads in sweat suits, and people wearing the bright purple-and-gold colors of a school like Alburnett or the red-and-silver of North-Linn. A high-schooler walks past, wearing a tie-dyed T-shirt that says on the front WRESTLING and on the back WHAT MEN DO DURING BOYS' BASKETBALL SEASON. It is a life of slogans, the wrestling life. It is a life of sayings and remembrances and little tiny pieces of information, like envelope scraps upon which have been scrawled the sundry secrets of success.

In the center of things stands Doug LeClere, and the man looks about as happy as he can be. In truth, Doug likes wrestling in general more than he cares for the kid programs anymore, though he used to be heavily involved in their organization and coaching. He is getting older, and his time is precious, and he hit a point a while back at which he just couldn't see the value in trying to teach wrestling to kids who were not of an age to get serious about it. The kids come in and goof around and laugh and mostly play, and while Doug can't find a thing wrong with laughter or play, he doesn't have the time to administer and oversee it. He wants to teach the sport to people who care deeply about learning it. "Too many people treat Little Lynx like day care," he says with a sigh. "Let me tell you: Wrestling ain't day care."

You hear this over and over from the coaches, the wrestlers, the parents, the officials: It is impossible to be a nice wrestler and win. The only winning wrestler is a whirling sonofabitch with a few good moves. There is no quality of mercy no matter the age of the opponents. To the uninitiated, this Sunday constitutes four mats' worth of child abuse: Little wrestlers running around getting their headgear yanked off, trying to talk tough in the hallways before a match and then bawling in defeat after it, parents themselves occasionally behaving at sub-toddler level. To those in the sport, it is simply basic training.

And it isn't all bad. There are scenes of genuine parental support, the good stuff. A few minutes after the ghastly matside episode with the mother and her young son, a disconsolate boy sits with his father in the tired-looking North-Linn locker room adjacent to the gym. The boy, 9 years old, has just lost a match that would have given him first place in his weight class, and he is taking it hard. His father will have none of it. "You're right there!" he tells his son enthusiastically. "You wrestled into the finals and you're one or two moves from winning. That's all you are!" The boy continues to stare down at the marble floor, unwilling to meet his father's gaze. The man moves closer, puts one hand on the boy's shoulder. "You've got to remember how good you really are," he says gently. "You've got to remember how close you came today. So you can use it next time."

Next time. You bet. There will be a next time for most of these wrestlers, whether they want one or not. This is the futures market, after all. You plant the crop as early as you can.

CHAPTER 11

Dealing with It

The wrestlers lie stretched out on the floor of the school hallway, trying to absorb the cold of the tiles into their overheated bodies. Brad Bridgewater has put his team through another ballbuster of a workout, which was the plan all along—three brutal days in the early part of this week, followed by a couple of tapering workouts leading up to the Class 1A sectional meet in Starmont. This is it: Early February, not even three weeks left before State. Bridgewater is pushing hard, trying to get the kids ready. On this day, even Dan looks like he's gassed; he moves ever so slowly through the hallways, searching for something to drink, knowing that the smart move is to drink only so much, to keep his weight close to the number. Dan is enjoying this season, relatively speaking, because he has mastered the art of keeping close to his wrestling weight of 140 pounds. He went through all of last year at this same weight while his body was growing, and he was hungry most of the time. This winter, he's got it pegged and isn't growing too fiercely anymore; his body is close to where it wants to be.

Even here at the end of the season, though, pounds matter. Just last week, Nick enraged his father by failing to make his 145-

pound weight for a meet in which Nick, still injured, wasn't going to wrestle anyway. It sounds warped, but the truth is that you don't forfeit until you have to—and in this case, had Nick managed to make his weight, he actually could have earned a forfeit from the other team, which didn't have anybody to send out at his class. Nick could have earned the Lynx six points just by walking out there. Doug was so furious that he sent Nick home from the North-Linn gym, but his act didn't play well with Mary. After stewing for a while, Mary finally walked by Doug and said tersely, "I think I'll go see how Nick is doing." "You do that," Doug replied with a dismissive wave, and his wife took off for the farm. Not too much later, Doug was slightly startled to hear his and Mary's names being called out over the public-address system to come to the mat and begin the ceremonies. It was Seniors and Parents Night at North-Linn. "Not the best turn of events," Doug says.

Now, though, it is Nick's time to round himself into shape, to see if he can yet pull something out of a year so abbreviated by his injuries that Dan jokes, "You can't really even call it a season." Limited in matches and held out of several practices as a precaution, Nick has wrestled barely a dozen times officially—yet both his brother and his teammate Tyler believe he can get it together and go all the way to State. Their faith is shared by the North-Linn wrestling community; Nick is a LeClere. Surely, before it's all over, he'll find a way.

Burkle, for his part, is right on his weight, and Ryan Mulnix was actually under his number at one point early this week, which is unusual coming out of a weekend in which a good meal might actually have been consumed. Of course, even the good meal can be harder to pull off than it looks. After one recent Saturday tournament, the North-Linn team and parents gathered at a country steakhouse, where Nick, to his dismay, left almost all of his meal on the plate. His stomach had shrunk so much that he'd gotten full just eating his salad and a roll.

But Nick and Tyler and Ryan are the sideshows. Dan is the show, not that it's necessarily something he wants. He's not a public speaker. He wastes no time or energy attempting to explain himself on the subject of wrestling or his dreams. Dan deals with his local fame mostly by not dealing with it, because that is easier and less draining. It is his way of forestalling the inevitable, which is that he is going to feel tremendous pressure to get things done at the Barn in Des Moines. His own pressure. The community's pressure. His dad's, of course. It is a pressure which he has slowly come to accept as a part of him, even as he sees now that it can be a quietly destructive force.

That part took a while, and it took his mom to see it, and looking back, both Mary and Doug wonder a little bit why they didn't spot it sooner. When Michael, their firstborn, abruptly quit wrestling after his sophomore year in high school, it never occurred to either of his parents to go seeking some complicated, deep-rooted reason why. Quitting wrestling makes sense on so many levels that it's a wonder more kids don't wind up doing it. Sometimes it feels like the hardest thing in the world just to do what's required to go out and have a match.

When Doug looked at his oldest son, he saw not a boy battling a clinical depression but simply a boy who had lost his love for the sport. Mike had made it clear that he didn't want to wrestle anymore, and his father just couldn't wrap his mind around that concept no matter how hard he tried, and so he stopped considering it. It was the thing that Doug loved perhaps more than any other in the world. It was, in so many ways, his way of pulling his family together and keeping it there. The LeCleres wrestle. That's life.

The rest is mostly work. Doug puts in his hours at the fire station, and Mary works at a long-term medical-care facility in Cedar Rapids, and Doug pulls extra duty inspecting acreage for the American Soil Conservation Service, and while all of that is continuously happening, there is the farm itself, 200 acres that Doug purchased from his father in 1991, connected to several hundred other acres of LeClere land around Coggon. The farm is hot, hard work in summer and cold, hard work in winter, and it never ends, and only sometimes does it turn a profit, and without government assistance it might never. The family farm is going down the tubes, not just in Iowa but everywhere else. Corporations have moved onto even the most sacred of old family grounds in Iowa, buying up land, controlling crop production, and thus more or less controlling the prices of things. In decades past it was not uncommon for family farms to run into the thousands of acres; by 2000, the average family farm in Iowa covered 339 acres, and the economic crises of the 1980s had effectively put an end to the notion of family farming as a sustainable business.

"That's why I'm a fireman," Doug says. "I don't farm for the profit; I farm for the net worth. I'm not doing it because I like it. I'm doing it for the land. It's a nonrenewable resource.

"Look," he adds, "nobody farms for fun."

But that isn't completely true, at least not for Doug. For most of his life, growing up in Coggon on the family land, he has had a relationship with the growth cycle of the earth; he enjoys the process of putting things in the ground and watching them come up. It is a business he knows and a tradition he respectfully carries on, and even if none of his four sons comes to adulthood with a desire to carry on farming, Doug won't mind, so long as they don't sell the land. They can lease it. They can sharecrop it. He just doesn't want them to sell it, because once it's gone, it's gone forever.

And the family farmer, getting screwed from every angle? "That's life. Nobody cares," Doug replies, neither his eyes nor his voice betraying any real bitterness. "They really don't. As long as the East Coast and the West Coast can have their steaks and pay twenty bucks a pop, they don't care."

So Doug plugs along with his corn and his beans and some hay, and he keeps cattle year 'round, but nobody is kidding himself about the deal. Like many other family farmers, Doug and Mary work their other jobs to actually pay for things. The farm has become almost impractical. It is for reasons of family and tradition that the LeCleres held on.

"And anyway," Doug says, folding a wrestling roster in his hands, "working at a fire station doesn't bother me. Farming doesn't get to me. What gets to me is this sport. We're just so serious about it—we want to excel at it. And it really bothers me when we don't, or when we lose, because it's the thing we do. It's right in the middle of everything we do in our family."

Thus, it made no sense to Doug that his son Michael would leave the family business. It took a long time to get over it. It took years, even after the rest of the story came out, about the depression that Mike had been dealing with, and suffering from, in that time. And it took Mary figuring out even that. Mary was the one who put the warning signs together. She could see that her son was continuing to excel in school, pull down great grades. He obviously still had friends. He was seldom, if ever, in trouble. But he had begun to change, especially around the farmhouse. Mike was suddenly moody, and quite a lot of the time. He began to rebel. He got annoyed so easily. He stopped smiling.

To Doug, the changes were subtle enough to warrant no further remarks. Doug had been a handful as a teenager himself. He still considers it a wonder that he and his father, Dwight, have remained so close (and, in fact, living almost side-by-side on separate family parcels) after all these years. It was Mary who finally got Michael to a doctor and received the diagnosis, and Mary who went on and got the antidepressants and always made sure the prescription was filled. Now she sees her oldest son happy and thriving, a young man who traveled the country as a student-manager of the Iowa football team, an artistic person who studied

English and was considering a future in architecture. It is the Michael she knew all along, and the one who left her briefly during those high school years, before she realized what it was that was dragging him down. Doug and Michael patched things up a while back. "I never want Mike to feel out of the loop because he quit the sport," Doug says now. "I told him, 'It's hard, if you love the sport, to wrestle, but if you don't like it, you just can't do it and ever do yourself or your team justice.'"

When it happened to Dan, he was almost exactly as old as Mike, a tenth-grader trying to deal with everything at once. His body was growing, and as a wrestler he was actively fighting that. He already had won a state championship, and the clamor for a repeat already was building around North-Linn. And, as Mary knows now, there was a family tendency toward depression.

Looking in upon the wrestling life, it's amazing that more kids aren't in full-blown depressions themselves. Theirs is a months-long experiment in deprivation: of food; of hydration sometimes; of normal interaction; of life-sustaining forces. The typical high school wrestler in Iowa has several days each week in which he drives in for predawn workouts, attends class all day and then meets in the wrestling room after school for another full-on practice. On Saturdays, the families pile into their weather-beaten vans and their pickups and head off for some dot on the map or other, leaving early in the morning, getting back home late that night. "They might only really see the sun once a week," Doug says. To Doug, that's just the wrestling life. To anyone else, it's a season-long visit to purgatory.

It was certainly eating up Dan in tenth grade, or at least something was, but this time Mary was prepared. She knew Dan's friends, because in a school district like North-Linn, everybody pretty much knows everybody, and of course they all know the LeCleres. The friends said that Dan had been acting a little strange at school, not quite himself. When her second-oldest son came home one day and announced that he wasn't sure whether he wanted to continue wrestling, she thought she had a pretty good idea of what to do. She sat down with Dan and asked him if he would like to visit with the doctor who had seen Mike, and to her mild surprise, Dan, an independent sort to begin with, said that he thought that would be okay. He has been taking Zoloft ever since, and he has ceased seeing his depression as an issue.

What seemingly began as an isolated thing—a wrestler dealing with what could be construed as the natural fallout of his severe lifestyle at such a young age—was eventually understood to be a family dynamic. For the LeCleres, depression became a real deal, a very plain chemical imbalance that affected just about everyone in the family to some extent or other. Mary began a regimen of antidepressants, and had them prescribed for her husband, who had always been prone to strong mood swings and who sometimes had trouble getting his temper under control. When Nick got old enough to wrestle on the high school team, she started him, too—enough to get through the season with his good nature intact. Doug, though he admits to dealing with "mild highs and extreme lows," still doesn't sound convinced of the effectiveness of the drugs, but he takes them. And Dan, though reluctant to speak when I ask him about the subject, finally simply replies, "I was never a person to run away from something." Mary knows the rest of the story: Her son found a roadblock to success in his depression; he dealt with it; the road opened up for him again. In her own reserved way, Mary is abundantly proud of herself and her kids for being unafraid to take on the kind of thing that, in a small town, could produce more than its share of coffee-shop gossip.

Mary has even summoned up her nerve a few times to mention to the parents of other wrestlers that they might be dealing with the same kind of effect in their households. The others mostly don't listen—it is, after all, a wrestling life—and Mary finds it re-

markable that so many people are so unwilling to admit the possibility of needing some help. "It's a medical condition," she says with
her usual candor. "The more you learn about it, the less there is to
worry about. But I can't get very many people to understand."

She is a wrestling mom; she has seen her share of boys suffering. But there is physical pain and then there is the other kind, and
for the life of her, Mary cannot understand her friends' kids being
made to suffer that way, when she sees an alternative right in front
of them. And from where Doug sits, Mary saved the family. The fact
that he was not present when Mary first told me of the LeCleres'
discovery of the depression in their midst does not diminish his
enthusiasm for it being discussed. "I wish we'd have known it a lot
sooner than we did," he says at one point, "and I wish some of these
other kids who wrestle would take a look at it. It's easy for parents
to miss depression in a wrestler because, let's face it, when you can't
eat, you're grumpy, and you avoid people so you don't get into an
argument or altercation because sometimes you lose it and all hell
breaks loose. It's easy to just stay in your room and be by yourself."

Mary, the girl that Doug has loved all of his adult life, the
one who lived barely five miles away from him in Prairieburg
when they were in high school and whom he fell for the first
time he met her—she saved his boys and got them back on track.
Michael says now that if he had been on antidepressants back as
a sophomore in high school, he might never have reached the
point where quitting wrestling seemed like the thing to do. Mary
helped Mike to the point where he could begin going forward
again—and she made sure that the rest of the LeCleres were taken
care of, too. "She was the best thing that happened to me," Doug
says flatly. "I hope I can someday repay her for her loyalty."

When Brad Bridgewater mentioned earlier in the week that Dan was
ratcheting up his workouts, I took it to mean he was putting in

more time than usual, which seems unlikely, since "usual" in the LeClerc vernacular is roughly equivalent to "most of the time" in the first place. In fact, Dan is going to put in more time, lift more weight, climb more rope than usual. But he also is going into game-day mode, or at least into a full-scale bear-down mentality, almost a full week before competition.

In the conference tournament the weekend before, in front of the home fans at North-Linn, Dan wrestled in the finals at 140 pounds against a kid from Starmont named Brett Moorman. He had won easily, an 8–0 major decision, and yet Dan walked away angry. In his opinion, Moorman was more interested in keeping the score close than in actually wrestling. It was all defensive movement from his opponent, and Dan, no matter how much he understands Moorman's position intellectually, just cannot abide it as a competitor.

"I've never wrestled defensively in a match," Dan says. "Never. Or at least never that I thought I did. I just don't get that."

Not that anyone associated with North-Linn would allow it, anyway. Bridgewater has always taught the attacking, aggressive style of wrestling. He wants his guys to force their opponents to do all the reacting. For Dan, such comes naturally. After all, he grew up with Doug.

By his own assessment, Doug had little in the way of style as a wrestler, but in his physicality he is a force, even now. And that force still routinely comes into play—at times, to demonstrate the genuine difficulty in coaching one's own son. On the subject of Doug dealing with both Dan and Nick, Bridgewater says, "Doug and Dan are getting along better now. Last fall they went through a whole stretch where they weren't talking to each other."

When I ask what had happened, Brad replies, "Doug can ride Dan pretty hard in practice." And that figures, after all. These coaches are driven people in general, and they're wrestlers on top of that, which makes them driven beyond what is probably reasonable or even sometimes healthy at the high school level. Put that together with the normal friction of a father-son relationship, install the father as a coach of the son, and you have yourself a recipe for an emotional explosion.

"No," Bridgewater says. "I mean he *rides* him. Hard. In practice."

Body on body, the coach means. Wrestler versus wrestler. This particular incident occurred months ago, the product of Doug's basic inability to dial it down on the mat no matter what the circumstances. On that day, Doug had Dan down and was riding him, using his weight to prevent Dan from escaping or getting up. It frustrated the holy hell out of Dan to have his father essentially sitting on him, working him over, and finally he just let loose with an elbow—"It was a cheap shot," Bridgewater says with a smile—that caught Doug above his left eye. Doug fired back with a fist blow into Dan's side, and suddenly these were not two wrestlers having a spirited workout: This was a father and a son going at it, sprawling and brawling around the mat, venting months and years of whatever was bottled up inside. Doug was bleeding from the elbow; Dan was seething from the frustration. It was the head coach who finally got them out of the room and into the hallway, where he laid down the law. "This can't happen ever again in front of those kids," Brad told them.

After that, things seemed to get better. "Of course," says Bridgewater, "I separated them across the room during drills for about the next three weeks."

It's probably not the perfect situation. No father-son relationship ever is, when sports are at the center of it and both people actually have a stake. There's too much competition, for one thing, and even if Doug isn't living out sports fantasies through his kids, it is undoubtedly true that he has such a passion for wrestling that he processes almost all of his emotions toward the children through it. It was a long time after Mike left the sport before

Doug could talk to him about anything, time lost that Doug now regrets. There was just suddenly this huge chasm between the two. How much of their fallout trickled down to Dan is hard to say, because Dan loved wrestling from the start and has never really burned out on it. Still, Doug cannot help but view his son first through the prism of the sport. And Dan's impending departure, off for the foreign world of Virginia Tech, is the signal that it is time for Doug to begin letting go.

"I've got to give my attention to Nick now," Doug says. "Dan's there. He's done. He's ready to leave the nest."

Dan's actions, not his words, make it so. It was a year ago, at the State Tournament, that the son began to create that distance between himself and his father. Prior to one of his key matches, as Dan prepared to go to the mat, Doug wandered over and began using his fingers and thumbs to rub deep into Dan's shoulder and neck muscles, a bit of a nervous habit that Doug has foisted upon generations of wrestlers. For years, Dan had tolerantly waited for his jittery dad to stop. On this particular day, he had to make the break himself. Very gracefully, without speaking, Dan reached up with his own hands and removed his father's hands from his neck. "It was like him saying, 'I'm ready. I don't need it,'" says Doug. "And he was ready."

Doug thinks for a moment. "And he still is. He's ready to go. And Nick is here, and Chris, and the other guys on the team. We have to go on here."

Over to one side of a practice mat, Dan's high school coach—the one who has been on board for three consecutive state titles and a lifetime's worth of fiery conversations and dented relationships and occasional family-on-family combat—takes it all in, and what Brad sees is a future for the LeCleres that may just work itself out. "I think the distance [from Virginia to Iowa] will probably be good for him," he says. "But I also think Dan's going to be surprised at how much he misses his dad. I mean, Dan's lived a pretty sheltered life. He has had his dad at almost every wrestling thing he's ever done—had his dad taking him around, driving him everywhere, all that. This'll be very different. And maybe that's good."

At the LeClere farm, out on Monticello Road off Highway 13, the hundred or so head of cattle huddle together in the frigid night air and gather near one corner of the fence line, within bawling distance of the family house. It is a simple and unfussy farmhouse, probably a time zone removed from anything approaching pretense. Mary likes it, but the rooms were all made small, and the living room just isn't big enough to do anything with. The kitchen she can work with. The chili is warm.

On the ride to Troy Mills to get gas and hot cocoa before the run out to the property, Doug discusses the evolution of the North-Linn program. He has already been candid enough to admit that the head-coaching thing was eating up his marriage and had to go, but that doesn't mean he is entirely happy with the way things are. In his heart, he longs to run his own program again. He has obvious respect for Bridgewater, one of whose first moves upon being named head coach was to officially make Doug and Larry Henderson assistants, so they could be thrown at least a few bucks for the time and effort they already were putting in. Doug's good feelings for the coach make it easier to accept the fact that it is Bridgewater, not LeClere, who really calls the shots. Doug's relationship with Henderson is clearly cooler and more distant; the two coach, but seldom together. Then again, it's a small room. You stay in there long enough, over enough years, and somebody is bound to get on somebody's nerves for something or other.

As Doug and Dan look over scrapbooks and photo albums, Nick drifts over and stands near, and what's amazing is the recall that all three LeCleres possess about tournaments and competitions that are years and years old. There is picture after picture of Dan on the medal stand, accepting a first-place award as a 5-year-old, now an 8-year-old, now 10. Doug and Nick and Dan are pulling last names out of the air, recalling wrestlers from years ago who have long since left the sport or moved out of Iowa altogether. This has been a family endeavor: Nick wrestled in those tournaments, and Chris, when his time came, and Michael, too—even the old man, at selected events from time to time. The family worries that the hardest part for Doug may come not when his kids leave North-Linn, but when his knees and his aching body finally won't allow him on the mat anymore. Already the joints and muscles are punishing him, yet Doug cannot conceive of coaching the sport another way. When someone mentions the name of a rival coach in North-Linn's conference, Doug snorts and replies, "Fat guy wearing a tie," and shakes his head. The man doesn't get out on the mat to coach, is what Doug means. That would be a life barely worth living, when wrestling is the thing you want to do.

Outside, it's bloody cold and pitch-dark. In here, the LeCleres are settling in for the night. Doug comes in from another round of chores. He will be up again hours before sunrise, doing the other things that need doing before he heads for Cedar Rapids and the fire station for another 24-hour shift, but for now it is enough to enjoy a bowl of warm chili. Dan heads for his spot on the couch and grabs a blanket, and he is back to looking small again. You figure he'll be easily lost in the crowd on that first day at Virginia Tech, surrounded by forty times the population of his hometown. It is only when he wrestles that they will realize they're in the presence of someone bigger.

CHAPTER 12

They Hand Out Roses

You get right down to it, it's a lousy deal. For years, the Borschels, along with these countless other families whose kids never did get the first-place payoffs that people like Jay and Dan and Kyle and Mitch and Joey got repeatedly, have arranged whole chunks of their years around the questions of when the boys would wrestle and where. And all of this traveling, all of these tournaments and this incremental improvement and advance—it all ultimately has brought the Borschels right back to Marion, to the Linn-Mar team of which Jay now is almost finished being a member. To heartbreak, basically.

For Carol, there was never going to be a way to make it easy at the end. She can be in denial with the best of them when it suits her purpose, and prior to this exact moment Carol has done a magnificent job of ignoring the reality that is creeping in around her where it concerns Jay. She is running out of chances to watch her oldest child do the thing he is the best at in the world.

A night like this, kids like Matt McDonough can scarcely process—it's so far away for them, beyond the scope of relevance. But Carol could tell you that it gets here faster than you think. A couple of days ago Jay was the freshman, making his first Linn-Mar varsity team, finding a niche at the lightest weight on the list. Now Jay is the senior who has grown beyond all measure, the one coming into the hallway to greet his mother and walk with her and Jim into the Linn-Mar gymnasium to shake Doug Streicher's hand and listen to the words spilling out of Kevin McCauley as the assistant coach rattles off Jay's astonishing athletic accomplishments—and the other things, too. He mentors an elementary-school student once a week. He maintains a 3.4 grade-point average. He's a founding member of the Tailgating Club, which is basically an excuse to goof around in the parking lot before football games. He can eat a full meal and still make weight. Some things defy the odds.

The Linn-Mar gym is a big, bright place, with huge bleachers that come way out without actually even getting close to the basketball court or the wrestling mats. Of course, for the wrestling team no such deep bleachers are needed; Jay is used to that and long ago stopped thinking about it. He has chosen a sport that, at Linn-Mar, has almost nothing to do with fans or attractive girls or mass appeal—that even living in Iowa, one can be a raging success at and largely anonymous at the same time. Of course, that was before Jay became the guy going for a four-timer while ditching his home state to go wrestle in the East. Now the people around here see him coming, for better and for worse. He can't help it: He wants to get on with this, and get it over, and get on out.

For years now, Carol and Jim have given Jay every tool at their disposal so that, essentially, he could one day make his escape. They found this place, in Marion, all those years ago, having come straight in from the West without even knowing what their new jobs might be, knowing only that Iowa was where they would raise the family. Marion had been the place where Jim had lived before moving to Illinois as a 14-year-old, and Carol had grown up in a twelve-child Catholic family on a farm north of tiny little

Lourdes, and Iowa was the place. Jim wound up inspecting low- and moderate-income family leased homes for the city of Cedar Rapids. Carol landed as an elementary school music teacher. The jobs are good and Jim's is almost perfectly flexible, and they have weekends off, and these jobs allow the Borschels to fashion their existence significantly around what Jay (and now Hannah) needs in the way of support.

And, inevitably, Jay is drifting ever so slightly away from them now, and as much as Carol has done to ignore that fact, there are some days when the truth of it has no place to go. Senior Night tends to be one of those kinds of days. Put it this way: When they walk you into the big room and hand you the rose, it means your son is going away.

Jim has to be retrieved and reminded to go join Carol and Jay for the ceremony, which also includes wrestling staff and cheerleaders and the other seniors—Mitch Benfer, Shawnden Crawford and Kyle Minehart. It isn't really Jim's thing. He's the kind of dad who somehow usually finds his way to the wrestling room while practice is still going on, one of those people who, before you know it, is out there with some jayvee kid, helping him learn one of the multiple variations of the basic moves that Doug Streicher and his staff teach. And Jim's rewards all come down there, in the room with the mats and the stereo. When he was in the tenth grade, weary of sitting the bench on the basketball team, he fell into wrestling; by the time he was a senior, he was a conference champion. He loved the work. He loved how much it hurt after a hard practice. He admired the ethic. Later on, as a dad, he ran the kids' program at Linn-Mar for a while. Now he's just sort of one of those guys who is always there, ready to answer a question or work a technique. He gets paid nothing for it. He asks for nothing in return. He pays the freight. The ones who really love it, they usually find a way to hang around.

The families file into the oversized gym, with its dozen

rows of overhead lights. Carol wears black slacks and a Linn-Mar cardinal-red top, her reddish-brown hair slightly tousled. As the Borschels enter, Streicher does his thing as the greeter, shaking their hands, shaking Jay's hand rather formally. Jay is stoic, trying not to take it too seriously for fear his mom will fall apart completely. Streicher, ever the coach, has a program of that night's lineup rolled up and sticking up out of his back right pocket, and the ever-present pen poised above his right ear like an unsmoked cigarette. The whole ceremony feels like it's over before it begins, which only fits: Jim once said that while the little-kid wrestling stuff seemed to go on and on, this entire high school experience has gone by in a blinding flash.

The one thing Jim ever really worried over, with Jay, is what they might talk about if they had no wrestling. On his own, Jim had asked himself that question. He made it a point to tell himself that when this was all over, he would take Jay and just head off somewhere down the Wapsipinicon River—"the Wapsie," they call it—and do some fishing, go somewhere where the phone doesn't ring. Jay's year has begun to fade into a series of calls and interviews and projections and evaluations, and the college thing has seemed like such an unbelievably big damn deal, and he hasn't even made it to the Barn yet. Jim can sense in his son the long, slow beginning of a burnout. He wants Jay to get through this thing in one piece, and get the hell out. They are speaking the same language without either one knowing it.

But it is Carol's moment, really, Senior Night. It is a mother's kind of a thing. Jay's relationship with his mother—and his father, too, really—is loose but not unstructured; Carol is the one whom both kids like to tease about her faulty memory, or press on the soft spots in her household politics. In his final year at home Jay has taken that liberty and stretched it about as far as it will go, crunching Carol with straight-faced insult after insult while eating the food that she painstakingly prepares for him at dinner.

He talks over her, tells her point-blank that she's wrong, needles her with intimations that maybe he'll head out this night for the strip club. He knows how to push her buttons, which is to say, he's a senior. But he does so completely secure in the knowledge that Carol will always snap back into place. Jay has the luxury of thinking that he knows the greatest secret about his mom, which is that she will be there for him no matter what. Carol Borschel has done nothing, so far as anyone connected with the family can tell, to ever discourage that kind of deep-seated security.

As for the here and now, Senior Night, Carol decided to fully contain her heartbreak. Walking along with Jay, she is every bit the proud parent. "I don't think it'll really hit her until after all of this is over and Jay starts getting ready to move," Jim says, and it's a compliment. Carol knows plenty about landing on one's feet. She joined her husband right out of school at his residence-hall management jobs on college campuses in Illinois and Arizona and made those places work, and she was with Jim when the two of them decided they wanted to raise their family back home and simply bolted for Marion. She went on faith. She is the product of a huge music- and art-loving family, growing up with virtually no interest in sports; she converted herself into a rabid wrestling fan to accommodate the reality of her own family.

And she will land on her feet through this emotional turbulence, because she does it every day, loses Jay a little bit more every day. And even though the thought of Jay actually leaving town is crushing, it is also indisputably true, she tells herself, that he is going *to* something and not just *from* something. Jay is heading straight into his future. The Borschels, no strangers to road trips themselves, can appreciate the quality of that adventure.

Carol accepts her rose and smiles as the gathered crowd— you would call it a decent crowd, not a huge one—brings forth its applause. A few in the crowd stand up in recognition of the wrestlers and parents who may be leaving the Linn-Mar program forever. Carol says, to no one in particular, "Next December is going to roll around, and where am I going to go? I've been coming in here for four years."

"You could always cheer on the other kids," someone answers feebly. It's ludicrous, naturally. Going there would only remind the Borschels that Jay is gone, and wrestling doesn't really work that way. Still, there are these kids to root for, kids like Matt McDonough, so good and so young, whose improvement from the beginning of the season until now you could see with your own eyes. (One night later, Jay will say of Matt, "He could place this year" at the State Tournament, a huge possibility considering that McDonough was barely on the rankings radar when the season began.) Matt is still way small and he got pummeled by the Iowa City kid, Nate Moore, just last weekend; but things can change, things can change. So there is Matt, and there is Jason Nelson, Jeff's son, another kids-club alumnus who could bring glory to Linn-Mar. And there is the athletic and quick Wes Shetterly, who with a little more strength could be tough to beat; and maybe Bryan Telgenhoff, the sophomore who has suffered through such an exquisitely crappy year, not always working hard enough or smart enough, knowing the moves but not always being able to execute them. Telgenhoff may stand as the most frustrating wrestler in the room to his teammates and coaches; they see the huge potential but not yet the results. But it's clear that Bryan is going to have to want success maybe 50 percent more than he did this season. He tells Jay that he is pondering entering some summer tournaments. Jay says, "That would be so huge for him. It would help a lot."

So there are all these kids to root for, kids like Colin Wolf, the 215-pounder who could return next year and form a core of solid seniors alongside Jon Obst and Alex Gansen and Casey Dunning and John Monroe. It's a new set of names, you see? There are stories next year for Linn-Mar yet to be told. Jim and

Carol know every kid, every family. They know where all the stories are going. The thing is, Jay Borschel's story is almost played out. What is a parent to do about that?

Carol takes her rose and walks back up into the stands. She is too lovely and too aware of the moment to do anything but smile radiantly, and then she commences cheering and gyrating and punching the air with her fists, almost wrestling an entire match herself as she goes through her usual motions and emotions of watching the Lions down there on the mat. She does this because it is what she does, after all, and when it comes Jay's time to wrestle, even though it is obvious to everyone in the room that he will win easily, Carol wrenches herself into impossible positions in the bleachers all the same, and shouts instructions and encouragements that don't quite make it all the way down out of the air and onto the floor of the gym, and screams with wild happiness when Jay inevitably concludes the Home portion of his high school life by pinning his opponent from Cedar Rapids Washington, a kid named Alex Grafft who wrestles his tail off and still winds up whipped. It is an appropriate ending to a career spent mostly beating people up in front of cozy crowds of devoted onlookers, people who really get it. Carol videotapes the match so that it will last forever, which is really the final line of defense for the parent who is fighting that losing battle against time and childhood. She videotapes her son the magnificent wrestler for one last time inside Linn–Mar High School, because she can take that one with her, and hold it, in the moments when other people go away and there is no one left inside the gymnasium but other people's children, and other people's stories. Save it for a rainy day. It will be worth gold then.

At times, it appears that wrestling runs in a direction counter to the rest of sport. In other endeavors—football, distance running, swim competitions—coaches often shy away from full-throated workouts as they approach the big finish or the championship game. The idea is that their athletes have had whole seasons in which to achieve peak physical condition; the thing now is to avoid injury and basically make sure nothing falls off or turns the wrong color between now and the moments of truth.

"I know some coaches who do that—and they're successful with it, too," Brad Bridgewater says, as the North-Linn wrestlers around him haul themselves off the mat and over to the scales, some of them about to discover they have just lost six or seven pounds during Bridgewater's final Monday workout before the Class 1A sectional tournament the coming weekend.

Bridgewater, that is to say, isn't a hundred percent behind the take-it-easy approach to the wrestling life.

The new place at North-Linn, if it ever comes, won't save the world, but it's a start. It will be larger than the current space and certainly better than the bad old days, when the Lynx wrestlers didn't even have this and instead had to shuttle over to the elementary school at Coggon for practice, a situation that resulted in very few kids from the far western side of the school district, around Walker, coming out for the team—it was just too far to scramble to practice every day. The new plan will build a 50-by-80 wrestling space alone, with more room for showers and exercise bikes and the like. It'll connect off the north side of the main school structure. The money is the issue, but that was to be expected all along. What may happen now, Brad says, is that the wrestling program will borrow a final chunk of money from the district, repaying it in installments of several thousands of dollars per year for the next several years, while the boosters contribute a few thousand a year over that same span. The boosters might ultimately be able to help to the collective tune of $40,000 or $45,000—and with that money in sight, "we may be able to turn dirt on the thing by next spring," the coach says. It is a glowing thought, as Bridgewater watches his wrestlers scramble around on the mat and a half available to them, trying to find enough room amid all the bodies to actually do some one-on-one work on takedowns and arm-bars and the like.

Still, it isn't as though the program has suffered for its surroundings. "This room has seen a lot of battles, a lot of blood," Bridgewater says, and it's the truth. North-Linn may not be where it wants to be just yet, but the wrestling program has been making noise for a while now, and the Lynx could send a significant number of their kids to districts out of the Starmont sectionals on Saturday: Ben Morrow at 103, Madison Sackett at 112, Wes Ward at 119, Ryan Mulnix at 125, Ben Fisher, both LeCleres, Tyler Burkle, possibly one of the upper weights. If Nick LeClere can get and stay healthy, he has a chance to join Dan, Ryan, Ben and Tyler with a shot at getting to the State Tournament.

Of course, Nick can't get healthy, and he sure cannot stay there. While Dan not only takes tremendous care of his body but also seems to have a knack for veering out of harm's way, Nick's season has been a series of pratfalls, one seemingly coming right after the other. There was the hip flexor problem, and then the hyperextended elbow, and then a wicked bout with the flu. Now, on this Monday, he finishes his workout, takes off his left shoe and sock and begins untaping his foot.

"What happened there?" I ask Bridgewater.

"Oh," the coach says, "this time he rolled his ankle doing something on Sunday. Just running, really."

Ben Fisher has a subpar workout, which is in keeping with his subpar weekend. For all of his athletic skill, Ben's confidence can be shaken so easily; he's such a perfectionist that he is easily driven to distraction. When he decided to give wrestling another shot in his senior year, Mike and Kathy Fisher both hesitated on behalf of their son. It wasn't merely that they worried he might do something epically hideous to his back, although there was that thought. It was more that they weren't sure he could shoulder the emotional burden.

Tyler senses as much in his friend. He says that Ben did a lot of the kicking on the football team, in addition to playing running back on offense and cornerback on defense. "Kicking wasn't his best thing," Burkle says, but the team needed a kicker and so Ben stepped up. "But then, if we lost a game, he felt like he was the reason why. He'd blame himself for it."

"If he missed an extra point he'd come off the field so frustrated there were tears in his eyes," Bridgewater says, and evidently it is the same with wrestling: Fisher was terribly emotional after last Saturday's performance at the conference tournament, where he reached the final and then lost 6–4 to a wiry kid named Alex Riniker of East Buchanan, and today it is clear that the unexpected defeat, to a wrestler he has beaten in the past, is preying on his mind.

Fisher is upset with himself, not so much for failing to win (though he clearly can't stand the idea of that) as for not really trying to. "I was nervous," he says. "I wrestled like crap. I was afraid of losing." It's a scathing self-assessment, yet when I mention this to Ben's old friend Jay Borschel, who knew the Fishers when they first moved to Marion from Nebraska, Jay nods his head in silent empathy. It is every wrestler's nightmare, after all, to go out on the mat and find himself constantly on the defensive, too tentative to make a move. Most of the really good high school wrestlers have spent their years experiencing the other side of that equation, sometimes to the point of trying to goad their opponents into actually engaging. This time, Ben Fisher engaged, but not fully. He was out there but not completely there. And he paid the price. All of which explains why he can barely bring himself to a full workout today.

"We've got to get him right before sectionals," says Bridgewater. No question there: Fisher, on his game, can storm through to the State Tournament. As Tyler Burkle said, "If the season lasted one month, Ben would win a state title. It's when the season goes on longer that Ben starts to go down, because he's so hard on himself." And the Fisher who is hard enough on himself to be just a little bit off his game might not even advance out of Starmont.

As Bridgewater sits against one of the padded walls of the wrestling room in the moments after his team leaves, watching the littlest of the Little Lynx spill around the mats under the eye of a coaching father, Dan reappears perhaps fifteen minutes after his full two-and-a-half-hour workout has ended. He walks slowly to a hanging rope and begins pulling himself up it, holding his knees spread apart so that he is using only his arm strength to raise himself. Hand over hand, he needs maybe a minute to ascend the rope and touch the metal hook that holds it in place at the ceiling. Then he lowers himself back down, length by length, again using only his arms. Then Dan does it again. Then again. And then once more.

"You can tell when Danny gets serious about it," Brad says, "because you start seeing this kind of stuff all the time." Dan clearly shares with his coach the notion that the week of the sectional tournament is no time to be taking it easy. In fact, Bridgewater says that in years past, as the district and state tournaments neared, members of the team would drive to Manchester to work out at the West Delaware High School, because West Delaware had climbing ropes that went all the way up to the ceilings of their main gymnasiums—basketball ceilings, basically. This sharing of facilities isn't uncommon. As time goes by and the field narrows, the surviving schools from different classifications will begin visiting each other in order for competitive wrestlers to work out with one another in preparation for the state tourney.

No one really asks all that often to come to North-Linn for the workout. In the muggy little room on this day, Bridgewater had wanted to end the practice with some rapid-repetition weight work—only there weren't enough weights to go around. It was time to improvise. So Dan and his brother Nick shared a weight doughnut that had slid off one of the barbells in the wrestling room, while other wrestlers traded off medicine balls or heavy bags of sand. Over to one side, one of Bridgewater's varsity starters got his weight work in by hoisting and curling one of the equipment toolboxes, the stuff inside rattling noisily with each repetition.

It is a provisional life in the program. And that is, in some ways, the bonding agent of the team. The wrestlers work out in this little sweatbox and crowd around taking turns on the mat and run those 46-foot sprints all day, and they and their coaches are the closer for it, the tougher. Theirs is the program that produces winners out of whatever raw material happens to be lying around. It is only just now that the generation of wrestlers who first brought the school a little statewide notice—the classes right around Doug LeClere's 1978 team—is bringing its own offspring through the program. The good news is that many of those wrestlers have stayed around, stayed in the area and the school district. The rest of the news is that there aren't enough of them to make a complete team, and Bridgewater finds himself trolling for talent all the time. He found Kirk Schmidt, the ninth grader with no wrestling experience, basically hanging around campus. Kirk was playing on the junior varsity football team, and he was tremendously big already, and so "I just walked up to him and said, 'Hey, we need a heavyweight,'" Bridgewater said. "And he has come such a long way in just this year—he has learned a lot about the sport in a short time. He was always kind of a soft kid, a video-game kid. To see him do this, do these workouts and everything—it's a huge step for him."

And wrestling is about that, sometimes. Kirk has been thrown on his back so many times he must know the shape and texture of every ceiling in the Tri-Rivers Conference, but he may yet see it through to a happy ending. He drags his big body up and down the wrestling-room floor, doing wind sprints that leave him soaked through with sweat and gasping for breath. He never says no, and he never asks out. He is a redheaded, chunky country boy who is probably too sweet-natured for his own good—but don't tell anybody connected with the North-Linn wrestling program that he can't someday be a winner for the Lynx.

"He's got a chance," Bridgewater says; but Brad's attention is suddenly diverted. Across the mat, over at the far wall, Dan hops onto the climbing rope and prepares to take himself up to the top again. What does that shirt say? HARD WORK SOLVES EVERYTHING. Dan already has put in his years of always showing up. He's just about ready to be the one they're all waiting to see.

The school is called Starmont, and although that sounds like an ideal name for a smaller town in a rural area, there is in fact no such town. There is a burg toward which Highway 13 winds and curves and eventually runs right into; this is Strawberry Point. Another town, Arlington, is nearby, and not too far away a third called Lamont. Put Strawberry Point and Arlington and Lamont together, and up comes the amalgamated moniker of Starmont, a middle-school/high-school megaplex that juts up at the table-top-flat intersections of Highways 3 and 187.

The Starmont gym has light-canary-and-crème-painted walls, bleachers on both sides, the school's colors of black and yellow forming the indelible image of a stinging bee as they meet on the wrestling mats to form the outline, the circle, and the start marks. The nickname of the school is the Stars. Doug Streicher wrestled here, and out in the hallway that leads from the gym past classrooms and on to the cafeteria, the school has carefully mounted a series of framed photographs of its Stars, with Streicher prominent among them. He stands in the photograph in a wrestle-ready position, three medals draped around his neck and hanging from their red–white–and–blue ribbon lanyards. The engraved plate beneath the photo identifies only two of the medals, for Streicher's state championships in 1986 and 1987. The other medal is a silver. No mention of that.

This is, in some important way, the day of reckoning for Brad Bridgewater and his program. For most of the season, the North-Linn team has battled its demons, which in very specific order have included injury (Nick, Ben, Ryan Mulnix), illness (Nick again) and the looming distraction of history (Dan's attempt at four titles). Bridgewater has once again bet his team's performance on the strength of its conditioning and aggressiveness; the past week's work was brutal, at times over the top.

Now that bet will be called. North-Linn did not wrestle well at its conference tournament, even though it hosted the event. Ben lost his 135-pound final in an upset; Ben Morrow didn't make it through to the championship match; Nick didn't wrestle at all because of his lingering flu; and Dan was conspicuously humiliated and angered by his failure to hammer his Starmont opponent, Bret Moorman. It was a result that raised a few eyebrows in wrestling circles and got people wondering whether Dan might be vulnerable after all. Moorman hadn't wanted to wrestle, or at least he was too smart to really engage Dan vigorously and expose himself to getting pinned. By "holding" Dan to just a major decision (as opposed to a technical fall or a pin), Moorman had helped prevent North-Linn from scoring more team points, and in the end Bridgewater's group finished a very disappointing fourth in front of its home fans—and, worse, had to watch Moorman's team be presented with the conference champion's trophy. Now the teams who finished 1-2 at that Tri-Rivers Conference meet, Starmont and East Buchanan, are among those on hand as part of the sectional. For Bridgewater and North-Linn, the deal is fairly straightforward and a little bit daunting: They're going to have to step up markedly from the weekend before, or say a disappointed good-bye to a season mostly notable for its continuous uncertainty.

Doug is worried primarily about Nick as the wrestlers begin their pre-match stretching and warm-ups, and it is obvious why. Nick wrestles with Doug's over-aggressiveness, an approach that gets him into trouble as often as not, but about which he does not appear inclined to do a thing—it's his style. But Nick hasn't been able to engage that part of his game, because he hasn't been able to stay healthy long enough to get in a groove with his sport this winter, in part because of the rollover effect of his football injuries. Doug doesn't mind football, but his passion runs strictly to this one sport, wrestling; and here Nick has a chance to be something special. He cannot win four titles like his brother, but that's not the same as saying he cannot be great.

Dan has his own thing to solve today. He spent his week stewing over his result against Moorman; he couldn't help it. To understand how a shutout could be viewed as a failure is to arrive at the heart of the matter with Dan. He didn't want a shutout; he wanted a massacre that would send a message of invincibility. He does not wrestle anymore at the high school level to win, but rather to purchase ownership outright. He is going off to college to wrestle the best in the country, eventually, and he does himself no favors by being satisfied with merely winning out at the end of his high school career. No, Dan wants to go out in a fiery storm.

Dan and Jay are exactly alike in this respect: They no longer see it as enough to get their hands raised in the air at the end of the match. They have identified levels of competition beyond mere winning and losing, pushed through to some parallel universe to which only the elite are admitted and within which only thorough domination is acceptable.

They don't want to win anymore, is the thing. Winning is for scorekeepers, and it has been done. Now they want to rule kingdoms.

As always, the early talk around the North-Linn sideline concerns which Ben Fisher will show up. Ben has become a notoriously difficult person to predict, alternately aggressive and uncertain. He went inexplicably limp in the conference finals the weekend before, succumbing to Riniker from East Buchanan, whom Ben had beaten during the season. It was a frustrating lapse; Riniker is a quality opponent, and yet the feeling among the North-Linn folks is that Ben on top of his game beats Riniker and beats him soundly. As fate would have it, Riniker is in the brackets at this sectional tournament as well.

"I hope Ben's ready," someone mumbles to assistant coach Larry Henderson.

"I hope so, too," says Larry, looking across the mat. "He sure does look it."

He does. And he is. For this is one of the days that the coaches often talk about—about the way Ben can look when he believes in himself and has the right frame of mind. Generally, Ben wears his uncertainty on his sleeve. With the best wrestlers, like Dan and Jay, it becomes difficult over time to distinguish a good day from a bad day in their emotion; they appear invulnerable no matter what the circumstance. With a good-but-not-great wrestler, the difference between those two edges of quality lies in that kind of confidence—and today, Ben is ready to rock. He strides out for his first match of the day at 135 pounds, takes a 6–0 lead after one period, pins his opponent with 46 seconds remaining in the second period and walks briskly off the mat. He's all business.

The Starmont crowd has filled up the parking lot by the gym with its cars, and the parents and fans have come inside and located the computer printouts taped to the walls above the bleachers, which designate seating areas for each school. North-Linn's folks wind up in the southwest corner, which is where they seem to gather almost everywhere they go. That fits: The overwhelming sense of events like these is familiarity. The schools have generally competed against one another for years, in the same conference or section. Old rivalries have stratified, and the teams that other schools want to beat don't change much from year to year. Wrestling, because it is so personal, intensifies all of those factors. The North-Linn athletes have been scrapping with East Buchanan and Starmont and Center Point-Urbana forever, and grudges build. "I hate them guys! Them guys are assholes!" Doug LeClere had barked to his wrestlers just a couple of days before, during a break in practice. "I don't want to lose to assholes!" Outside of the North-Linn wrestling room itself, he could've been talking about anybody.

Doug says he wants Nick to wrestle early in the day, on the theory that it's always better to get going soon and get breakfast off the stomach. In truth, Doug is so knotted up that he needs to see Nick wrestle in order to believe it'll be okay; but instead Nick has drawn a first-round bye and will head straight for the sectional semifinal. The same is true for Dan, who has been placed on the opposite side of the eight-man bracket from Bret Moorman.

It's hard to say exactly what makes a team come together in any given moment. The North-Linn team wasn't great the weekend before, and it will not be as good as it wants to be a week from now. But for today, in this time and place, it is just about as good as it's going to get. This will be the day when Madison Sackett, a 112-pound freshman for whom Brad, Doug and Larry have great hope, gets over his disappointment at being pinned in the semifinal and wins his last match to qualify for the district tournament. This will be the day when Tyler Burkle looks unstoppable, pinning his way through his 152-pound bracket. It will be a day when Kirk Schmidt comes back after getting pinned in his first match and ends his season by pinning his final two heavyweight opponents. Despite having no chance to move on to district competition, Kirk stays focused enough to take fifth place and win points for his school. It's worth the trip to Starmont to see the bear hug in which he envelops Doug LeClere coming off the mat after that last match, and the ovation he receives upon passing by the North-Linn portion of the bleachers. Good feelings in packages large and small.

And it's Ben Fisher's day. He is in control throughout, and he plows through with a 13–0 major decision in the semifinal and a completely satisfying 7–2 victory over Alex Riniker of East Buchanan—"East Buc" to its supporters—in the final. He's into it.

For Ben's dad, Mike, that part—Ben's focus—is almost always the question of the moment. Mike brought the family to the Marion area about a decade ago, and not long after that he sought land out in the country, taking the Fishers away from the Borschels and into the North-Linn district. From the beginning, Mike knew he had athletes in Ben and his older brother, Adam. Adam, in fact, was a strong wrestler for North-Linn, whose exit from competition his senior year is still spoken of with genuine sadness; he was leading a match solidly at the district tournament when he suddenly got spun onto his back and pinned by a wrestler whom he had beaten earlier in the season. It was over for Adam just like that, after a career at North-Linn that included a hundred victories and more than eighty pins. "There was not a dry eye in the house that day," says Mike Hageman, the North-Linn fan who manages to make most of the duals and all of the tournaments despite not having a child on the wrestling team. "It was so awful for the kid. He was a great wrestler, too."

So Ben has Adam's shadow there, his legacy not only of tremendous accomplishment but also of a dramatic exit. More dangerous, he has the LeCleres, standard-bearers for the kind of performance he believes he should be able to replicate. "He thinks he should be *that*," Mike Fisher says, pointing over to the action one mat removed from where we stand, where Dan LeClere is warming up. "You see the issue."

But for this day, all is well. Ben is on his game and able to walk away satisfied. Ben Morrow has found his way through the 103-pound bracket and will move on to districts, and so will Madison Sackett, and Ryan Mulnix with the bum shoulder at 125.

And, of course, now comes the meat of the order.

At 140, Dan is majestic, completely dominant. There is no question of his being ready here. There is certainly no question of his being the best wrestler in the building. And yet he manages to have an unusual day, and to be tested in ways that are more emotional than anything else.

In his first match he wrestles a boy from Central City, a community not far from Troy Mills, and it immediately becomes clear that the boy took some notes from a week ago. Dan is attacking, almost stalking his opponent, who in turn does everything he can to avoid getting into a tangle with the top-ranked wrestler in the state. His name is Tony Nolting, and his aim is really just to finish the match without getting pinned. Dan swarms Nolting from every angle. He's simply vicious in the pursuit. He hits Nolting high up on his body, using the strength in his chest and arms to fling him down. He slams into Nolting on the lower end, deftly picking up a foot and using it to hammer him to the mat. But Nolting isn't interested in wrestling, only in successfully eluding the pin. He isn't really even attempting much in the way of an escape; he is essentially being ridden by Dan while figuring out ways to keep his shoulders from being flattened against the foam rubber. And when the match finally is declared finished, with Dan recording a 16–1 technical fall that stops the action, it is Tony Nolting who receives a standing ovation from his team's crowd—for not getting pinned.

In the hallway a few moments later, still breathing hard, Dan retreats to a corner to deal with the results. He knows he isn't going to pin his way through the rest of his life, and for that matter he expects to have a match at some point this winter that he is simply happy to win—but not like this. This is no way to get things done. It's no way to get prepared for State.

Walking by with friends, Nolting sees Dan, goes toward him and extends a hand. "Nice match," he says.

"Get the fuck away from me," Dan hisses back.

Nolting, the smile fading from his face, moves on with his friends. Dan doesn't look after him, and he never gives the exchange a second thought; he has to be reminded later of what he said to the wrestler. In Dan's mind, there is no need for an exchange of pleasantries with someone who just ran away from him from the opening whistle forward. He isn't much for the post-match small talk.

As expected, Dan is pitted against Moorman in the finals. Moorman is a fine wrestler who, later this month, will find himself headed for Des Moines. He doesn't need to apologize to anybody for his talent or effort. But he will never be in this match, never. He has made the mistake of staying within eight points of Dan LeClere, and for that he will be made to suffer.

It's over when it begins, and it is merciless. Dan repeatedly takes down Moorman and lets him up again, the better to shoot and stick and take him down again. He comes flying at Moorman and grabs a leg on the back side of the kid, moving around behind him to better ratchet him to the mat. After several seconds of grinding him down on the pads, Dan lets Moorman escape, as if to say, "Let's try this one more time." It is a pattern of playful torture that probably won't find its way into the State Tournament, where things get more serious and the object is to win as quickly as possible and get off the mat. But on this day Dan is toying with Moorman. It is an intentional punishment, and it is delivered with a touch of either anger or frustration.

"I didn't want to leave any doubt," Dan says afterward. "I didn't like how it went last week."

With a little less than a minute remaining in the second period, Dan wrenches Moorman onto his back, rams his shoulders against the mat's surface and records the pin. He stands up, accepts his victory with a handshake and walks expressionlessly away.

It is a nice victory, a satisfying one, but neither Dan nor his father takes a moment to enjoy it. Instead, the two share a quick hand-slap and then anchor themselves at one corner of the same mat. It is Nick's turn to either announce himself as a force to be reckoned with or begin making plans for next year.

Doug's influence is especially felt here. During the semifinals, he had remained in Ben Fisher's corner on one mat while Dan wrestled his match on the other mat. But as soon as that match ended, Doug bolted down to where Nick was about to follow his brother for the 145-pound semifinal against a wrestler from Starmont—and this was Doug as a coach and a father, alternately rooting and barking out strategic commands, pounding the mat and pantomiming with his arms the moves Nick was playing out in real time in the match. All of that had come in the service of a 16–1 rout, but those were just the semifinals. Now Nick has his match, his test, against Cascade's Alex Ressler, who recently has battled injury problems of his own.

And, in one of those unscripted nice moments, Nick LeClere is ready to go. He grinds out the most difficult 3–2 victory imaginable, basically riding out Ressler after gaining the lead in the third period, hanging on, denying the Cascade kid a chance to get an escape or late reversal that might swing the balance of the match. It is a good and tenuous victory, almost the film negative of his brother's pummeling of Moorman. Alex Ressler fights to the final seconds, desperately trying to keep his win streak intact. In the end, Nick is just a little tougher, a little more technically sound. He never does allow himself to be driven into the mat. He takes that 3–2 lead and carries it home, the North-Linn fans roaring their approval as the final, seemingly endless half-minute of wrestling time winds the match to a close.

In the end, Nick gets his victory, and Tyler Burkle wraps up a typically smashing day with a pin in the finals at 152, and North-Linn advances eight wrestlers to the district tournament at Midland-Wyoming. The Lynx are announced as the team winners of the sectional meet. Bridgewater stands off to one side, watching his individual champions take the podium to receive their medals, and he is informed that by virtue of winning here, the North-Linn team will host a dual against Belle-Plain on the following Tuesday, with the right to advance to the March state dual tournament on the line.

Someone mentions that the basketball team is supposed to play a home game Tuesday night in the gym. For the first time in forever, that team will have to give way to the wrestlers.

"Tough," Bridgewater says with a broad smile. "It had to happen sometime."

It happens out here, on a Saturday that goes from nearly balmy to spitting snow in the span of the six or seven hours that it has taken for North-Linn to work this magic inside the Starmont gym. And some of the day does have a magical feel. Nick's match, in fact, is the one that produces for him the strangest sensation of the season; even after giving up a reversal to Ressler in the second period, "I never even felt in trouble for one minute," Nick says, shaking his head at the thought. "It was weird. I felt the whole time like I was going to win, even though I knew how close the score was."

And it is close, as close as the score would make it seem. It is exactly close enough to temper Doug's praise, though it's obvious that the father has just experienced something like a state of grace while watching both his sons perform to their capabilities in critical moments.

"It's too early to celebrate—three-two for Nick is too close," Doug says, watching his sons accept their congratulations. "But he's got it in his head now that he can do it."

It might just be enough.

CHAPTER 13

Moving Day

The district tournament format in Iowa is as stark and unforgiving as the landscape itself in February. Only four wrestlers at each weight advance to the meet, meaning their first district matches are semifinals. The two semifinal winners then wrestle each other for the title, and the winner is guaranteed his ticket to the State Tournament. The two semifinal losers also wrestle, and whoever is defeated there is finished for the season.

Thus, after two matches at districts, there is a 2-0 champion, a 0-2 eliminated wrestler, and two kids with 1-1 records. If both of those 1-1 wrestlers suffered their losses to the new district champ, then they will wrestle each other, their third match of the day—this time to determine who is deserving of the other State placement in Des Moines.

It is a brutal and emotionally wrenching process—and it will happen all over Iowa. In wrestling, the format is called competing for a "true" second place, because it ensures that every possible combination has been matched along the way to the finish. No one gets a free pass simply for winning his semifinal. Des Moines is not given. It is earned.

North-Linn has sent eight wrestlers to the district tournament, again at the overcrowded Midland-Wyoming gym, and, just one week removed from the celebratory feel of Starmont, it becomes evident early on that the struggles will be real. In the first match of the day, Ben Morrow loses his 103-pound semifinal, a difficult contest in which he never leads. Immediately after, Madison Sackett loses at 112 pounds, and it isn't until Ryan Mulnix takes his wounded wing out there and punishes Jason Enlow of Camanche for three periods that the Lynx have a district finalist.

Ben Fisher is next, and although he wrestles too cautiously and looks at times uncertain on his feet, he wears down a kid from North Cedar before finally pinning him in the third period. It isn't a classic win, exactly, but Ben is in control, leading 12–5 at one point before putting the thing away. Coming off the mat, he wears an expression not of happiness but of relief, which tells the story not only of Ben but of the district format. Win your semifinal, and the worst that can happen is that you will wind up with a chance to wrestle for second place and a trip to State. Lose your semi, and suddenly the future no longer is something that you altogether control. You need help. For the moment, Ben need not ask.

By the time Ben is winding down, Dan LeClere already has put himself through his paces, literally. He is warm and ready to attack, and he will not allow his attention to waver even if, as he suspects, the competition is not stellar and he may not get the kind of state tune-up match he would like. He may need to use his time in the Midland gym more to prepare for the road that is opening up before him, to make winning here into an exercise in getting ready for Des Moines. Still, there is more than one aspect to his pacing, the back and forth and the serious effort to control his emotions. Dan knows that the people at North-Linn don't just want him to win, they already have banked on his winning. Dan is their sure thing. They have marked him down in the book as their four-time champion. Now it is left to Dan to take care of the details, the actual wrestling. Is it harder in sports to do something that no one expects you to, or something that everyone already assumes you will?

By the time of his match, Dan has spent about thirty-five minutes pacing back and forth, all but wearing grooves into the wood floor of the gym. It is almost thirty-four minutes longer than he will be on the mats themselves. As he storms after his opponent, Dan is all arms. He waves them in a constant motion, as if searching for the opening that will allow him to find a grip and make something happen. After a few seconds, he finds just such an opening, and it takes no more than an eyeblink for him to close in on the kid and slam him down.

In the stands, Mary looks on expectantly; she knows the other boy on the mat isn't in Dan's class and that this should be over quickly. At the same time, she has seen enough wrestling to understand that nothing in the sport is safe. Even very good wrestlers have been known to inexplicably let up in the middle of a match, perhaps thinking they had things under control. An upset is always one significant screwup away. Of all Dan's traits, this may be the most admirable: He virtually never supplies that opportunity to an opponent who doesn't deserve it.

He won't supply one now. Once he gets the boy down onto the mat, Dan battles furiously for the kill. It's an electrifying kind of physical domination, and as Dan wriggles his hand in between his opponent's arm and the boy's side, the North-Linn fans come to their feet—not to shout or scream, yet, but to see the finish more clearly. Once his hand is through, Dan nearly shoves the rest of his arm into the small space, then uses the leverage and his pure upper-body strength to turn the boy over. Seventy seconds after it has begun, the match finishes. Dan has another pin, and a spot in the finals. And now the North-Linn fans have something to scream about.

Now it is Nick's turn, and judging strictly by his presence at this moment, you'd never guess he has spent most of this season hurt. As Doug and Dan both sit in his corner on the mat, Nick engages North Cedar's Luke Bader in a taut, physical semifinal. It's no surprise; coming into the tournament, Nick's weight class was considered perhaps the most loaded four-man set in the entire state. Included are Nick and Bader, a strong senior, and Cascade's Ressler, who had such a close second to Nick at Starmont. There is also a defending state champion, Ryan Bormann of Tipton, who is generally thought to be the favorite here. Despite the family lineage, Nick is the wild card in this group, the one opponent about whom none of the others can safely draw any conclusions. Generally speaking, this time of year favors the wrestler who has been getting matches all winter, against opponents of every quality, from inferior to competitive to pure evil. Wrestling is not much about being "fresh." "Fresh," in wrestling, doesn't stack up next to "match-ready," and it never will. To be match-ready implies a different kind of toughness, the mental kind. It implies that all those weeks of constant work in the practice room and regular exposure to the overhang lights of the dual matches in distant and foreign gyms—that all of that experience has taught the wrestler about working through pain, and refusing to yield to difficulty, and finding the right combination of moves against a particular opponent, and how to deal with the sick feeling of having lost a match because one wasn't actually ready to rock when the first-period whistle blew. It is not about having a rested body; it's about having a trained mind. And the reason Doug didn't sleep last night, or at least one of the reasons, is that he recognizes that difference. He can't help himself: He is worried for his son.

But Nick is the sort of wrestler, like his brother before him, who never forgets how. He may, as his father suspects, love football beyond all sports, but he understands wrestling beyond all things. He is a genuine product of his family. His recall is staggering. That evening at the farmhouse, as Doug began referring to a photograph from one of Dan's national-competition matches, it was Nick who casually swooped in and provided the details: the opponent's name, where he was from, the score of the match. A glance at the photographs makes it clear that Dan couldn't have been more than 8 years old, meaning Nick wasn't but 5.

Nick is steeped in his family history in the sport, which is to say he knows everything about his two older brothers, including the one who has stayed with the sport long enough to flirt with transcendence. Nick knows all that stuff. It is time for his own story to begin playing out.

Stationed in the far corner of the bleachers, the families don't need to be told the significance of Nick's match: Bader can essentially cripple Nick's shot at State right here. As the opponents walk out to begin, Doug sits in his plastic coach's chair as if he were anchored to the floor. He allows himself only small physical movements of his hips and shoulders, the real muscle strain coming through his neck and face. It's almost as if he doesn't trust himself to let loose.

In the opening period, Bader sweeps in and gains control, sending Nick to the mat and earning a two-point takedown. Nick struggles for position and then, with Bader seemingly hanging on to every limb, somehow manages to pry himself free, stand up and separate himself—a one-point escape. Now only fifteen seconds remain in the first period.

"Attack him! Attack him!" Doug screams, Dan sitting beside him almost impassively. Doug is leaning nearly all of the way off his little chair. With the seconds winding down, the risk is obvious: If Nick takes a shot and misses, Bader might be able to establish some quick control during the ensuing scramble and get takedown points of his own, right before the whistle. They are points that could be crucial in such a close match, and if they go against Nick, it's a hole that will be difficult to climb out of. But

Nick won't think that way, not this early in the match. He wants points now. He's going for it.

Shooting down low, Nick spears one of Bader's legs and quickly drives him to the mat, then hurries to establish his control by getting most of his body on top of Bader's. The official sees it and declares it enough control to matter, raising his hand to signal a two-point takedown. It's a 3–2 lead for Nick just as the period ends.

"Now, be smart," Dan implores in the corner, and then the grinding begins—two full periods' worth. In the second, Nick spends the entire two minutes attempting, unsuccessfully, to free himself from Bader's grasp. Nick has started in the down position, on all fours, with Bader on top of and controlling him, but Bader is unable to score despite his repeated tries at turning Nick onto his back or exposing his shoulders to the mat. It's still 3–2 heading into the third period, and now Nick is the wrestler in the top position. Bader bucks like a bronco, trying to shake Nick off his back. Nick has to be careful; he is searching for an opening through which he might trap Bader into a near-fall, but he cannot expose himself to too much risk of letting Bader get free of him. All Bader needs, after all, is a one-point escape to tie the score and force overtime—and in overtime, Luke would get to choose whether he wanted to begin in the top or bottom position, since he scored first in the match. The odds would be in his favor there. Nick can't let that happen.

With Doug and Dan now screaming their encouragement, Nick rides Bader for a full minute, then ninety seconds, and then into the final seconds of the match. Around the Wyoming gym, followers from several different schools have diverted their attention to the LeClere-Bader match—a one-point lead in the final seconds, after all, is one of the most electrifying scenes in the sport, and Nick hasn't been tested this severely in what feels like forever. Bader thrashes and yanks in his effort to get the match back to even, his fans screaming encouragement. Nick won't budge. He has locked on to his opponent and decided simply to ride out the storm. Bader strains; he claws. His mule-kicking is not enough. Nick is taking this one home.

The referee's whistle blows to end the match, and Doug flies off his chair to congratulate his son. Nick, even though he has another huge match to wrestle today, willingly accepts his father's hug. "OK, then," Nick says with a smile. It is, after all—and considering everything—a hell of an accomplishment at a critical time. It isn't too late for Nick to do something wonderful this season.

Taking the mat after Nick, Tyler Burkle goes into the third period and then pins his opponent, earning himself a championship match against Ryan Morningstar. But after Burkle, another trial faces North-Linn. Shannon Hocken, a senior at 171 pounds who has never made State, runs into trouble in the form of a Tipton wrestler, who locks Shannon up and puts him on his back for a pin almost before anyone knows what has happened. Shannon, a good wrestler who has had a good season, gets up stunned and hurt and walks back to the sideline to sit down. He needs to figure out what went wrong, because he needs to get it right in time to salvage this last chance to wrestle in the Barn. Alas, he is going to spend this day learning precisely how distant Des Moines can feel.

Around the North-Linn team, Doug is manic. He can't sit still, isn't comfortable standing. He paces for a while and then goes back to sitting for a few seconds, repeating the cycle through the day. Doug worries over his sons, Nick more so than Dan, but he's also a North-Linn guy through and through. He wrestled here. He was part of the first great migratory group of Lynx wrestlers to the State Tournament. This is his program. Oh, sure, Brad coaches it, and it is clear that Doug has good feelings not only about Bridgewater but also about the job Brad is doing in planting and growing the North-Linn program. As Larry Henderson remembers it, it wasn't but a decade ago that the school district considered the wrestling team so diminished that it discussed combining the program with some other school's to produce one presumably more competitive unit. Such mergers now are common among the smaller programs across the state, but the transaction would have driven a stake through the heart of any true North-Linn fan.

Doug also nods approvingly at Bridgewater's practices, so lengthy and demanding. "Our guys know that every time they go on the mat, they can wrestle the full six minutes if need be," Doug says. "That's a big advantage as you go into the third period and the other guy's breathing hard." It is Brad's system that has made sure of that; still, in so many ways, this is Doug's place. He doesn't just coach at North-Linn, and he isn't merely the father of North-Linn wrestlers. Doug feels the program. He frets over the LeCleres, but also over the Fishers and the Mulnixes. He worries over a young and promising wrestler like Ben Morrow, who needs to catch a break today if he's going to see the inside of the Barn dressed as a wrestler. Doug would love to see a kid like Ben get the reward that he has clearly worked hard enough for. But wrestling isn't about what you deserve, it's about what you get. Almost everybody tries. Almost everybody wants it bad. They only raise one arm when a match is over, and the plain truth is, sometimes it's the wrong one.

In his loser's bracket match on this afternoon, Ben Morrow gives up a takedown in the opening seconds of his 103-pound consolation match and spends the rest of the three periods trying to get it back. He is young and small, even by 103 standards, and while he's doing almost everything right, he lacks the strength to muscle his way out of the hole. When the final whistle blows, Ben is on the short end of a 6–3 score, his freshman season coming to its conclusion on a cold, gray day in Wyoming. He has wrestled well. It is a respectable loss. But beyond that, it all has to be about next year now.

A wrestling tournament, for anyone deeply involved with a single team, is basically a recurring emotional whiplash. For North-Linn, this includes going from the disappointment of Morrow's elimination to the surprise and elation of seeing Madison Sackett, wrestling right after Morrow, get another chance by winning his second match at 112. But now it is Ryan Mulnix's turn to twist hearts. He does so in shocking fashion, failing to score at all in a 5–0 winner's bracket defeat by East Buchanan's Derek Lentz, a wrestler he has beaten before. Ryan leaves the mat confused and hurting. His shoulder, the one that always pops out of joint, is aching like hell again. He can't understand how he could fail even to score on Lentz, and he somehow has to get his game back in time to wrestle in the 125-pound second-place match, this time with a trip to State on the line. Doug follows Ryan over to a cool brick wall, where Ryan slumps against it, sweating and panting. "Forget about it, starting right now," Doug says into Ryan's ear. "I know it hurts. You've got to come back now. You'll be fine. You've just got to come back now, that's all."

Ryan's stepfather stops by. "Are you okay?" the man asks.

"No," Ryan replies flatly.

You know what? At a time like this, that'll have to do. Because what Ryan doesn't realize is that Ben Fisher is about to make his experience look like a night at the opera.

Ben's 135-pound winner's-bracket match is familiar enough to set teeth to grinding all over the gym. Again it is Alex Riniker of East Buc on the other side, and after the last two weekends of the boys trading blows, it is obvious that there's almost no difference between them in terms of their physical ability and their technical precision. What that means is that the edge on any given day will be mostly mental, which is generally trouble for Ben. And this match is going to be something close to a replay of the conference finals; it is scoreless after the first period, and 1–0 in favor of Ben after the second only because he chose the down position to begin the period and then earned a one-point escape. Neither wrestler has been able to do much with the other. It's just one giant standoff.

In the stands, Mike Fisher's emotion runs from hopeful to charged to frustrated and, increasingly, annoyed. He grows more and more agitated; the strain shows in his clenched jaw and his rigid back. It's hard to watch. "Move, Ben! Keep moving! Get in on him!" Mike screams. Sitting there with his wife, Kathy, surrounded by friends and family and yet utterly alone, Mike cannot stand the idea of Ben leaving the fate of this match to the final two minutes—or, worse yet, to his opponent. He wants Ben to be better on his feet, wants him more aggressively pursuing takedowns. He knows what everybody on the team knows, which is that Ben can do this. He could always do this. It's not a question of ability. But Ben has to want it first.

On the mat, Ben is clearly tentative. He's afraid to go for the shot. Whereas Nick had been willing to take a risky move in his semifinal in exchange for the promise of a couple of points if he succeeded, Ben is headed the other way; he seems to want to simply make the rest of the match go away. Riniker is too good for that. He finally escapes Ben's hold early in the third period for a point that ties the match at 1-1, and now it is Riniker, not Ben, who is willing to take the chance and go for the win. With Ben almost backpedaling, trying to wind down the clock, Alex suddenly shoots in after him and drives Ben to the mat with barely twenty seconds left. "Move, Ben! Move!" Mike screams. "Get up! Stand up!" But Ben, on his belly on the mat, goes almost limp. He appears to concede his defeat with several seconds left, and it is clear that the emotion of the moment has overcome him. He looks almost too surprised, and too bitterly disappointed, to go on trying.

In the stands, Mike Fisher has had enough. As Ben makes the long walk from the far mat to the North-Linn team area, a vacant look on his face that his teammates and coaches know will soon contort into spasms of self-loathing about his performance, Mike comes down out of the stands. He knows how good Ben can be when he is mentally prepared to wrestle. He knows the sacrifices Ben has made to get himself to this position, the guts it took to even consider coming back from his injury. And yet guts, right now, appear in short supply when they're needed the most. Mike decides, in this moment, to make sure that if Ben doesn't get all the way to State, it won't be because he hasn't been given sufficient emotional firepower.

"You've got to wrestle smarter than that," Mike says, his compact frame putting him at about eye level with his son.

"Get out of my face," Ben says.

"This isn't going to get it done!" Mike says, raising his voice. "You've got to go harder than this!"

"I said, 'Get out of here!'" Ben says, now yelling.

Mike explodes. "YOU'VE GOT TO WRESTLE HARDER THAN THAT! YOU'VE GOT TO WRESTLE SMARTER THAN THAT!" His screaming voice suddenly galvanizes the corner of the gym that comprises the North-Linn wrestlers and cheering section. He is perhaps two inches from Ben's face, jabbing his index finger in the direction of Ben's forehead. The veins in Mike's neck bulge visibly as he pursues his son. Ben is screaming back, bellowing at his father. "Get away from me!" Ben shouts, but Mike is only closing in—and so Ben begins edging toward his father as well, the two screaming at each other in this volcanic emotional vent, two frustrated perfectionists taking defeat out on each other. Bridgewater and Larry Henderson and some parents quickly come between the two and push open the gym's exit doors for Ben, who storms outside into the frigid cold of the Wyoming day, wearing only his wrestling singlet. Mike, still raging, stomps off in the other direction.

In the North-Linn corner of the gym, a heavy silence falls. It isn't as though no one here has witnessed such a thing before—the truth is, it's hardly a unique event in the sport. But this is an awfully big moment, and Ben is an awfully fragile wrestler. "Tough day for something like that to happen," one of the fathers says on his way back to the bleachers.

Around this emotional hailstorm, the rest of the tournament hums along, oblivious. Most of the people in the gym neither saw nor heard the moment, and they might not have thought about it for long even if they had; they're too wrapped up in the fates of their own wrestlers. It isn't as though an anguished cry inside a wrestling room is breaking news. Fathers and sons, coaches and wrestlers locked in screaming matches are as commonplace as injury timeouts—you'll see them in every gym, sooner or later, and never more so than when the stakes are the highest.

Around the North-Linn section of the stands, though, this feels different, because Ben is different. Wrestling exacerbates whatever problem one may happen to have, be it small or large, and Ben is one of those people for whom the sport brings his insecurities and his personal demons to the surface—not every day, perhaps, but often enough. He goes into that little wrestling room at North-Linn, knowing he is taking himself down a path that likely will end in some cataclysmic event. He signs up for his own emotional exposure. Before this season began, it was Mike and Kathy, not Ben, who had felt ambivalent about his taking up wrestling again. They worried about his ability to survive on every level, not just one of them.

But that was then, of course, back when the decision needed to be made. Once it was made, there was really no choice about how to proceed—it had to be full tilt, or it had no chance to work. Now Mike's only concern is that Ben leave it all out there on the mat, every ounce of energy and emotion available to him. Ben has just lost one chance at Des Moines because he wrestled scared, because he gave up his own aggressiveness in favor of a re-active style that not only runs counter to his strengths but counter to what North-Linn preaches throughout its program. Ben will have one more opportunity to put into play the approach that serves him best. And Mike is going to have something to say about making that happen.

Still standing on the floor of gymnasium several minutes later, Mike appears calm. "He'll be all right," he says of his son, and then he smiles. "Things get a little intense sometimes."

The words are offered as an explanation, not an apology. "Ben has got to know that he has to come back hard," Mike adds. "He can still qualify for State, and he should. He deserves to be there."

Stepping through the doors outside, I spot the potential State qualifier in the Fisher family. Ben is sitting, nearly naked in his little wrestling singlet, on the frozen dead grass near the front of Midland High School, tears streaming down his face. From the door that leads to the gym just across the way, Mike Hageman emerges with a long coat, crosses the lawn and drapes the coat around Ben. Then Hageman retreats quietly. It looks like a good time to let Ben work out his pain on his own.

By the time Ben and his father are getting into it at the far end of the gymnasium, Dan is already out of his warm-up clothes and onto the mat to face the same opponent for the third time in three weeks: Brett Moorman of Starmont. From Moorman's point of view, wrestling LeClere is as good a preparation as he could hope for the State Tournament; he won't necessarily be surprised by anything he sees in Des Moines, having already faced the tough-est kid on either side of the bracket.

Dan, on the other hand, appears to have grown emotionally in only a week—or at least to have altered his methods. After
needing to get revenge on Moorman at sectionals with a convinc-
ing pin, he wrestles a little more in control in the district final.
Coming right out of the opening whistle, Dan dives in and gets
Moorman's leg on his way to a quick takedown, but after watching Moorman shut tight physically to prevent being turned over,
he proceeds differently. He withdraws almost carefully, allowing
Moorman to stand upright again, and then goes in and takes him
down a second time, trying other combinations, experimenting
with the ways in which he attempts to latch on to Moorman's
arms and drive them behind the boy's back. Although Dan is pil-
ing up points and a lead—it is 12–5 after two periods—he realizes
that Moorman is actually a good matchup for him. The opponent
is difficult to pin and tough to move around the mat, and even
though Dan can take him down at will just on quickness, the
Starmont wrestler has earned his respect. He has reminded Dan
of something, too: There are times when the right thing to do is
to collect your victory and move on. In the end, Dan's repeated
takedowns earn him a 16–5 major decision and the district title.
He receives both with only the slightest flicker of satisfaction. Still
getting warmed up, as it were.

"He doesn't smile much," I say to a North-Linn mother.

"He will a week from now," she replies.

A few months ago, *The Predicament* published a cover photo
of the top seniors from the eastern part of the state: Borschel,
LeClere, Mueller, Anson, Morningstar, Slaton, Beatty. On an inside page were thumbnail sketches of each of the wrestlers, including the opportunity for them to recall their most memorable
matches. Every wrestler chose a breakthrough performance or
a landmark victory, something that either defined him as a high
school success or cemented in his own mind the possibility that
he could achieve greatness. Every wrestler but one.

"Dan's the only one who talked about a loss," Mary LeClere says. "He was still upset about getting beat last year."

Some champions are driven by a love of winning, some by the hatred of losing. Dan LeClere, at the heart of things, really is his father's son.

After shaking hands with Moorman, Dan walks off the mat and then right back onto it, circling around the edge so he can get over to Nick's corner in time for his 145-pound final. For the second time today, though, Dan is mostly a spectator; Nick doesn't need the help. He goes out against Cascade's Alex Ressler and is simply in charge from the start. Nick is so good, so active and aggressive and yet controlled, that after a little while even Brad and Doug sit back a bit in their chairs. "Is this the kid who wrestled for us all year?" Brad wonders aloud, a smile creasing his face.

It's sure the one they wanted. Injuries or no injuries, Nick hasn't forgotten how to attack. He blasts in and grabs Ressler for a takedown in the first period for a 2–0 lead, and in the second he pushes the lead to 4–0; and as the seconds and minutes roll by, you begin to suspect that Ressler, a very, very good athlete, isn't going to score a point. He searches for an opening, and none appears. He struggles to break free of Nick's hold around his waist and arm, but Nick is a step ahead, constantly switching his defensive position, forcing Ressler to start over again, draining the strength out of him move by move. Nick is having his day, and at the finish even his dad and his brother need do no more than stay in the corner and let him do his thing.

When Nick reverses Ressler in the third period to make the score 7–0, Mary LeClere allows herself a smile. She knows what it means. Unless Nick screws up royally and gets himself pinned, he is going to punch his ticket to Des Moines; and Nick isn't going to blemish this effort. He concludes his victory the way he began it, totally in charge. There will be two LeCleres on the podium today. And Doug is going to walk into the Barn, the place for which he has such a reverence, in the company of both of his State-qualified sons. Even amid the chaos of the Midland tournament, Nick's victory is a moment of clarity.

Tyler Burkle will go to Des Moines, too. He wrestles Ryan Morningstar again in the 152-pound final, and although Ryan is again the winner, this match feels closer than the one the boys wrestled just a few weeks ago—and Tyler isn't fazed by the defeat. He promptly goes out and wins his next match to secure second place and the State Tournament spot. Ryan Mulnix will go, too; Ryan pushes past the pain in his shoulder and needs only 24 seconds to pin his opponent for the "true" second place and his invitation to State. Madison Sackett's dream ends in his wrestle-back, where he loses his match and thus the shot at Des Moines; still, Madison has proved out well. He loses to a wrestler who, everyone can agree, deserves his place in the tournament.

The same cannot be said for Shannon Hocken, the senior from the family with deep roots in Walker and North-Linn High School. Shannon's consolation match at 171 pounds, against Matt Stiefel from East Buchanan, is a brutal struggle to stay alive. The boys trade reversals in the second period, neither able to contain the other. Shannon knows what he wants to do, but he can't seem to stay on course. He's erratic on the mat, showing flashes of strength and speed but then, just as quickly, losing his concentration and allowing Stiefel to take the upper hand.

Shannon takes a 6–4 lead into the third period, but Matt scores an escape to make it 6–5, and then he seizes the lead with a 2-point takedown. Now trailing 7–6, Shannon needs an escape of his own to tie the score and force overtime—and, for that matter, he could win right here, on the spot, with a late 2-point reversal. But with the clock counting down on the period, Shannon appears to yield to the moment. He gets stuck on bottom, pressed against the mat, and cannot seem find a way back up. "Get active, Shannon!" Bridgewater screams from the corner. Up in the stands, the North-Linn parents become increasingly animated, their voices rising and rising. But at some point, they seem to sense that Shannon just isn't going to fight his way out. Slowly, their cheers begin to recede. It's a weird shift of emotion, and as the final half-minute ticks away on his wrestling career, Shannon appears almost incapable of movement altogether. The seconds crawl by, and then it's over.

It takes a moment after he shakes the hand of the winner for the reality of this exchange to settle in on Shannon, but when it does, it comes in a fury. Sitting propped against one of the metal exit doors, slumped in his defeat, Shannon suddenly raises his right arm above his head and slams his hand, knuckles-first, against the door, a pounding that resonates even inside the packed gym. A few seconds later, another slam. And then again, as the frustration begins pouring out of him, as the truth about his situation sinks in. He was maybe one great burst of effort away from keeping his career going. He didn't have it. Now it's too late.

As Shannon begins to crank up, pounding his hand again and again into the metal door, I am reminded of that conversation with the mother at the little kids' tournament at North-Linn, who had watched a boy put his hand through the glass after losing and thus ruin his own season. Now Shannon has no season left to wreck, and so he's basically just taking it out on himself. Sensing the trouble, Larry Henderson comes hustling over to try to put an end to the scene, but Shannon becomes even more agitated, trying to push away anyone who comes close. Finally, lacking any other alternative, Henderson grabs Shannon, picks him up and shoves him through the door, out into the cold, gray afternoon.

"Cool it! Cool it! That's stupid!" Henderson screams.

"Get the fuck out of my face!" Shannon screams back, swinging at the air, not his coach.

"You want to punch something? Punch me!" Henderson says. "Huh? Punch me!"

But it is clear that Shannon's anger is completely inward-directed. He doesn't want anything to do with anybody right now. He wants to suffer, probably needs to suffer, and he wants to do it by himself.

"I wrestled like a bitch and you know it!" Shannon finally wails, and at that Henderson realizes he's going to have to give the boy some room. He backs off, a step at a time, and leaves the senior alone to sob. He knows the obvious thing to say, and he won't say it, because he loves Shannon and doesn't want to see him hurting. But the obvious thing to say is this: All that anger and regret, all that emotion, could have been put to use. And if even a small bit of it had been used a few moments earlier, in competition, then Shannon Hocken wouldn't be having this moment outside right now.

When I last see Shannon as a North-Linn wrestler, he is sitting in the same spot on the same dead grass that Ben Fisher had occupied a while earlier. Ben's story, though, does not end there in the cold. It continues on through the next hour or so, as the boy slowly rewinds himself from his semifinal defeat and the blowup with his dad, and at the same time lets his emotions flow, at one point coming back inside the gym and sitting on one of the wooden bleacher seats and simply crying. Teammates and cheerleaders and parents mill past and either offer a short word of encouragement or pretend not to notice. But that's not what is strange. By now, they're all accustomed to seeing gut-churning scenes played out in almost complete obscurity, despite being in plain sight.

What is strange is what happens next: Ben gets something to drink, loosens up, goes out to wrestle in what could be the final match of his life, and just utterly dominates it. I don't mean he wins. He does, but this is more than that. This is the Ben Fisher whom his coaches were waiting to see, whom his coaches sometimes wait weeks at a time to see. This is the Fisher who attacks and can almost always get the takedown when he goes for it, and who doesn't lay back and wait for something to happen. He is quick on his feet and storming around on the mat, flying in for leg-holds, using his strength to overpower his opponent. He just kicks the crap out of a kid who was also trying to get to Des Moines; the win is so dominating that it would appear, to just about anyone in the gym who isn't a North-Linn follower, so routine as to never be in doubt. In the bleachers, Mike Fisher is back to being any other rooting parent, standing next to Kathy, clapping and shouting encouragement to their son, the one who suddenly looks like he'll never lose another wrestling match in his life. It is an emotional transformation—for Ben, for his father—that took barely an hour to occur. It only felt like it was a lifetime.

At The Heights, a restaurant in Monticello on the way home, Dan takes a few bites of beef and tries to relax. It has been a productive day; he has gotten what he went to Midland High School to obtain. But of course Dan's senior year was never about making it to the district finals. He's just getting warmed up. There is no joy, for him, in reaching the Barn; the only joy will be in conquering it. "I'll feel better when I've won the fourth," Dan says, and that's the tricky part about excellence—there's almost nowhere to go with it, after a while. Dan has been so good for so long that he has probably forgotten how to experience a simple joy like winning, even though there are kids all over Iowa today who would trade places with him in an instant. They just don't see it the way Dan sees it. They don't see up to the horizon line like Dan does, so they don't know what Dan knows, which is that the only way he can approach this thing is as a person who is still just getting started on his journey. Getting to Des Moines is just another stop on the road. It's a barnstorming life, from one plateau to the next.

Up at the other end of the long table at which the North-Linn wrestlers and their families sit, a cell phone call comes through. Jim Borschel is on the other end with news: Dan will not be alone next week. In Waterloo, at his Class 3A district tournament, Jay has pinned all three of his opponents. He was on the mat for barely two minutes in all. It was an utter domination, and only Carol and Jim noticed anything worrisome in it: Jay seemed to be breathing a little harder than usual, and he was taking longer to recover after his matches. To anyone else observing, it was classic Jay Borschel wrestling, on the attack and eager to lay everything to rest. And Jay will have teammates with him in Des Moines: Shawnden Crawford has overcome his injury and reached State at heavyweight. Senior Kyle Minehart, in a pleasant surprise, has had a wonderful district tournament and also is moving on. And Matt McDonough has come all the way through in his freshman year, finishing up strong, earning the second-place spot in his district at 103. Matt is going to Des Moines on his first try.

As he is riding home from Waterloo with his teammates, Jay's voice is scratchy and his cough low and long. He doesn't sound well, but that isn't so uncommon in winter in the Midwest. Colds and flus happen, and the ethos of the place is that you accept it and keep going. Jay is fully prepared to pretend nothing is happening on that front right now, because a weakening ailment would be too inconvenient to really even consider. "It's nothing," he says dismissively when I ask. "Got a cough." In his mind, there will be no getting sick at State. He has come too far for that. He won't let another human knock him off trail, much less his own lungs.

Back at The Heights, the word spreads down the way that Jay will be joining Dan. Ben Fisher, whose family has known the Borschels for years now, smiles at the news; but, then, Ben has been smiling for two hours now. He has been smiling ever since he walked off the mat in Wyoming, off the mat and straight into an embrace with his father, a hug that lasted awhile and seemed to stand as more than simple congratulations. Now, Mike and Ben talk and joke a little, and laugh lightly as though nothing unusual has happened today. It is all a means to an end, perhaps. It is as though the entire scene from the semifinals has shrunk into but one blurred corner of a much larger photograph. Ben is calm, tired, happy. He is not thrilled, exactly; it is different than that. This is a deeper sort of satisfaction. He fought the gods and the demons today. For Ben—for Dan, for Jay—it won't be the last time.

CHAPTER 14

Barnstorming

Just north of the clustered center of downtown Des Moines, at the corner of Fifth Street and Crocker, set well back from the sidewalk, sits the Veterans Memorial Auditorium. It is a large, plain building, 50 years old, with a roof that rises to its point as a sort of gigantic upside-down V, and it is said that, were one so moved, one could fill the arena with 58,400 tons of baled hay. A local writer once described the place as "practical, efficient, unadorned, like Iowa." It was fully intended as a compliment.

But, of course, this is not how Dan sees it. When he glances at the face of the creaking old event center, Dan sees a thing that looks an awful lot like home. "It just feels like where I should be," he says one day; and it is the peculiar attribute of an elite athlete that he can come from a town of 700 people and yet feel at ease inside a building that soon will fill with upward of 11,000, each of whom will sound quite confident that he knows better than Dan how to do the thing Dan has been doing, with great success, his entire conscious life. Which is to say, it'll become a sports venue.

Still, it's the vast, cool, unconstrained space of Vets that feels right to Dan. "I've always liked it here better," he says, meaning better than the stuffy gyms in which he has been honing his craft these months. Dan has wrestled in so many big venues before, lots of times, in lots of states, in front of lots of people. He has won important things inside huge buildings. Those smaller places, the ones inside which he has spent the majority of his wrestling life—they serve the purpose now of an elaborate warm-up act, the prelude to the show. When Dan walks into the place in downtown Des Moines that they long ago and so appropriately nicknamed the Barn, it is exactly what he wants, and where he wants it to be.

It is the same for Jay, that feeling. Although the Borschels live a little more than two hours away, there is no point in their traveling to Des Moines for any reason other than the State Wrestling Tournament. They come here for the one thing, and for the memories it creates. When Jay thinks of Veterans Memorial Auditorium, he sees not a collection of old plastic seats that rise too steeply and weren't really all that comfortable to begin with, but rather the rewards of his era. This is the place, after all, where the good stuff began to happen. His relatives have made trips from different parts of the country in order to see him stand on top of the podium here. Jay began to forge his identity as a dominant wrestler by succeeding here. "It's hard not to feel good about a place where you win," he tells me on Wednesday, the first day of State; and this is such a place. Jay has never lost here, at least not yet. His teammates and school followers have been able to walk right down to the side of the wrestling mats here—despite the fact that it was the State Tournament they were tramping through—and essentially track his every move, grunt, mouthpiece adjustment and brutalization of opponents through the years, from a mat-side distance of maybe two full body-throws.

That's standard wrestling-lunatic behavior, by the way. Everybody at Vets does it. It is practically a birthright of the ticket holder to crash the party going on down on the floor. Once you hear, over the vaguely corroded PA system, the name of a wrestler you want to cheer from any vantage point closer than your upper-level seat, you basically just tear downstairs and elbow your way past the folks standing stump-like around the retaining ropes; and on any night other than Finals Night you can, within perhaps a minute or two of decent scrumming, find yourself within a few feet of the wrestlers themselves, going at it on one of the multicolored mats spread about the floor. You can see and hear everything, even amid the din of eight separate matches and a series of announcements all going off at the same time. You can shout very specific instructions—"Single leg! Single leg! Work it! Drive him!"—at your guy. You can wildly and profanely insult the other team's wrestler without any real concern over retaliation, a fact which Jay already understands pretty well, considering the number of times through the years he has been called a faggot or a queer—or sometimes, even, an overrated wrestler—by the various loons in the crowd. At the Barn, you can pretty much do as you like.

But best of all is this: If somebody either achieves the pinnacle of his fantasies or flames out in a spectacular, soul-crushing defeat, you are right there to witness the kill. You don't need to strain in order to hear what comes out of the losers, the people who have just had their hearts ripped apart with their parents looking on. You get to hear the testosterone-fueled screams of the winners, the ones moving forward—the kids who still can see the horizon lines of their hopes. You can watch young people uncontrollably burst into tears right in front of you, or leap into the arms of their coaches in a post-victory delirium. Maybe, if you are extremely fortunate, you will see a boy quietly remove his wrestling shoes and leave them in the middle of the mat—a compelling and emotional symbolic announcement of his retirement from the sport, right there on the spot, seconds after completing his final struggle.

And if either Dan or Jay should somehow screw up this time—well then, the Barn will bear witness to his failure and, simultaneously, to that great moment of ascendance in some other young wrestler's career. Whoever beats one of these guys is going to be anointed a star.

For early arrivals at the State Wrestling Tournament (and they're all pretty much early arrivals), the sense of time having slowed a little is always near. The fans file inside to the sounds of Foghat and Van Halen being pumped through the building. The tickets cost seven dollars, and with the exception of Finals Night they cannot be purchased beforehand. The people drive from their hometowns, Wapello or Mapleton or Council Bluffs, and check in at the hotels they have had to reserve months in advance. They find a place to park downtown and walk through fat, wet flakes of snow into the grand foyer of the auditorium, and go stand in the box-office lines alongside hundreds of other wrestling people dressed in T-shirts bearing slogans such as PAIN IS WEAKNESS LEAVING THE BODY. Once handed their general-admission tickets, they quickly engage in a sort of semicivilized land rush, a full-on—but mostly polite—scramble inside the doors in order to secure their schools' traditional group of seats in the Barn, their unofficially staked claims in Section 220, or Section 103, or Section 4, or wherever.

Section 4, by the way: Horrible seats. A lousy view with a bad angle to the mats, stuck right at the northwest corner turn of the building. But that's where the families and fans of Marion's Linn-Mar High School have sat for years' worth of State Tournaments, and the most recent group isn't going to change now, not with Jay bearing down on history. Says one parent, very seriously, "That's just tempting fate."

The lighting isn't much at Veterans. The upper-level seats arc heavenward at an instant-nosebleed clip. The announcer generally comes through the loudspeakers sounding, to borrow a descrip-

tion from long ago, like geese farts on a muggy day. The concession lines curl sideways in snakelike patterns to accommodate the
extra floor-level bleachers that are jutting their way backward
from the mats; the bathrooms show their age in leaks; and when
you want to go over to the wall by the entry doors to have a look
at the painstakingly hand-drawn brackets for each weight class
that over the course of four days here will become the living history of the tournament, you find yourself pretty quickly stuck in
the middle of a human traffic jam, too many folks packed into far
too small a space. You can't move left or right without needing
to circumnavigate a fellow who, from appearances, might still be
wrestling today if his high school eligibility hadn't expired sometime last century.

In short, it's just about heaven. As Doug LeClere puts it,
"Every time I step inside that building the hairs on the back of
my neck stand up. Look: It just happened. And all I did was talk
about it."

And they will miss the Barn when they go. They will miss
the history and the stories and the reserved "unreserved" seating
and the mat access, fifty years' worth of good stuff. What they
gain in the move down the street to the shiny new place, the
one under construction now and bearing the Wells Fargo bank
logo on the outside, they will lose in institutional value and the
dependable sameness of the years. The new place is to be thoroughly modern and much more stylish, substantially larger, emi-
nently comfortable, full of bells and whistles and climate control.
It ought to suck just about completely.

They say nothing much happens in Iowa, but for a half-
century-old, nothing-special-by-design building, Veterans Memorial Auditorium has done all right for herself. Ozzy Osbourne
bit the head off a dead bat here during a concert in 1982. Antiho-
mosexual crusader Anita Bryant was struck in the face at Vets in
1977 with a banana cream pie tossed by gay activist Thom Hig-

gins during a preconcert news conference. Larry Bird scored 45 points for Indiana State one night against Drake. *Beverly Hillbillies* star Irene Ryan appeared at a country concert in 1964, prompting the rather unlikely headline—"3,578 Roar Welcome to Sexy Granny"—from the normally staid *Des Moines Register*. Elvis Presley played the auditorium five weeks before his death in 1977.

And in 1976, Jeff Kerber, a 98-pound strongman from the town of Emmetsburg in the northern part of the state, very quietly and without fanfare won his first Iowa High School wrestling title here. The next year, Kerber, having moved to 112 pounds, won another. The next year, another. And in 1979, before an audience which by then understood what it was witnessing, Jeff Kerber, now filled out to 126 pounds, won it all again. It was a victory little noted anywhere else in the world but one that caused the walls of Vets to reverberate with the applause of the people inside it, because in so doing, Kerber achieved the distinction of being the first four-time state champion, the first of the new Iowa kings to be crowned inside the Barn.

It was the kind of scene Jay and Dan find themselves so close to now that they can almost see it. Of course, that assumes everything goes according to plan.

The hacking actually had begun in the days before the district tournament in Waterloo, and by that weekend Jay was feeling perfectly lousy. He couldn't get a clear breath. It was annoying as much as anything, because he wasn't ready to be worried. He slammed his way through the district, recording three pins, the kind of performance that is so on par for him that no one outside his family and coaches had the slightest idea what was going on. His entire goal that day was to get off the mat and go take a steaming hot shower. He took four of them on the Saturday of districts alone. There was something building in his chest and he couldn't shake it. What can you say? Timing's a bitch.

By the time of that long bus ride back to Marion from Waterloo, Jay sounded like a sea lion. It was clear that whatever he
had gotten was going to settle in and completely screw things up,
or at least become a major distraction. He didn't know then that
he had bronchitis, but he knew it was lousy. All of which made
it all the more galling to Jim that Jay immediately went out and
made things worse.

Getting off the bus from that trip, Jay and Shawnden hopped
in a car and headed for Woody's, a local juice bar/strip club in
Cedar Rapids out on the other side of the interstate, toward the
airport. They stayed for a while, maybe an hour, maybe two hours.
Jim only knew Jay wasn't home.

Finally, Jim grabbed his cell phone and got hold of Jay.

"Where are you?" Jim said.

"With Shawnden," Jay replied.

"Get your ass back to the house!" his father barked.

Jay considered it an unremarkable development at the time.
He was 18, after all, and not doing anything illegal. "It's not like I
went out and got in a fight," he said the next day, sounding a little
defensive. "We just went out for a little while."

Jim, on the other hand, was beside himself. "It's just flat-out
the wrong place to be," he said bluntly. Setting aside every other
implication for a moment, Jim couldn't believe Jay would lapse
into such ludicrous judgment when he knew his body was in a
fragile state. It wasn't as though Jay didn't understand he was sick.
He certainly could read a calendar. What part of "bring your best
to Des Moines" didn't he understand? Was this another challenge
the kid needed to set out for himself?

Still, Jim knew he had to be careful about what he said, and
how much. Des Moines was approaching, and what was done was
done. The focus had to be on getting Jay better as quickly as possible.
Jim had yelled at Jay on Saturday night, but by Sunday afternoon
his thought process had gone back to basics: They had to get Jay

some help. Jay spent two stultifying hours sitting at a clinic, waiting to be seen and then being prescribed something for the infection in his lungs. "Just sitting here," he said at one point upon answering his cell phone. To Jim, this was almost an acceptable punishment in it-self. He was willing and frankly happy to stop lecturing. Jim, above all others, understood how many days and nights Jay had pounded himself into superior condition—all on his own, all from his own internal motivation. Jay had pushed himself when the other wres-tlers wanted to go home, and Jay had been the one who, night after night, found it in himself to head back out after dinner for another run or weight session. Jay had proved so many times to be a worthy guardian of his own aspirations. He had spent years perfecting his craft. Jim was respectful of all of that. He knew what that took out of his son, what his son gave up willingly to make it happen. That couldn't be diminished, even if his son had just done something only a knucklehead could love.

Jay, on the other hand, was pretty clear in what he wanted from his father, and criticism wasn't high on the list. He could take it from Streicher, because Streicher was the coach who had wrestled at some of the levels Jay wanted to reach. From Jim, Jay wanted high fives and not much else. Of course, he knew full well his father, in the end, could never offer only that much. Jim had been a wrestler, too.

"I've never just come out and say, 'Fine, you're the best,'" Jim says. "It could be because there's always another something to reach for. If somebody tells you you're the best, where do you go from there? Even now, if Jay is the best in high school, what does that mean? He's going to college after this—he's got to wrestle up to that level. It'll be starting all over again."

Still, Jim understands that with Des Moines a couple of days away, it is pointless for him to go too hard on Jay for screwing with his health. A few hours out late didn't start the problem. It's a problem. Jay has to deal with it.

Carol, on the other hand, feels no such constraints. She is enraged not only by Jay's carelessness but also by the message that it sends to anyone who might learn where Jay had gone in the hours following the Waterloo tournament. It isn't just putting himself at risk; it's sleazy. It is beneath him. He has a girlfriend he genuinely likes and a mother whom he admires (despite his deep love of teasing and testing her), and something like this just doesn't fit. Marion is a small town. Carol cares about her family's position in it. She didn't raise her son to disrespect women.

At dinner that Sunday evening, Carol sits across the table from her son, fuming. Jay, trying to lighten the mood, uses the moment to needle his mother on the topic.

"How am I disrespecting women?" he says with a playful grin. "Aren't I supporting their jobs?"

"You know what I'm talking about," Carol shoots back.

"But that's their business," Jay says. "I'm supporting their business."

"That's not support."

"But if I'm giving them money—"

"Jay," Carol suddenly says decisively, her voice flat and firm; and that is the end of the conversation. Even Jay, it turns out, knows when to back off. Some challenges are not meant to be met. Besides, every time he draws up a breath to conjure up another argument in his favor, his coughing spasms shoot him down. The visit to Woody's may or may not have had the slightest effect on his condition, but about the condition itself there is no question: He looks crappy and feels worse.

Jay has taken three pills designed to work over ten days, but now, here on Wednesday, the first day of the State Tournament in Des Moines, it is clear that there will be no easy fix. He arrives at the Barn looking pale and feeling listless—not that you can necessarily pick him out of the crowd. Wrestling is a sport that produces tremendous, superbly conditioned athletes, some of whom nevertheless appear almost constantly in danger of passing out while standing upright. In part that is due to the ongoing weight-cutting regimens, in part to the fact that the athletes spend the majority of their free time for months indoors, under fluorescent lights, shortchanging themselves on fluids about half the time. And they are notorious for involuntarily sharing germs and viruses of all types throughout their season, which explains why you see the freshmen and non-varsity wrestlers out there disinfecting the rubber mats at the coaches' insistence at every available opportunity—pure punishment for not being on the A-list, but also as a practical matter of keeping the team as healthy as possible. Earlier in the season, the Linn-Mar team suffered an epidemic of impetigo that even took Streicher out of action, and after that, the flu-like, deep-cough-producing stuff started going around. Half the room has had it, and assistant coach CJ McDonald has got it right now, and the doctor says Jay has bronchitis. In other news, it's the State Tournament.

"I'm feeling a little better," Jay says.

"You look terrible," someone replies.

"Yeah." Jay smiles weakly.

He will wrestle, of course. No self-respecting wrestler would even consider bailing out at State because he feels lousy. As Jim says matter-of-factly, "Even if he throws up during the match, it's just an injury timeout." But Jim, a man who tries not to sweat the small stuff, is worried all the same. Carol is worried outright even though she knows the truth, which is that Jay already has been treated and that, sooner or later, he'll get better, and there's nothing to do about it now. The Borschels have seen their son wrestle so well in so many different situations that it is almost impossible to imagine any result other than a good one, and yet everyone around Jay recognizes the crushing magnitude of what he is trying to do. They hate the fact that he quite evidently will go through his final State Tournament with what feels like a hundred-pound bag of seed lying across his chest.

And on this first day, in this first match, it becomes apparent that health is going to play its role. On the same day he appears on the front page of the *Des Moines Register*'s sports section alongside Dan, Jay is paired in the brackets with Craig Abrahamson from Boone, a town north of Des Moines in the central part of the state. A junior, not quite filled out yet, with nine losses on his record this season, he's the kind of opponent Jay normally toys with before pinning. Any other day, Jay would use the mat time the way Dan sometimes does, to work on certain moves or experiment with a new series of maneuvers that might lead to a pin. It would be experimentation in the middle of a match, the kind of thing only the advanced wrestler would really try.

This day, though, is not like any other day. Jay, so used to wrestling in this huge place, comes out with no nerves and no indecision. He stalks Abrahamson from the opening whistle and gets a quick takedown, then another. He looks himself, basically. But it doesn't last. As Jay reaches across Abrahamson's body late in the first period, looking to get the boy's arms behind his back and begin the process of wrenching him over onto his shoulders, he loses his grip. Abrahamson tries to squirm free, but there's nowhere to go. Jay steadies his opponent, locking him back down, and then he reaches for Abrahamson's arms again. But he misses again, and this time the crowd around the mat begins to murmur. Jay is trying, but he can't seem to wrap this thing up. It's as if Abrahamson were dipped in oil. If you didn't know better, you'd swear that Jay just wasn't concentrating hard enough to get it done.

And then something almost shocking happens: Jay appears to reconsider, right there on the mat. He backs off a bit. He stops trying to pin Abrahamson. The period ends. Jay looks tired—and not just tired, but gassed. And just like that, we have taken a sharp left turn into the land of You Sure Never Know.

It isn't just that Abrahamson is lanky, although that helps—for a wrestler to be longer and leaner means that while he may not pack the raw power of some of his weight-class counterparts, he can cause them problems with his range and his reach. But right now, it's more about what Jay can't do than what Abrahamson can. As the second period begins, it becomes obvious that Jay is struggling to get his breath. He's moving slower than at any time in recent memory. Abrahamson, who does not stack up as a serious threat, suddenly finds himself able to get his hands on Jay and actually gain leverage—and then, to the shock of the people watching, he simply wrenches Jay down to the mat and gains control of him for a takedown. No one can remember the last time a wrestler scored offensive points against Jay, and even though Jay quickly rights himself and gets back on top of Abrahamson, the significance of the moment hasn't been lost on anyone here. What they just saw was a chink in the armor.

For the first time since I arrived in Iowa, Jay spends the rest of his match watching the clock on the scoreboard that has been wheeled out to the edge of the mat. He is actually hoping to grind out the time. As the second period gives way to the third, it is obvious that he just wants the thing to end; he no longer cares about sending a "message" with a vicious pin, or anything of the sort. What he wants is to be done.

In the corner, Doug Streicher is screaming for Jay to continue scoring as the time runs down. Despite his inability to finish, Jay has managed several takedowns and a few escapes, and has piled up a 21–9 lead. If he can get to 24–9, the 15-point margin will constitute a technical fall and yield Linn-Mar more team points. But Jay flat-out hasn't got it and doesn't want to use it, whatever "it" is that normally fills his tank. He rides out Abrahamson, watching that clock, and he accepts his major-decision victory, perhaps Jay's least impressive win of the season. He has made news simply by failing to obliterate his opponent. It is the last thing Jay cares about right now. He's too busy trying to get a breath.

Jay shakes hands with Abrahamson, who then turns to celebrate with his coaches that he kept things so close against the great Borschel. Jay, meanwhile, grabs his gear and heads downstairs to the dressing area. He begins lightly going down the steps, and then he pauses. Jay grabs the handrail. It's getting fuzzy. He abruptly sits down, right there on the cold cement stairs. He cannot stop panting. He doesn't feel as though he can make it down even one more short flight. Day One of the biggest tournament of his life, and the three-time state champion, the wrestler called one of the best in Iowa state history, sits.

For twenty minutes.

"This sucks," he says, and that's the right word. Normally, Jay is back to a resting heart rate within a couple of minutes of finishing a match. For the past few days he has been playing the role of high school kid, ignoring the thing in his chest in hopes that it'd just go away. He took his three horse pills from the doctor and figured he'd go on with his life. But now Jay sees that he is going to have to deal with this thing. He wrestled fairly effectively for a few minutes with Abrahamson despite his limitations, and then he realized that he could not breathe. He was wheezing to the finish, trying just to hang on. Streicher, ever the coach, was arguing for the points, and later he would note that, even allowing for the illness, Jay wasn't technically sharp at all. But Doug knows this is serious. He screamed at Jay so much from the corner because he wanted him to wipe out Abrahamson and get off the mat; staying out there for the full three periods was the worst that could have happened. The thing is, Jay didn't have it in him to finish—and both he and his coach know it.

"The tournament just got interesting," Jay says half an hour later, studying the big 171-pound bracket taped to the wall. The best wrestler in his class—the best in the state—is in a dogfight against the toughest opponent he will face this week: himself.

Unlike just about everything else connected with the Barn, the basement doesn't really have a name, which is too bad. The basement at Vets is the place where, over thirty-odd years, thousands of wrestlers have readied themselves for thousands of matches, jogging around the cement-floor perimeter of the huge, fluorescent-lit area in five layers of clothes, trying to sweat off enough water to make weight, dashing to the bathrooms to empty stomachs and bowels, using one of the quarter-mats spread around to warm up and deal with the nerves, coming down here to cry after terrible, season-ending defeats and to celebrate after great, transcendent victories. Three decades of this sort of grand theater should have produced a classic nickname, or even a workable one. No such luck.

And so everyone just goes "downstairs," to the place that is their final refuge of the year, where fans and families are not allowed to tread and cameras and reporters seldom follow. It's like the biggest rumpus room in the country. The Barn, after all, covers an area of roughly two acres, and this basement looks to account for almost all of it. It is accessible from stairwells on either side of the ground above, meaning that as soon as a wrestler loses a match, he is free to make a wild dash for the stairs in order to suffer his pain more or less out of the public eye, and that as soon as a wrestler wins he can hurry down the stairs to let out the kind of whoop that might appear unsportsmanlike if he did it out on the floor of competition. When the tournament came here in 1970, it quickly became apparent that with this many wrestlers, there was a crying need for a significant warm-up area, and the space just didn't exist upstairs. Downstairs was pretty much wide open. You could say it worked out.

Doug Streicher isn't a big downstairs guy; during the opening round of the Class 3A competition on Wednesday, his four wrestlers spent most of their time up on the main floor, off in one of the officially protected cement corners of the building just away from the eight wrestling mats of competition; they didn't go downstairs unless they really needed to. On Thursday, by contrast, the North-Linn team and coaching staff have basically taken over a downstairs warm-up mat for themselves. Dan and Nick, and Ben Fisher, and Ryan Mulnix, and Tyler Burkle—they'll all kill time down here before they are called to the mats.

Doug LeClere paces around the room, which comes as no surprise. Doug once described himself as "the doom and gloom guy," but what he really appears to be is just a good old-fashioned worrier. He's in the right place. At the high school level, coaching is basically one sustained exercise in dealing with the limits of one's ability to impart fireproof information to young athletes. Wrestling is actually better than most, because if a kid doesn't listen to instruction, he's likely to get an arm or a nose or a brain pan twisted exactly the wrong way by some kid who *was* listening when his coach delivered the speech on chicken wings and cross-faces and the like. But high school coaching, at the heart of it, is still working with young people who have other things to do besides come to practice—a million other things to do, sometimes. And because of that, there really is only so much one man can control.

At this particular moment, Doug has at least three reasons to be nervous. The first two are the members of his own family, his two State entrants. The third is standing about forty feet away, stalking around the downstairs area in his sweat suit, a physical specimen by the name of Joey Verschoor. It is Verschoor with whom Tyler Burkle has had the horrible luck to be paired in the first round. It's nonsensical; after Ryan Morningstar, Burkle and Verschoor are widely considered to be the two best wrestlers in the entire 1A field at 152 pounds. Because they face off so early, one of these highly rated wrestlers will be eliminated from championship consideration on the first day of competition, which is patently ludicrous. But because the State Tournament's entries are not seeded (the Iowa State High School Athletic Association says it cannot come up with a fair ranking system), matchups like these sometimes occur in the early rounds, and frequently top wrestlers will meet in the semifinals, not the finals.

While the Burkle-Verschoor winner will have a path toward meeting Morningstar in the final, the loser will have to win five straight matches just to finish third, with no chance of reaching the championship. It is widely agreed that Tyler has drawn the harshest first-round pairing in the entire field, and just now that opponent is limbering up what appears to be a wildly oversized frame for just 152 pounds of body weight.

"Look at him," Doug says, muttering under his breath so that Tyler won't hear. "That kid's one tough kid." It's the highest praise imaginable from Doug, a man who absolutely hates to compliment the opposition and who generally views other wrestlers strictly in terms of how they can be beaten and what tendencies they reveal each time they perform.

Once the two boys get upstairs and square off, Verschoor gets Tyler back on his heels in the first few seconds of the match. It's easy to see that Tyler, who appeared cautious this season only when wrestling Morningstar, is wary of even locking hands with Verschoor. But Tyler never gets the chance to gain his bearings. Within a couple of seconds of the match beginning, Verschoor shoots in for a takedown, and he is so quick and so strong that he pulls off the move without even a hitch in his motion. Perhaps a minute later, he wrenches Tyler over onto his back. Tyler appears shocked at what is happening; he is trying to process what to do, but there's no time. Verschoor isn't going to miss this chance. He sticks Tyler on his back and records a stunning fall in just a minute and a half of wrestling time. Even those who championed Verschoor wouldn't have predicted it. It's no fluke; Verschoor is too good for that to be so. But it's also something that might not happen if the two opponents wrestled a dozen times more. Of course, it doesn't have to—it happened this time, when it mattered most. On this day, for the only time this season, Tyler gets caught and pinned. In his corner, Doug and Brad Bridgewater and Larry Henderson don't appear terribly surprised, but it's clear they are struggling for what to say to their beaten wrestler.

If there is any good news, it is that Tyler seems more confused by the turn of events than hurt or emotionally flamed. He grabs his gear and runs off the mat, but downstairs, just a few moments later, he is neither hanging his head nor trying to be alone—he's around the other North-Linn wrestlers and coaches, talking, going back over the sudden sequence of events. Learning. Tyler isn't ready to anticipate the end of his tournament—he's just getting started. He also knows that, outside of Morningstar, Verschoor is the toughest wrestler he could have faced. It isn't over yet for Tyler as long as he won't let it be—and, seeing him now, it is clear that he won't.

The disappointment of Tyler's match aside, the day is not lost for North-Linn. Ryan Mulnix wins his first-round match when his opponent gets hurt, the boy eventually requiring a gurney to take him off the floor with his neck in a brace. Ryan, who has endured that season-long pain in his shoulder, looks on impassively. He knows how it feels.

Ben Fisher's tournament begins at 135 pounds with an opponent whom his coaches think he should be able to beat. Easy to say from the side of the mat, of course, and with Ben there is seldom anything that feels predetermined. The two wrestlers struggle, each looking a little nervous and a little conservative, afraid of making a fatal mistake so early in the tourney. With the score tied 2–2 going into the third period, Ben escapes from his opponent (1 point) and then gets him on a low takedown (2 points) for a

5–2 lead—but with 16 seconds left and Mike and Kathy screaming their encouragement from the nearby bleachers, Ben seems to
let up momentarily, and his opponent squirts out of his grasp for a
1-point escape. Now it is 5–3, with the clock counting down and
both wrestlers back on their feet. Ben is forced to play keep-away
for the remaining seconds of the match, avoiding his opponent's
attempts to get a takedown and tie the score. Nothing easy about
it, actually.

When the time comes for Dan LeClere to reenter the world
of the State Tournament, he is ready. A half-hour of pacing in the
downstairs room has had its intended effect; Dan is set to go. He
likes for his first match to be a good workout, so he attacks for a
quick takedown, then lets his man back up. He takes him down
again, lets him up. His opponent is big, certainly bigger-looking
than Dan, and he will successfully avoid getting pinned, although
at the cost of being dragged around the mat for most of three
periods. As time winds down on the match, Dan finally scores
the points that will give him a technical fall and thus a bonus
score for his team, a 22–7 victory that announces him as ready to
pursue the fourth title. He feels good. "This is how I started the
tournament last year, with a tech-fall," he says. It's funny: Dan has
captured his match by only a few points more than Jay did his,
and yet the two have had almost opposite emotional experiences.
Dan clearly won; Jay walked away feeling as though he'd lost.

And that is the talk of the tourney, of course—how Jay felt,
or looked, walking away. Wrestling is a close-knit society, and everybody understands the stakes for LeClere and Borschel. It is the
reason that Jay's opening-round victory has become such news; the
word has leaked out that he may be sick ("Jay Borschel gets out
of his deathbed and wins!" one broadcaster intones half-seriously
later that evening), and there is talk that Jay may finally be vulnerable in his field. It's a hell of a time to suddenly appear mortal.

Dan, too, is having his every move scrutinized. After all those weekends in lost towns and moldy gyms, he has come back to the place where they know him. And though he has passed his first test handily, the questions from the interviewers afterward are almost strictly directed at what might happen on Saturday.

"How do you feel about becoming a four-timer?" one asks.

"Well," Dan says, "I haven't gotten there yet. I just want to keep going and get it done."

Dan, by now, has been through enough interviews to answer the questions almost by rote, which he prefers to do anyway; and his low-key style and apparent lack of emotion serve him beautifully in one respect: The TV people don't keep him long. "I just wanted to get it done," he says of his opening match at one point, adding nothing. The interviewer waits for an elaboration that isn't going to come. Dan is not suddenly going to burst into a flurry of enthusiasms.

Finally cutting his losses, the interviewer thanks Dan and moves on. Dan is officially dead air. It may save his life this week.

By Thursday evening, the storylines are falling into place. Dan and Jay have found their way into the newspapers, their quest formally announced to the masses, and Dan has responded by winning his first match handily. Under the 1A system, he will wrestle twice on Friday and need those two wins—one earlier in the day, one later—to vault him into the finals.

Jay, meanwhile, wrestles his second match of the tournament Thursday evening against Robbie Kramer, the Cedar Rapids Prairie kid whom Jay has dominated at points earlier in the season. This time, though, Kramer takes a different tack entirely. Standing upright, refusing to lean too far in and get yanked into a low tussle, the Prairie wrestler stays a pace away from Jay and spends his time trying to anger and annoy Jay to the point that Jay might make a mistake based on emotion. When the two boys get

close enough to one another to reach in, Kramer uses the prox-
imity to slap the sides of Jay's headgear with his heavy hands, jerk-
ing Jay's head around in the process. The rest of the time, he uses
his strength to push away Jay's arm every time Jay tries to reach
under Kramer's midsection and find a hold on the side. It's an
interesting strategy, coming on a day in which Jay still feels horrible and might be tempted to try and shortcut his way through
a match. Jay absorbs the blows and keeps on coming, but at a low
hum. He is working with a cautious referee who disallows one of
Jay's signature moves, in which he wrenches his opponent's hand
behind his back in an effort to get him turned over and ready to
pin. The official blows his whistle and re-sets the wrestlers, saying
Jay's move is too close to being a physically dangerous one, just as
Jay is about to apply it and try to finish off Kramer.

But it might not matter anyway; Jay looks, sounds and wrestles as though trapped in a fog. The weight on his chest simply
will not lift. He hacks, heaves, blows out his nostrils, spits some
more; and though he is still dangerous enough to score points, he
cannot finish.

From his corner, Doug Streicher is again riding Jay verbally,
trying as he did on Wednesday to help his wrestler snap back into
form. But, just as he did the day before, Jay already has come to
understand that he is in a survival mode. "Cut him! Cut him!"
Doug screams, meaning he wants Jay to turn Kramer loose so
that he can take him down again and pile up extra points for the
Linn-Mar team. But Jay already has made his decision: conserve
and move on. He clings to Kramer down the stretch, again moni-
toring the clock. "This is fun," he deadpans during one break. The
final score is a serviceable but unimpressive 8–2, and coming in
the second round it does nothing to suggest that Jay is ready to
dominate his way through the rest of the week.

The stuff inside Jay's chest is glowing all sorts of colors as
it leaves his body. All in all, it could be the worst time ever to

be answering questions about reaching for wrestling immortality, which Jay nevertheless is asked to do as he meets with a pack of reporters after defeating Kramer. "You suck, Borschel, you fag!" one of the Prairie students shouts from the thick of a crowd, behind the retaining ropes. Jay doesn't even have the energy to look back. "I need to go sit down," he says, and his eyes glance out across the arena and up into the stands, where his family is seated.

It feels a long way off. What Jay would like to do is crawl up someplace and pass out for a week. Says Jim, a few moments later, "It'll have to wait."

The Friday of State is moving day—moving up, or moving out. For the North-Linn kids, it is a day in which everything feels tantalizingly close and the emotion runs near the surface: Win both matches today and a wrestler suddenly has reached the finals, the biggest stage of the year. Lose either one, though, and it is a long, slow journey to the consolation bracket, from which the highest possible finish is third place. And early in the day, Ryan Mulnix begins that journey, dropping a tough 7–5 quarterfinal decision to a boy from Ogden who manages to hold Ryan scoreless for the entire third period. Ryan wrestles well; he's just slightly overmatched. This isn't the conference tournament anymore.

Still, there are greatly encouraging signs. Ben Fisher trails 4–3 in the third period, but he manages an escape and then gets a takedown for the lead, and holds on for the 6–4 victory that gets him through the morning. Rather incredibly, considering what has happened the last few weekends, that's Ben in the state semifinals. And Dan will be there, of course, and his brother, too. Dan wrestles a senior from Don Bosco, perhaps the most revered program currently in the state. Dan is ready for him. He scores his first takedown 18 seconds into the match and keeps attacking for three periods. He is relentless and looks fresh, and the Don Bosco wrestler, who had only returned from injury fairly recently, just can't hang. It's a 14–3 major decision for Dan, to go along with the 8–0 shutout that Nick posts right after that at 145 pounds.

So Dan and Nick are there in the semis, and Ben; and in the loser's bracket, Tyler Burkle already is beginning his comeback with a solid victory. For the most part, it's setting up pretty nicely. Of course, it's early.

Sure enough, the semifinal session that evening plays a cruel joke on Doug LeClere and the rest of the North-Linn fans. As if by some cosmic design, all three of their kids—Ben, Nick and Dan—will be wrestling at the same time. Their assigned mats are close together, but the parents and fans are still going to have to try to track all three matches simultaneously, and that means they may well miss important parts of each. It seems almost like a punishment, considering the drive they've all made and the money they're putting up at hotels this week.

Ben's week begins to turn the other way as the pressure ratchets up. With Doug coaching in his corner, Ben repeatedly takes his shots in the first period, trying to get an early takedown that will put his opponent on the defensive. But he can't get it and can't get it; and then his opponent begins to assert control; and Ben gets that look in his eyes that says he knows the way this is going to go. He doesn't run out of fight, exactly; he just suddenly seems unable to get anything started. It's a long six minutes of mat time, and Ben never really appears completely into it. He ends the match down 4–1, and even though it's respectable, the defeat knocks the wind out of him. Ben seems shocked by the result. He has to come back in a few hours and win another match just for the right to try for third place; but this is no Midland-Wyoming, and these are no district-level wrestlers. Downstairs afterward, Ben already is starting to look like a guy who is envisioning the rest of his life, the part without wrestling in it. "We're losing him," one of Ben's teammates says. He's right: Ben is going to be defeated in his evening match as well, a match he is never close to controlling. He will go to the final competition of his high school career on Saturday, wrestling for fifth place, when he had begun Friday just six minutes removed from a shot at the finals.

By the middle of Ben's semifinal, Doug has switched places with Bridgewater and Larry Henderson so he can scurry over to Nick's corner, where Nick, for the first time since coming back from his injuries, is beginning to show the effects of not having wrestled the full season. "Get on top!" Doug screams. "Get over on him!" But it's obvious that Nick is laboring to find a balance against Mitch Norton, a finished product from Nashua-Plainfield. Norton is just strong all over, and he doesn't make mistakes. Even though he can't do much with Nick, he is able to get two reversals for points. Still, going into the final period, Nick trails only 4–2. He has a crucial strategic decision to make: It is Nick's choice whether to begin the period in the on-top position (and thus try for a pin or for near-fall points) or the down position (and try for a 1-point escape, then a 2-point takedown to win). Nick looks to his corner for guidance. Doug, straining to be heard over the din of the crowd and all these other matches bursting with sound around him, tries to hand-signal Nick that he can choose whichever position he feels better about—but Nick only sees his father make the "down" motion with his hands. Nick starts on the bottom, but his fatigue is setting in, and almost as soon as the period begins, Norton is able to break down one of Nick's arms and get one shoulder of Nick's to the mat. Nick fights to break free, but Norton uses his top-position leverage to finally roll both of Nick's shoulders onto the mat. Not quite a minute into the third, Nick is pinned.

"I did that to him," Doug says later, downstairs. "He didn't see my sign. I should have yelled it, too." Doug is disconsolate. It's no use telling him the truth, which is that it probably didn't matter, that Nick was fading physically and stuck in there against a really solid wrestler. After having spent so much time on the sideline this season, Nick cannot summon his A-game on command, and over in the cool-down area, he looks spent. He is. He will go on to lose his consolation semifinal as well. After such a great run through the section and district tournaments, this isn't Nick's year, after all. As Dan had earlier observed, it was barely a year at that, and at the finish it was too much to ask to get all the way there. But Nick is only a sophomore. There is still time. There is more LeClere to come.

By the time the excitement on the other mats begins to taper off, the crowd inside Veterans Memorial has almost completely turned its attention to an eye-popping scene more or less in the middle of the auditorium. There, down on his hands and knees, is the great Dan LeClere. Stuck.

The other wrestler on the mat is Klint Kersten, one of a number of strong entries from a well-coached program, Logan-Magnolia, that will finish this weekend with the top team score in Class 1A. And Kersten has decided, in this semifinal, to put on the match of his life.

Dan has stormed the mat with his usual fierceness to begin the contest. He is so ready for this; he has paced himself into his usual frenzy downstairs and come up to this great roar of applause from the North-Linn fans in particular and many in the crowd in general. As the wrestlers circle each other to begin, Dan suddenly springs forward, so quick and so light on his feet, and dives down to spear one of Kersten's legs. He holds on and gains leverage for a single-leg takedown and a 2–0 lead. And there it stops.

After allowing that solitary lapse, Kersten suddenly locks himself in, using his strength to more or less suspend the action. Choosing the top position in the second period, Kersten spends the entire two minutes of clock time riding Dan around the mat. It's the damnedest thing Doug LeClere and Brad Bridgewater have ever seen. On the one hand, Kersten is unable to do anything with Dan, who isn't much on being moved and most certainly will not be turned over. But on the other hand, Dan, despite all of his experience and his own considerable brawn, can do nothing with Kersten, either. He cannot forge an escape no matter how he tries. For most of the second period, in fact, he doesn't even appear able to move. There is enough action on the mat to prevent either wrestler from receiving a warning for stalling, but only that much, no more. Now, as the third period begins, Dan chooses the down position, confident that he can finally wrench an escape and add a point to his lead. He is wrong about that—and how often is Dan wrong about anything when he's on the mat? It just doesn't happen. But it is happening now. He is being ridden again, this time hard. And as the Vets crowd watches more and more intently, Dan LeClere, two matches from history, suddenly appears to be in a real fight.

Deep down, Dan feels no fear; as he says later, it is only the frustration of not being able to do what he wants that bothers him. It never occurs to him that he might lose, because it is obvious, from early in the second period on, that Kersten can't do anything with Dan besides stay on top of him. But what he can do is stay on top, and as the final seconds of this match begin to count down, a low buzz makes its way through the crowd. Kersten is achieving something thought nearly impossible this season. He is making LeClere look mortal.

This match is going to finish 2–0, essentially the way it began. And 2–0, even against a state semifinalist, is the kind of match Dan swore he would not allow this year.

"He just fricking rode me," Dan says afterward, his eyes blazing with frustration. "Everything was legs. I couldn't reach."

He is pacing again—but *after* the match, this time. He can't seem to come down. It cuts too close to the bone. It takes his mind back to that loss to the Minnesota kid, the one in which Dan felt like he did all the work but wound up losing. It's like a blueprint for how to fluster him: hunker down, clamp on and refuse to engage.

Dan couldn't reach across Kersten. He couldn't do anything, really. Kersten was long and strong. And, boy, will they talk about this match. They will talk about it all around Vets, because this is the match that reminds the wrestling world that Dan isn't yet one of the gods. It is, in fact, a match in which Dan never imposed his will. If they hadn't seen it, the wrestling fans might have forgotten such a thing was even possible. Now Dan has to prepare for his championship knowing that it is.

Late on semifinals day, the grand plan, the one hatched all those years ago in the Little Hawkeyes' wrestling room, is playing itself out again. The super-seniors have a chance to run the table again. Jay is sucking wind, but nobody in the place is going to bet against him in a State semifinal. Joey Slaton is on his game. Mitch Mueller is all energy and physicality; he just looks so capable. Kyle Anson is rolling over people, throwing them out of the tournament. Dan has done his part, no matter how unhappy he is with the match itself. Ryan Morningstar is slicing through his bracket. This day, Friday, is the day they are going to move on to the finals together.

Around the Linn-Mar team, Doug Streicher has noticed a change in Jay this week, though he would never say a word about it to anyone. But this is, without question, the Jay that Streicher rarely sees, the one who remains somber rather than the buoyant, intentionally immature Borschel that the coach has known all these years. Jay's way of dealing with any of this—or all of it—has always been not to take it too seriously, to stay loose, make jokes, reserve his focus for the few minutes on the mat or practice room when they are truly called for. On opening day in Des Moines, he showed up wearing headphones and sweats and walking around with the tunes blasting in his ears, stopping occasionally to talk to Matt McDonough, looking—at least at a glance—fairly easy with it all. Now, though, things are happening fast. Jay's teammates Kyle Minehart and Shawnden Crawford, though wrestling reasonably well, have both gone out of the tourney in two straight defeats. Matt, the one they might be talking about in seasons to come, scores a huge overtime victory in his second-round match, but in his semifinal he runs into Nate Moore of Iowa City West, and falls, 8–3. It's no shame in losing to one of the highest seeds in the tournament, and Streicher can't help but see good things ahead for McDonough. But his loss leaves Jay as his school's only remaining wrestler with a shot at the finals.

It is as Streicher and Kevin McCauley and the other coaches, Jason Haag and Curt Hynek and CJ McDonald, had figured all along: When push comes to shove, they will be watching Jay, watching him try to get through something none of them have experienced as wrestlers—something that almost no one ever experiences, not even in the cradle of wrestling. It is a thing to watch and to marvel at without completely understanding; and so, while Jay gradually becomes quieter as the week progresses, Streicher and his staff let it go. "You don't know how he'll react, because you don't know how anybody would react," the coach says simply. "This is not a normal situation."

Not on any level. Jay's chest still hurts; he cannot find a comfortable way to breathe. There's no use talking about it, and so, Jim Borschel has stayed with the rest of the family, with Carol and Hannah and Jim's folks and everybody else, on the other side of the team hotel and away from Jay and his teammates. There wasn't so much to say anyway when it came to the bronchitis, because wrestlers deal with shitty stuff all the time. It is, to Jim, part of what makes them so worthy, that they simply deal with things. Surely it is part of the reason why wrestling has such a hold on people, and why they believe that it is a sport that reveals character as much as shapes it. It's the good part. They come to see heroes, no matter the circumstances. Who is Jay to fail to deliver? Who is he, really, to even ponder failure at all?

He breathes in and wheezes out, and Jay thinks he knows what they're thinking out there. They are thinking that they might be about to witness an upset, something that will shake the Vet to its foundations. They come inside this holy place looking for a thing to remember, and it might just as well be something catastrophic as something magnificent, because it's all sports, and it is all drama. Jay knows that Tom Brands, on hand to be inducted into the High School Wrestling Hall of Fame on Saturday, is watching from the stands, checking on his futures market. Jay knows that other people have come, that the great Gable will be on hand, that the officials and the families and most of the modern history of the high school tournament will file into the Barn today and tomorrow. They will come wondering if they might not see something truly wild, truly shocking. They will come wondering if this is the year in which they see something that jolts everybody in the place at the same instant. They come looking for a memory, looking for a giant to be felled. What Jay doesn't know, standing here quietly in the downstairs, waiting his turn, is that they will get exactly that.

When it happens, it all happens in such a flash that you can't be blamed for wondering if you have seen what you think you've seen. When it happens, the world feels upside down for just those few seconds, which is all the time it takes for the auditorium to seize upon the moment, register its thrill, and let loose the screams.

The wrestling fans, that is, know beyond question and almost immediately what it is they have just seen, and it is an upset. It is an upset born of bad strategy: a naturally aggressive wrestler trying desperately to cling to a thin lead by riding out his opponent. It is a natural attacker essentially being coached to adopt a defensive, do-nothing, just-get-to-the-finish posture, with disastrous results.

"That's not even what he's good at," Jay says minutes later, in the stone-silent aftermath, when Mitch's dream gets punctured.

It is, for Mitch, a 1–0 lead that gets destroyed in the final seven seconds of mat time, after three full periods of championship-caliber wrestling—the kind of match that is almost tailor-made to such an event as a state meet, where it can be properly appreciated. It is six minutes of fury and failed attacks and successful defenses and constant grinding, with the one single point to show for it, that point awarded for an escape in the second period. Then the lightning strikes. As he looks on from his seat, there is a part of Jim Borschel that cannot actually believe what has just transpired. It wasn't in the plan.

No, the plan was for everyone to go off into their glory together, Jay and Kyle and Mitch and Joey. They would stand together on Saturday night as champions in Class 3A, just like last year, and then Jay and Dan would go off to stand together as the two newest rare breeds, the 15th and 16th four-timers in history; and it would be one giant celebration, smiles all around. It would be the warm, perfect ending to things.

Instead, this match ends in shock. It ends in a 2–1 score that no one sees coming, because it comes so late and with such a stunning fury. It is a reversal in those final seconds, Zach McKray suddenly finding his way around Mitch and not merely getting away, but getting on top, 2 points, end of match, end of high school career, end of glory. And Jay never sees it coming.

And Joey never sees it coming.

And Kyle—he never sees it.

They don't see it because they are busy still tending to their own dreams—because it happens so fast that Mitch is already sprinting away from the mat, his headgear clutched in his hands, his defeat already searing into his insides, by the time the officials finish raising McKray's hand and declare him the winner in the 135-pound semifinal. Mitch is running now, running for the downstairs, away from the noise and the disbelief out there on the floor. Upstairs, still on the mat, it is Zach who seems unsure how to proceed. He had lost six straight times to Mitch, lost by close scores and lost by more than a few points. It had been almost a given that he would wrestle his tail off and lose yet again—but not this time. This time, it is Zach who finds deep inside him the one move that he needs, and Zach who astonishes the Vets audience by pulling that move on Mitch as those finals seconds trickle down. Now it is Zach, not Mitch, who bursts into tears of joy, stumbling around the mat, looking for somebody to hug. There is no shortage of takers.

Down the flights of stairs, away from the screams and the pandemonium around McKray, all is quiet shock. How could Mitch, of all people, lose this one at such a critical time? Kyle has already won his semifinal at 125 pounds, and Joey follows right behind him at 130. It had been a given that Mitch would be joining them any second, ready to go give Jay a quick thumbs-up before Jay's match gets ready to go. Now Joey Slaton looks across the basement, under the harsh light, and he spies his friend doubled over against a tile wall. Mitch has retreated to the loneliest corner he can find, but there is just no place even inside this massive old structure to really be alone. He will suffer in public, or at least in the public company of those who have always known him, and it is such a deeply personal moment that, as the reality of what has happened sinks in, the other wrestlers begin moving away, giving Mitch a wide berth in his misery as they walk past in an exaggerated curve.

Dan LeClere once said he didn't think it would be the end

of the world to him if he experienced that kind of defeat, then thought for a moment and added, "But ask me again if it ever happens." It isn't so much that losing is beyond the realm of possibility; everyone understands that. But it is simply beyond the scope of what any elite athlete is really willing to process. Now, Joey, already weighed in for his Saturday championship match, finds his way quietly to Mitch's side and leans in close, and the two of them share that moment of common disbelief. It is pure silence. Old friends.

Across the way, Jay absorbs the news. There are no great lessons to be learned at this stage, and he doesn't waste a minute in trying. Jay can't believe that Mitch's coach would have him wrestling so defensively for so long when it goes against Mitch's natural character on the mat—but, on the other hand, it isn't as though anyone needs to remind Jay that anything can happen. He has felt ready to cough up a lung now for the better part of a week. Of *course* anything can happen.

Now, as Jay moves upstairs in the Barn, he soaks up that collective crowd energy and the leftover buzz from the Mueller-McKray match, and he takes it inside of him, and he will wear it like a black hat. He will assume the role of the unpopular favorite, the kid from Iowa who won't bow to an upset, who won't stay in the state to go to college, who won't let his own wobbly health and lack of stamina come into play for even one more moment's worth of actual wrestling time. He has spent his life learning how to be a champion, and he will make the Iowans respect him, even if they never do wind up loving him.

So they came to the Barn to see an upset? An upset they already have been given. And that is all they will get.

By the time Jay takes the mat, that is, he has thought the whole thing through, and he has concluded that he is sick of feeling sick. His opponent is Chris Dunkin, from Knoxville. On this night, it couldn't possibly matter less.

At the opening whistle, Jim and Carol lean forward from their perches high up in the Barn to get a close look at the action, and then, as the early seconds of the match unwind themselves, Jim slowly leans back in his seat. He suddenly realizes that he doesn't need to worry. Down there on the mat, his son has decided to go wild, and it's the Jay of old. As Dunkin begins moving around, Jay just appears to lose all patience with the idea of being patient. He storms in, grabs Dunkin down low. He slams Dunkin to the mat before anyone has the slightest idea what is going on, and then, after a bit of scrambling and positioning, Jay simply locks up Dunkin's arms and sits him up high and pins him. Just like that. The Vets crowd is barely focused on the mat before the whole thing ends. It's over in 1 minute and 14 seconds.

This was a state semifinal, and Jay has just made it look like a throwaway match from last fall. In reality, though, it's the kind of match for which Jay seems to have prepped for years, an almost prototypical Borschel-dominated event. He gets bigger as the moment gets bigger, and that is the part of Jay that his father long ago came to understand. What Jim knows is what he has seen for most of Jay's competitive life, which is that Jay is generally the most easily overlooked person in a wrestling room most of the time. "He doesn't always walk like a wrestler, talk like a wrestler or even look like a wrestler," Jim once said. It's only when it is time to actually compete that the truth about Jay starts making itself apparent.

On this night, there is nothing left to chance or circumstance, or hacking cough or rasping breath. There is no Mitch Mueller ending. It's only Jay, in command. And he is not alone: On a nearby mat, in the other 171-pound 3A semifinal, an undefeated wrestler named Austin Boehm has pinned his opponent in even less time to earn his spot against Jay for the state title. Boehm is from Urbandale, a Des Moines suburb, and he will take the local goodwill along with his season record of 38–0 into Saturday night. Jay has been around the sport too long to put much stock in an undefeated record, because, in Iowa as everywhere else, the issue is almost always quality of competition. All Jay really knows is that Boehm is good enough to be the other last person standing, and that, somewhere, there will be someone who thinks Boehm can take down Borschel in the biggest match of Jay's life. And, once again, that is all Jay needs to know. It's enough.

They begin wrapping things up on Saturday afternoon inside the Barn: Stories, careers, endings. The people file in and out of the freezing cold, some of them standing in the lobby trying to get their hands on tickets for the evening finals session, the only one of the State Tournament to which a reserved seat is necessary. Naturally, all those seats were sold last fall, and so now it'll be a seller's market. "But they won't scalp—you'll get the ticket for face value," says a father from Glenwood, a man looking, however improbably, for five seats together for Saturday night. "It would be unsportsman-like to scalp at an event like this."

In the afternoon consolations, some of those wrestling stories are being told. With the full North-Linn crowd in the stands, Ben Fisher, still in the aftermath of his two Friday defeats, goes out for the final match of his career and finds himself wrestling for fifth place against his old nemesis, Alex Riniker, the boy to whom Ben lost at conference and districts but beat at sectionals. Considering everything, Ben appears surprisingly ready to wrestle; it's not until the match begins that it becomes easy to see how physically depleted both boys are. From the start of the match forward, it is a grim struggle for position on the mat, two wrestlers who know each other's moves well enough to blunt almost every offensive maneuver. Each time Ben tries to dive for Riniker's ankle, Riniker deftly moves backward. Riniker, in turn, can't get a decent hold on one of Ben's legs, because Ben knows better than to let his opponent beat him with that move. It's exhausting to watch. Three full periods of grind produce a 1–1 tie that spills into overtime, and then Ben makes the mistake—he has made it before—of appearing for just an instant to stop wrestling as the two boys near the edge of the mat. It's a tiny let-up, almost nothing, but Riniker notices. He summons up the energy to maneuver around Ben for a blink-and-you'll-miss-it takedown, and that is the end of it. Ben finishes in sixth place. He shakes Riniker's hand, jogs downstairs, reaches the North-Linn warm-up area and collapses into Brad Bridgewater's arms. Ben's shoulders heave as his emotions come all the way to the surface. It isn't merely that he believes he could beat Riniker; it's that there are no more chances to make that true. It is officially time for Ben to put wrestling aside and get on with his life.

Only later, when he returns to his hotel room and finds a handwritten note from his father, the one that conveys in loving language the pride with which Mike Fisher watched his son fight through his fears to complete the season, does Ben receive the real payoff for his year of work. Mike will almost come to tears talking about writing the note. It's the finality of it all that hurts. Some things you never do get fully prepared for.

A few moments later, the quality and depth of Bridgewater's North-Linn team asserts itself one final time. Nick wrestles the last match of his fractured, injury-abbreviated sophomore season, and he does so with his father and his brother in his corner. Having looked out of sorts the day before, Nick comes back strong and in control, and it is a great finish, the best that Doug could have hoped for. Nick dominates in a 7–0 victory that earns him fifth place in the state and the raucous applause of the fans in the stands.

Tyler Burkle, meanwhile, completes one of the brilliant comebacks in the tournament, albeit one that almost nobody outside of the North-Linn cheering section notices. His dominant 8–1 victory in the consolation finals gives him a third-place finish and marks his fifth straight win through the weekend, following that crushing pin by Joey Verschoor. Tyler has his medal and the admiration of his coaches, who still recognize the real deal when they see it. Put Tyler and Nick together with the rising young talent on this team, with Madison Sackett and Ryan Mulnix and Ben Morrow and the rest, and the Lynx will be ready to wrestle again in the winter of 2006. Doug LeClere is already making plans: He will have Alex Burkle, Tyler's talented brother, in ninth grade by then. Chris LeClere will be a freshman, too. Another Burkle and another LeClere. It's probably worth sticking around to see.

Between the afternoon and evening sessions on the final day, the State Tournament gets dressed up and formalized, and the eight mats that have been handling nonstop action all weekend are now stripped down to a bare three. They are placed side-by-side, across the middle of the cavernous auditorium; and it is there that the state champions will be decided, one weight class at a time, the 1A, 2A and 3A finals being wrestled simultaneously. On the floor, TV cameras are slid into position. Along that far tile wall near the entrance, the hand-lettered brackets all have been removed; the wall again is bare. By tradition, the winner of each weight class is presented the bracket on which his name appears. The kids walk off the podium looking like they're holding giant ceremonial paychecks.

Downstairs, the coaches struggle against the constraints of the coats and ties they have donned specifically for the finals. More to the point, it's getting mighty quiet. Near the south end of the space, Scott Morningstar, who went through this evening four times himself as a wrestler, helps his son warm up; Ryan will be trying for his third straight state title. On a practice mat, a single wrestler from Don Bosco High of Gilbertville finds himself surrounded by six or seven teammates and another slew of coaches. On finals night, it is virtually impossible to go unnoticed.

Into this atmosphere pass Jay and Dan, and it isn't as though anyone around them fails to grasp the significance of the moment. Still, no words are spoken to either wrestler; it is a traditional, respectful sort of avoidance. Upstairs, the Grand March is about to commence, and a bizarre scene it is. On the one hand, it is a mass celebration, with nearly 350 wrestlers proceeding onto the main floor; they are the boys who have survived the week to become one of the eight place-winners at each weight, and they enter to thunderous, gooseflesh-raising applause. But among their numbers are Dan and Jay and the other championship finalists, the only ones in the building who don't yet know what place they will take in this last, loving turn through the Barn. It gives the moment a sort of electric edge. Last night in the old place, and there is still some mystery left.

Along a catwalk, a high-schooler wearing a Cedar Falls shirt says loudly, "Jay Borschel ain't gonna win four, because I'm personally gonna kick his ass." It's a remark that sounds familiar. Two summers ago, Jay, with his soft features and his deceptively pretty eyes, had tried his hand at construction, a job offered him through a coaching connection. After a few weeks, Jay went to his boss and thanked him for the opportunity, but told him that he had decided to give up the job in order to put in more time training for the coming season. The man never knew the real reason Jay quit was that he had grown weary of the casual taunts by the veteran construction workers and worried that he might react by hurting somebody. "I guess there's a part of you that would just like to take them and kick their ass," he says one day, speaking of the average heckler in the wrestling crowd. "But it wouldn't change anything. They'd come back with something worse tomorrow." Jay has long since discovered his truth: The only chance he ever has to put in the final word comes on the mat. Everything away from it, no matter how much he feeds on it to drive him, is just talk.

Back downstairs, Dan takes up residence on the same mat where the North-Linn team has been for most of the week. With the triumphal music from the loudspeakers up on the main floor trickling through to the basement, he gets up and begins to pace, joined almost stride for stride by his father. Doug and Dan pace in circles that come near one another but never quite intersect; they are pacing for totally different reasons. For Dan, it is time to begin envisioning the match, from the first takedown to the final escape. He sees his hand raised in victory, sees himself on the medal stand. He sees it all the way. In the vision, the opponent is nothing more than a singlet, a blur of color; he's just the guy who keeps getting knocked to the mat and thrown around. Dan sees the match as though he were looking through a viewfinder; and as he paces those circles, it's only his physical body, really, that is there. The rest of him has already won.

As much as Doug would love to join that vision, the worrier in him won't allow it. He paces because, as he says, "It's nervy time," and most of the nerves belong to him. It's funny: For weeks, if not months, Doug has done a brilliant job of concentrating his time and his emotional energy anywhere else, away from Dan; now, there is nothing left but for him to come face-to-face with Dan's destiny. A couple of years ago in this basement, Doug and Dan were sitting on a mat, waiting for Dan to wrestle; all of a sudden, Doug got up and shot past Larry Henderson and made for the men's room. "I think Dad just went to puke," Dan observed dryly, and then went out and won his second straight title. But of course Dan, at the time, only wanted a championship for himself, the same as any wrestler who is made to stand alone on a mat. Doug wanted the title for his son, for his family, for his school and a sport that he loves pretty much unreservedly. It isn't always so easy to know who has the most at stake.

A few mats away, Jay sits in a tight cluster of chairs, playing cards, coughing frequently, saying as little as possible. Everything but the cough is by design. When Jay won his first title as a freshman, the year he pinned his friend Joey at 103 pounds in the finals, he had played cards with his coaches before the match, and they have recreated that scene every year since—along with everything else from that year's routine. Jay has taken a ninety-minute nap today, because he takes a ninety-minute nap every year on finals day at State. He will wear his black Linn-Mar wrestling singlet because the only time he wore his red one in a postseason tournament, he suffered his only defeat, to Joey at the conference championships four years ago. He will not allow Kevin McCauley to sit in his corner on finals night. He insists instead upon Jason Haag alongside Doug Streicher, because when he won that first title it was Haag who was sitting there. McCauley, that year, sat in the corners of two other Linn-Mar finalists, and they both lost. "He won't admit it," Haag says, "but Jay's a superstitious guy."

By the muted cries of the crowd above, it is easy to tell that the event has finally begun; up there on the floor, champions are already in the process of becoming known. But Dan can't hear them; he has already gone deep inside. They won't get to him. This is the vision he has pursued for three years, since the February night on which he won his first title; it was then that Dan believed he could become a four-timer. He has pursued the vision in his head through what feels like a million days in moldy rooms, weekends on the road, food left uneaten. He waited for the real time. This is it.

Soon Dan is upstairs on the mat itself, pacing a little faster, now, his dad walking grooves into a space nearby. That blur in Dan's vision has a name, Brett Rose, a wrestler from Woodbury Central High School in Moville. But it doesn't matter; it doesn't matter. Mary LeClere and her family and her friends and her supporters sit up there in the stands, and Mary holds her breath and looks down upon Dan. She got to Dan in time, saved him on the inside so that he could pursue something as emotionally loaded as this. The son she sees now doesn't need anything, really. Just set him down and let him go.

Dan is all fury and certainty, same as he always was. He doesn't wait for a better opening; he takes the first one he sees as soon as the match begins, grabs one of Rose's legs and scores a quick takedown. After trying and failing on a couple of turning moves, Dan allows Rose to escape and then immediately takes him down again. Now Rose tries to grab Dan in a headlock; Dan pulls out of his grasp, but he looks across at Rose with a slightly different expression on his face. He has just realized that, unlike his opponent the day before, Rose is going to actually wrestle him. The boy from Woodbury has come to scrap.

And that scrap is Rose's only chance. And that chance, as it turns out, sends a jolt through the Barn like an electric fence.

After pushing Rose around the mat and gaining near-fall points for getting him dangerously close to a pin, Dan suddenly appears to lose his balance. It's a tiny thing, really, barely a noticeable wobble from his position atop Rose, but Rose seizes the moment—it's his time to just go for the entire match. With a shocking twist and the strength in his upper body, Rose brings Dan down on his head and spins Dan's legs and torso up, so that at one point Dan actually appears to be perpendicular to the mat, his wrestling shoes sticking up in the air. The auditorium Vets crowd reacts as though a shot has been fired through the building. It's a stunning breach in the middle of a championship match.

Over in the corner, Doug jumps from his seat, but he is helpless to do anything but watch. Dan could come down in any number of positions. He could land on his shoulders and get stuck there for a pin. He could come down awkwardly, not seeing the mat clearly, and injure himself—a wrenched neck, a strained shoulder. Rose tries to react to this instant with a quick flurry of moves, and it's the right idea. Rose is doing everything he can to exploit the chaos, searching for a place to grab and hang on. He is searching for his own moment of glory.

The only person inside the Barn on Saturday night who isn't worried about his position is the guy who happens to be in it. Deftly, almost instantaneously, Dan breaks down out of his high spin, kicks away from Rose slightly, and comes to the mat on all fours. He immediately regains his balance, and with it his control. Upon further review, what just happened may have been the only moment of the entire match that Dan didn't anticipate in his mind's eye, but no matter now. The moment has passed.

Now, as he piles up points and continues hammering away at Brett Rose, Dan sees the finish. He hears the crowd, hears it before the crowd has even risen to acknowledge him. He is ready for the moment. It is Dan's father who cannot process it.

As Dan comes off the mat, a 16–8 winner, Doug stands stock-still in the corner of the mat. He is out of his chair but not moving, because he cannot move. He can't. And so as Doug stands there, letting the jolts go through him, it is Brad Bridgewater who wraps up Dan in a huge bear hug and lifts him toward the ceiling of the Barn, and spins him around while the camera flashes light up the building, allowing the crowd to see what a four-timer looks like fully illuminated. And later, when Doug steps forward during the medal ceremony to drape the gold around Dan's neck—only then does Doug begin to cry. He lets it go, the same way Dan's youngest brother, Chris, has done a few minutes earlier in the safety and privacy of the downstairs. They cry not so much because they are losing a son and brother to the rest of his life; it's more that there are some things even the dream doesn't quite get right. Every once in a while, it is not the imagination that's so hard to fathom. It's the reality.

When Jay finally puts down his cards, loosens up and walks upstairs, Austin Boehm is already there, waiting. In the time since his semifinal, Jay has learned a little about Boehm. The word is that he likes to brawl a little bit, likes to throw it around on the wrestling mat, get a little sloppy, maybe goad the other guy into a mistake. Boehm, the son of a coach, wins a lot and pins a lot—that's the word.

He also isn't averse to attempting a little pre-match mind game. As Jay comes onto the main floor in between the bleachers, waggling his head from side to side and jogging in place to stay warm, Boehm hovers just off his right shoulder, perhaps ten feet away. The Urbandale wrestler wears a tan ball cap tugged low on his forehead, headphones covering each ear. He strolls forward and back, forward and back, each time bringing himself into Jay's peripheral vision—just for a second or two, and then back out. Boehm wants to appear oblivious, too focused to care about anything, but with each pass back and forth, he steals a quick look at Jay. Jay doesn't once return the glance.

Boehm, that is, is trying to get the best of a wrestler who cannot be had. Jay looks at Boehm's undefeated record and sees nothing; the numbers bear no meaning. This match is not about anyone but Borschel and the people who wondered whether he could win it. As is often noted around the Linn-Mar wrestling room, if you took a poll over the years about potential four-timers among the super-seniors, the answers would have come back in this order: Morningstar, Slaton, LeClere, Anson, Mueller and then Borschel. It was widely considered a surprise when Jay won it all at 103 pounds as a ninth-grade kid. No one has ever gone from 103 to 171 while winning titles at every stop; it's the largest weight gain ever by a potential four-timer. And Jay is wrestling for that, for the fact that it's considered such an arduous thing to do. He is wrestling to put it in the faces of the people who say good riddance as he goes off to Virginia Tech, and to tweak the folks who don't want to put him on a pedestal. It isn't so much that Jay thinks he belongs on one. He just loves the idea of it.

And he is still sick, and there is still no doubt about that, what with the coughing and the spewing and all. In the end, it doesn't matter in the slightest. Austin Boehm, though he doesn't immediately know it, is beaten within the first two minutes of the Class 3A 171-pound final. Jay attacks from the opening whistle and he goes in hard—it's just a furious pursuit of the goal. When he looks at Boehm, he appears to look through the wrestler. Austin becomes a thing to be gotten out of the way, because for Jay this is not a duel but a proving ground.

Boehm begins the match by trying to grab one of Jay's legs, but Jay brushes him off with an almost regal air. Instead, he flashes around the side of his opponent and drives him straight into the mat. Jay already is ahead 2–0 and could probably ride Boehm all the way to the finish—but he won't. This time there will be no letting up, no matter what is happening inside Jay's lungs. It's time for Borschel to make his closing argument.

Wrenching Boehm's arm behind his back in the classic chicken wing that Streicher taught him years ago, Jay forces the Urbandale wrestler onto his side and then over on his back, exposing his shoulders to the mat for a 3-point near-fall and a 5–0 advantage. The first period ends there, and Jay chooses the top position to begin the second; and he's just going to grind Boehm down. There will be no relief. Jay wrenches the boy over again for 2 more points and a 7–0 lead, and he is laying it on thick, punishing Boehm into the mat. Up in the upper deck nearest the 3A mat, Jim and Carol rise out of their seats together, Carol with her usual spontaneous motion and Jim in transfixed concentration. But Jim doesn't need to shout tonight. He can see that his son, in the end, is as good as his word. Jim can see the wrestler he raised. He doesn't have to worry tonight. The only thing to fear is some sort of catastrophic mistake, but of course champions don't make those kinds of mistakes, do they? The Jay whom Jim has come to know would never dream of letting this one get away. He would never allow those people, whoever they are, to tell him they knew he couldn't do it.

When the match ends and his 12–1 victory is official, Jay looks up toward the crowd and raises both index fingers to the sky, a brief exultation that looks more like an expression of relief than anything else. But the Barn has at least one memory left. As Jay rises from the mat, the 11,000 people assembled there rise with him; and as he walks over to see his coaches, their applause follows his every step. Two years before, it was Jay who jerked his head up in the middle of his own match, wondering what that noise was before he realized that Mack Reiter was getting a standing ovation for having become a four-time state champion. It was Jay who had witnessed that scene and said to himself, "That's me," and so it was. And in this moment, right in this place, you suddenly realize there is no friction, no antagonists or doubters. They cannot be found inside the Barn. There is only the state of Iowa and its abiding love of the sport—and its true champions. The one thing Jay probably never counted on was the idea that these people might appreciate the moment as much as he would. Go figure.

And later, after the ceremonies and the love, after Dan Gable stops by for photographs, and the TV cameras and reporters' notebooks go away, the Borschels' extended family, twenty or so in all, heads out to a Bennigan's near the Linn-Mar team hotel to celebrate. Jay is presented with a poster signed by Cael Sanderson congratulating him on the four titles. Food and drinks are ordered all around. And then Jay, the center of all of this, stands up and says, "Thank you," and very quietly excuses himself, and hugs all the folks at the table; and he takes his ravaged body back to the hotel and passes out, leaving Jim and Carol and the coaches and their wives and girlfriends to carry on the party by themselves. They sit in the hotel hallway drinking Curt Hynek's homemade

Swisher moonshine; and inside, Jay sleeps, just as happy not to be part of it. Nobody has to tell him it's a great thing he did, after all. Nobody has to tell him anything, unless perhaps they want to say that they wonder how he'll do at the next level, with the next challenge. If they want to say that, Jay will listen.

CHAPTER 15

Making Things Grow

The day always starts at the same location. "We'll meet at the gas station in Walker," Brad Bridgewater had said the night before, by way of imparting the complete and total set of directions. Sure enough, all that is needed is to spot the sign that says WALKER while heading north on Troy Mills Road, and then to take that left turn. After a few miles of gently undulating corn fields and cattle pastures, there begin to pop up a few homes and then a few more; and finally, over there on the left-hand side of the road, there appears a little station with a couple of gas pumps and plenty of parking and hanging-around room. There's a place inside where you can buy chips and soda, fast food, mostly. It is called Hocken's, after Shannon Hocken's grandfather, who has owned the place for a long while—decades, really. In one of those signs of the times out in the country, the Hockens have run out of people who want to keep the family business going, and they're selling. The store and station will be called something else pretty soon, for the first time in most of these kids' lives.

Over by the mud-spattered LeClere minivan, Mary is handing out chocolate-covered mini-doughnuts and marveling at the state of the world today—specifically, the fact that when he pushed her small load of groceries across the counter just now, the store manager refused her money. "You've bought so many things here over the years," he told her. "You're not paying today." Another parent, standing nearby, hears the story and says, "I've been buying stuff in that store for twenty years and I've never seen him give anything away to anybody." Even in a small town, there are still surprises waiting to be sprung.

It's a grayish day, another winter day. The rain will come first, later this afternoon, and then the temperature will drop all of a sudden and the snow will fall in majestic, king-size flakes of white. It will ultimately be a wonderful day to stay indoors. But for now the sky is dry; and the volunteer fire trucks are waiting down at the intersection; and it is time to take a ride, because that's the way it gets done here on the day after the State Tournament.

As the cars begin to roll down the country road, they switch their headlights on. The windows of the vans and trucks have been painted with enough slogans and signs to make it clear what's happening, with congratulations to the wrestlers and listings of the weight classes, and kids popping up through the sunroofs of some of the trucks and vans, waving huge foam-rubber fingers at people, screaming out into the cold air to no one in particular, which is good, since we are in wide-open country.

At points all along the road, though, there are cars idling in driveways pointing out toward the road, the people inside them killing time reading the paper, waiting for the parade. When the procession finally comes past, they honk their horns and wave, and then they fire up their motors and fall in line, and the whole group heads down toward Troy Mills Road and the waiting fire trucks, which then switch on their flashing lights and crank up the sirens and lead the ride through town, around through the city blocks, honking and waving at whoever is willing to come out into the cold February air and wave back, which, it turns out, is just about everybody—old men, little girls clutching disposable cameras and standing in their front yards, people waving handmade signs lettered with slogans such as DAN LECLERE 4X STATE CHAMP and WAY TO GO STATE QUALIFIER RYAN!. They come out into their cold yards and shout a greeting, and the kids sticking out the tops of the sunroofs shout and wave back, and the parents honk their horns; and then some of those people hop in their cars and race ahead to the North-Linn School, headed for the gymnasium, just ahead of the victory parade that makes its way eastward to Coggon before looping back and coming to a rest in the high school parking lot, having touched all the bases.

Inside the building, the entire left side of the bleachers is full. There are the usual bunches of parents and friends, of course, but also wrestling fans, and fans of the kids in general, and people who love the community and feel like celebrating after a hard ride. The little school pep band fires up the North-Linn fight song, and, as if on cue, a couple of hundred people rise and begin clapping along. The team, the coaches and the parade are actually still en route. It doesn't matter. You stand for the school song.

And then it's time for the program to begin, and one by one the coaches are brought before the crowd, the waves of applause washing over them—first Brad, and then Larry, and then Doug, and the middle-school coach, too. And then the boys are called, each in his own turn. There is state qualifier Ryan Mulnix. State sixth-place winner Ben Fisher. State fifth-place winner Nick LeClere. State third-place winner Tyler Burkle. And the four-time state champion, Dan LeClere. It is a huge, huge roar from a small crowd, which makes this, officially, a Class 1A moment. The entire field is made of programs like this, programs that are run almost completely by handfuls of people who won't let them slip away: moms and dads who work the concession stands and take the tickets, and drive everywhere and bake the stuff for the fund-raisers. From where they sit it is a long, long way to the kind of money it would take to build that new wrestling room. But those somedays have a habit of coming around. You just wait long enough, and work.

Bridgewater offers his congratulations to the kids, eventually bringing the entire wrestling program, varsity and JV, down onto the floor. With North-Linn having finished fifth overall in Class 1A, he says, "We didn't come back with the team hardware that we were looking for, but we're on our way. We're making progress." North-Linn has sent five kids to state, come within a whisker of sending another (Shannon Hocken), and might with a touch of luck have gotten Madison Sackett there, too. There are all sorts of encouraging signs. Despite the massive hit that the Lynx will take with the loss of Dan, this is clearly a program poised to do good things. North-Linn was a legitimate contender for one of the team-title placements in Des Moines until the semifinal round. As it was, the team finished just 4 team points behind third-place trophy-taker Eagle Grove. Now consider Tyler Burkle returning, and Nick LeClere, provided he can get through football season in one piece. Consider that people like Ben Morrow and Madison and Ryan and Wes Ward all will be a year better and healthier, and Mason Cook, and Andrew Happ, and Luke Benning, and Kirk Schmidt. Add in Chris LeClere, ready to inherit the family legacy, and Alex Burkle, for whom Doug has such hope.

It is a group ready to continue making North-Linn a program to be reckoned with. Bridgewater can see that, absent Danny, his team may not produce the kind of individual firepower it has had over the past couple of seasons, but as a dual opponent the Lynx are going to be deep and good. The future, standing here looking straight at it, is legitimately bright. There is momentum at North-Linn again.

Momentum for Dan, too. And it is clear, as each boy is asked to speak, that Dan himself is perhaps the least emotional about seeing his high school career in the rearview mirror. He just can't bring himself to think of it as anything other than the beginning, and maybe what makes Dan the kind of winner he is is the fact that he whirs to the cadence of an inner clock that no one else can hear. Dan wanted to be a four-time champion, dreamed of it. He visualized it, of course. He saw it coming in the moments leading up to the final high school match of his life. But he also bore it as a weight, as its own form of gravity. It was a burden lifted off the entire family—a thrilling thing, of course, but a burden nonetheless. Doug says he felt it, "usually in my stomach," but the result was just so sweet, especially the part back downstairs at the Barn, the private moment with just the coaches and wrestlers, when Chris burst into tears, so overcome by the enormity of the thing. Now, not even eighteen hours removed from the moment of his greatest achievement, Daniel LeClere is done reminiscing. It's time to move on.

"The last four years have been great," he says. "I've got to thank my parents, my dad for getting me started . . . It's probably not as emotional for me, knowing that I'm not done in this sport. I'm just getting started. Thanks, everybody, for supporting me."

He was never much of a speaker, but the applause is warm and full all the same, coming from the fans who love the team so much and who don't mind leaking genuine tears at seeing the seniors go. Just last year at this time, Mike and Kathy Fisher had to deal with the reality that their older son, Adam, was finished—and brutally so, failing to qualify out of the district tournament and seeing it all end right there. Now Ben is going, too, and during his emotional speech to his parents—"It was worth it, huh?"—it is all Mike can do to keep it together. But he does, and for a reason: With the kids' speeches concluded, the soon-to-be-former wrestling parent stands up from the bleachers and walks to the floor.

"I think it's time for us to start a new tradition here," Mike says, and with that he calls all the eighth-grade wrestlers out of the stands, the guys who are going to go out for the varsity and JV teams next season. One by one, Mike has each boy walk through the line of outgoing seniors, shake their hands, and promise to try to maintain the increasingly strong presence that North-Linn wrestling has become. It is a presence that helps to define the school, the area. They wrestle around here, and it makes North-Linn good.

The young boys move slowly down the glossed hardwood floor of the basketball court, looking people like Ben and Dan in the eye, saying out loud, "I'll do my best." The parents, the coaches, the existing teammates look on mostly in silence, and then begin a slow and sustained applause, even though they know the truth: Only time and the turns of events will determine whether Mike's idea becomes one of the rites of winter.

Cake is served in the foyer, and leftover pizza from the banquet in Des Moines the night before, and pictures are taken in groups and little breakout sessions; and slowly, one by one, the wrestlers and their families drift out into the Sunday afternoon and away from the season. They shake hands and hug, and promise to see each other soon, which of course they will. It's a small enough place, this part of the world, and you'll see everybody again eventually. You could probably hang out for a day or so at Hocken's gas station, at least until they change the name, and wind up seeing half the people from the entire school district. They will see each other again. But it won't be the same. Shannon is going on, now. Dan will take his medals and the example he set for the other North-Linn wrestlers and he will go on into his shimmering future, until maybe, someday, if the pieces all fall together, he will find his way back to Coggon, back home, that is, to the farm. It isn't the most farfetched thought in the world. Maybe someday Dan will return to take over the LeClere land, although Doug and Mary have more realistic hopes that either Michael or the young one, Chris, will ultimately want to work the property. But maybe Dan will find his way back all the same. Maybe Dan and Leah will hang on and get married, and maybe Dan will return to this place and work alongside his father and Brad Bridgewater and Larry Henderson and all the other people who love it too much to leave, the people who could go out somewhere else in the world but who really, honestly choose to stay—their choice, not the world's. They will stay, and they will teach and coach, and work the tables, and sell the stuff at the concession stands, and design the T-shirts, and fix up the mini-vans, and make all the drives, and gossip about the local politics, and carry on the old rivalries, and take over the banquet rooms at the chow houses on the nights after tournaments.

They will provide the light and the space and the warmth and the discipline, all of it; and they'll suffer along when something goes wrong. They'll look for the greater meaning when it doesn't, such as the time a couple of years back when Dan and Leah and a friend were driving to Cedar Rapids for a night out and got hit by a train as their car crossed the tracks. They somehow escaped unscathed, after which Mary remembers telling her son, "I don't know what God has planned for you, Daniel, but it must be something very special." And maybe Dan will go on and do great things, Olympian things. He could, anyway. You look at him here, now, with this aura of invincibility about him, these other wrestlers gazing upon him with an odd mixture of longtime friendship and recently devel-oped awe, and you see Tom Brands down the road waiting to mold him, and you realize that anything is possible. And Dan could do those things, special things—become a national wrestler, or even an international one. But then, after it is done, maybe Doug and Mary's son will find his way back to unpaved roads and icy bridges, farmhouses, big fields, little wrestling rooms. Maybe, when you get down to it, special is in the eye of the beholder.

At the LeClere family farmhouse, the one in which Doug's parents live, where Doug's father was born upstairs and now uses an electric chair-lift to get up and down those stairs, the kids lounge around on the couches and chairs and on the well-padded carpet. Outside, the light rain has begun to fall. Snow is on the way. Dan and Leah are stretched out, both still small enough that they don't even take up the full couch, and everyone else—Nick, Chris, cousins—is either fully prone or headed that way. Nobody slept much last night. Dan, in particular, looks completely wiped out. It may be the most well-earned rest of the year.

Quietly sneaking away from the group, Doug's mother goes upstairs to show the scrapbooks she has put together for her grandson Dan over the years: dozens of photographs of that little kid, maybe 5 years old, standing on the winner's podium and collecting his little medals. Some kids just grow up expecting to win. And there are photos of Dan doing other things, playing baseball, fishing, going to Bible school, even running cross-country or track, although she says, "Wrestling is pretty much what he's done." And ever so true. Dan is not just a guy who wrestles; he is, like his father before him, a wrestler. The seed took only partial root in Michael, who had dreams in other directions, to writing and drawing and architecture. It took partial root in Nick, for whom football has been really the first love; only recently has Nick told Mary that he might consider wrestling in college, since he has slowly come to realize he will be on the small side for a football player. It's too soon to know about Chris, of course, although he has been with it all along and seems so completely ready to officially join up, as it were.

But in Dan the wrestling grip is complete. Dan was born to do this, and he knows it; he has the temperament and the smoldering fire of competitiveness, and the self-discipline to remain basically at the same weight for three years, and the strength, and the mental toughness. And he wants to wrestle probably more than he wants to do anything else in the world, even though he could refocus his intensity elsewhere. In any number of areas, Dan might be successful. But he was born to wrestle, and if you were projecting things out for years and years, you would see

Dan in roughly the same shape he is in right now, in a workout room somewhere, teaching other people how to try very, very hard to make themselves into some approximation of what he was as a wrestler. Which would make him, really, Tom Brands. Or Gable.

Out front of the house, Doug is taking a look around, seeing the weather ready to turn, making sure things are secure. Everything worked out in the end, really. Dan is moving on, and Nick finished up strong enough to nurse big dreams for this summer and next season, and what Chris experienced in Des Moines, the aftermath of Dan's victory, almost surely will lock him into a wrestling track for years to come. Doug looks out over his 200 acres. It's February. Never too early to begin thinking about making things grow.

Doug's mother puts out some things to eat and drink in the kitchen, and the kids come by and nibble on shrimp and crackers and Whoppers and carrots and celery and the like, and you are reminded again that wrestlers are not proponents of waste. They come through and take a few little things to eat, and put them on their plates, and that's that.

But maybe there is room for one more thing. As folks stand and sit in the kitchen, drinking coffee and trading stories with the grandparents, Dan pads in, in his stocking feet. Wordlessly, he pulls off the top of a plastic tub of vanilla ice cream. He selects a tall glass. He gets the ice-cream scoop, puts a couple of scoops into the glass. He reaches for a bottle of root beer, opens it. And ever so slowly, he pours a small, continuous drizzle of the root beer over the ice cream and into the glass. You figure when a dessert has been four months in the making, a few more seconds aren't too long to wait. The float begins to take shape, there in the warm kitchen, in the old LeClere house, on the old LeClere land, in the dead of winter. Dan looks up across the kitchen and smiles. Some things probably are worth waiting for.

• • •

At first glance inside the Borschel house in Marion, fatigue and sickness appear to finally have just pounded their way through the family—but more to the point, this is simply the Big Exhale. Jay, still battered by his bronchitis, seems finally past the constant coughing spasms, now that he isn't trying to perform at athletic peak levels for days at a time, only to see his place in the hacking line taken by his grandfather Jim, who wraps a red blanket around his shoulders. Everybody else is wiped out: Jay's father, Carol, Hannah, Jay's grandmother—it has been a long road and a longer week. They sit around the living room, comfortable, unusually low-key. It's a recovery day.

While Dan and his teammates are feted as heroes at North-Linn, Jay returns home to a nice photo on the front page of the *Cedar Rapids Gazette*, a decorated front door at his house, some toilet paper in the trees, and not much else. When I ask whether there will be something at Linn-Mar to celebrate, his face briefly twists into a look that suggests he has inhaled paint thinner. "When the basketball team wins, there will be," he replies, "and maybe during that, they'll call me down to the floor." (In fact, Jay will be proved correct almost to the detail; it will be more than a month after his historic victory that he is honored at a winter sports assembly at school.) Jay once said that he knew early on wrestling wasn't the most popular sport around his school, and now he has four years of largely empty home gymnasiums to prove it. He never cared in particular; he does not care in particular right now. There is a part of him, and even he is forced to admit it, that thoroughly enjoys being so dominant and so underrated at the same time.

On the Internet, the post-tournament chatter is in full swing. Message-board posters debate what might happen if Chad Beatty of Wilton, the Iowa-bound wrestler and undefeated state champion at 171 pounds in Class 1A, were to take on Jay, and already a couple have suggested that Beatty just has so much heart for the sport that there is no way he could possibly lose. Jay sees the postings; he chuckles. It's unclear by what path of logic a four-time state champion who along the way has consistently beaten a horde of other former and future state champions—Joey Slaton, Kyle Anson, Ryan Morningstar—can be deemed an underdog in his own weight class.

In fact, though, Jay will inadvertently stoke these conversations just a few weeks later, when he appears in a seniors-only exhibition tournament and is soundly beaten by Beatty. There are reasonable explanations for this, among them the fact that Jay didn't rest after the State Tournament as he should have but rather went off to compete in a national tournament, but there is no denying the result. The Iowa diehards crow, seeing in the final score a vindication of Jim Zalesky's decision not to pursue Jay more vigorously; it looks to them like Beatty was the one they should have been coveting all along. The two may eventually see each other, be it at a national tournament or around the NCAA. Maybe Jay should make a printout of some of the message-board sentiments, just in case.

Then again, it is possible that Jay won't be spending much time worrying about it. He is already drifting ahead, mentally, to Brands and Virginia Tech, to becoming a national power as a wrestler, one who beats other nationally ranked wrestlers. He is most likely to redshirt his freshman year, spend it in the wrestling room with the super-charged Brands getting ready to be an NCAA ass-kicker. Jay might well be too busy having a wrestling career to worry about having one.

It was last week that Carol Borschel took note of the fact that no one had stopped by to decorate the family's lawn or front door, curious only because cheerleaders had done so during the first couple of years that Jay headed for the State Tournament. "I

guess they decided not to this year," she remarked to Sandy Mc-
Donough, mother of the 103-pounder.

"Oh, they did Matt's," Sandy replied.

As it happened, the cheerleaders went to the wrong house,
in a different part of town, the evening they set out to decorate
Jay's lawn and door. Four straight trips to the State Tournament,
and Jay still finds himself unknown by his own school—even by
people who are trying to love him. It'd be funny if it weren't
true.

"That's pretty good, though," Jay says from the couch, a real
chuckle coming from him. On second thought, maybe it's funny
because it's true.

The really great ones, deep down, just don't give a damn.
Dan LeClere dealt with his depression and got past it, and he
dealt with his family dynamic and never let it slow his drive. He
suffered with fairly good humor his week of inordinate attention in Des Moines, but the fact of the matter is, he was relieved
to get out, get through the great homecoming in one piece, get
back to his family's land and maybe just not really talk much for a
while. He never wrestled for any reason other than the love of it
and an epic winner's urge, which makes him more like his father
than he would be likely to admit. Jay loves to use the doubts of
total strangers as motivation for him to be what he wants to be as
a wrestler, which isn't the same as saying he ever actually listens
to the criticism. He uses it, is all. He is aware of most everything.
He's a wired, plugged-in high school senior. But Jay has made
peace with two very basic facts that seem to have accompanied
his life in sports: Most of the time people have no idea what he's
actually up to; and when he is the subject of public interest, it is
often for the purpose of someone explaining that he isn't really
as good as people make him out to be. It only matters as much as
he needs it to matter.

If the ultimate honor is working hard at something for no

reason other than to master it, Jay figures, then wrestlers really are better than other athletes, because their suffering is so removed from the everyday world. They sweat and cry alone, with their teammates and their coaches, and even in the heart of the wrestling universe they really only are brought out for full inspection a few times in a year. The rest is just work. And that is what makes it so great, and what makes them special. And maybe they need to know that, and to be reminded of it—that there is a nobility in the idea of laying it all out there, every day, in a little box of a room with crappy ventilation, losing fluids, denying themselves the simple pleasures of food and drink, subjecting their bodies to real pain and full exhaustion, and then dragging their wilted, diminished selves off the mat, showering, going home and falling into bed in order to get up and do it all again tomorrow. There is supposed to be a cosmic reward in that.

Jay and Dan long ago came to believe that the reward was always there to be savored. The reward is yet to come; it renews itself in their blood and their ache. They are champions and gods, and they will start all over again in college, as nothings. They will have to prove everything again. The day after it all ends, it begins itself anew. That's not a warning. It's the good news.

Epilogue

In the late summer of 2005, Jay Borschel and Dan LeClere packed up their gear, made sure their cell phones and laptops were close by, hunkered down in their families' cars, and blasted out of town. It was a 900-mile drive from eastern Iowa to the Virginia Tech University campus in Blacksburg, and the wrestlers had someone waiting for them. Though school wasn't yet to officially begin, Tom Brands didn't plan on wasting time.

Joey Slaton also made the long trip East. Brent Metcalf, the incoming star from Michigan, was meeting up with his new teammates as they hit campus. T. H. Leet, a three-time state champion from Georgia, would be in Blacksburg as well. The second-ranked recruiting class in college wrestling was converging on its future, and Brands was one step ahead of them.

Despite his team having won an Atlantic Coast Conference title and seemingly built instant momentum in his first year, Brands had already penciled things out for the coming season, and it added up to a difficult but forward-thinking conclusion: His new kids were going to have to sit out their freshmen years, no matter how much he wanted to see them on the mat. Using his own college and international competitive career as a guide, Brands recognized the value in giving Jay and Dan and the others a year to figure out how to make campus life and wrestling life work together, to learn to live away from home, to get stronger, quicker, tougher—to do all this the Brands way, without the pressure to win immediately. The year could be invaluable. It could set up Brands's charges for four years of sustained success, and Brands believed both in his wrestlers' talent and his own ability to harness it, even if it meant a season that, in some respects, would be invisible. His incoming freshmen would be able to train with Brands and the Hokies team, and they could enter national competitions as "unattached" wrestlers; but what Brands's decision meant was that none of them could officially represent Virginia Tech in an NCAA dual or tournament. On the team scoreboard, in the context of the 2005–06 season, they would not exist.

To Brands, this was a necessary sacrifice—and a sacrifice it was. Absent his incoming class, he didn't have the overall talent on the mat to compete on a team level, and after having lost some seniors and chased off a few holdovers from the previous Virginia Tech squad, he was almost certain to run out of decent wrestlers before he ran out of ambition. Without the freshmen, the Hokies, not good enough and not deep enough, were going to make loud sucking noises as a group for a year. Brands, a win-or-go-home obsessive, was going to have to deal with it.

And he would, because Brands understood the bargain he was striking. In exchange for possibly losing every dual match his team had all season, Brands was giving himself and the program a chance to be very, very good in the winter of 2007 and for the three seasons beyond that. Brands wasn't thinking about mere improvement; he was thinking about national contention for a program that had produced four All-Americans in its previous 84 years of existence. He was going to come roaring out of the gate a year from now with this group, Borschel and LeClere and

Metcalf and Slaton and Leet. His wrestlers—by then they would be called "redshirt freshmen," meaning they were in their second year of college but only their first year of NCAA athletic eligibility—were going to be ready in 2007 not just to wrestle, but to win. Virginia Tech suddenly was going to jump into the national spotlight, and Tom Brands was going to be the coach who had made that happen. It was worth the humiliation of sustained losing that might very well have to precede it.

Brands had foreseen this possibility, and had said as much during the recruiting process, in conversations with Jim and Carol Borschel, and Doug and Mary LeClere, and Joey's dad, Matt Shaver. Even the Metcalfs, who knew Brent initially had wanted to wrestle as a true freshman, came to see the value in keeping everybody together, training as a group and waiting for the fall of 2006 and winter of 2007 to debut in unison. It could be one of the great coming-out parties in college wrestling, but for it to happen, everyone had to agree to spend this first year on the redshirt list—and Brands would have to resist the competitive temptation to activate any of them, no matter how dire it got out there.

Jay, having thought it over, was on board. He didn't mind the wait. The redshirt season was simply another year spent in the wrestling room with Brands, learning how to compete at a national and international level. Dan felt the same way. He saw in Brands a person who could make Dan better than he was, and Dan didn't need to be wearing an official Virginia Tech singlet for that to be the case. The same was true for Joey, and for Metcalf and Leet. They all ultimately agreed it was the right call, in part because they had so little problem envisioning the payoff. In the end, not one of them, not even Tom Brands, would be around to see it through.

By the winter of 2006, Doug LeClere was his usual nervous wreck. The Iowa State High School Wresting Tournament had made its move out of the Barn and into the new Wells Fargo Arena, but the old wolverines still gnawed at Doug's insides as he watched his team, and his kids, hit the mat.

The loss of Dan to college had perhaps left North-Linn without a headliner, but as a team, Brad Bridgewater's group actually looked deeper and tougher than before. With more than thirty athletes now crowded into the little wrestling room, Bridgewater was grateful that the school board had agreed to kick in $50,000 toward the cost of the new facility that would more than triple the size of the current place. Still, what that sweat in the old auto shop had produced this year for Bridgewater was five state qualifiers, including a motivated Tyler Burkle and two LeCleres, Nick and Chris. There was a chance for a strong finish in the team standings.

It wasn't to be easy, and that felt especially true around the LeClere house. From the beginning of the season, Doug had noticed a different Nick on the mat, and over time he came to believe that his son was suffering from Dan's absence. Nick had been so used to having Dan in the wrestling room—as much as he did at home, perhaps more so. Nick had had to answer to Dan's level of effort and Dan's ability to ignore distraction; these were qualities to be met, if not actually exceeded. Now, with Dan gone, Nick needed to summon his will and find his inspiration mostly from the inside—and he had to do this while dealing with his father's expectation, the expectation that Doug had shifted now from Dan fully to Nick. At one point during the season, Doug explained that Nick "just doesn't have the speed, the quickness and the determination that he showed last year. I really think he misses Daniel that much." Nick was 14-0 with eight pins at the time.

In Des Moines, Nick managed to become an integral component of perhaps the greatest team in North-Linn history *and* leave himself and his father wanting more. The Lynx finished second to Don Bosco in the Class 1A standings, earning the school's first team trophy from the State Tournament, and they sent three wrestlers to the finals of their respective weight classes: Ryan Mulnix, Tyler Burkle and Nick. Chris LeClere finished his freshman season with a promising eighth-place showing, with teammate Ben Morrow going seventh at his weight class. Burkle capped an undefeated season with a 12–0 rout of his opponent at 152 pounds, earning the championship in his senior year. But Nick, after turning in an inspired effort in winning his semifinal match, went flat in the 145-pound finals, losing a 7–1 decision that left him hurting and Doug both disappointed and determined. "Nick has one last chance to be a state champion [next season] and I will do everything to help him get that done," Doug wrote in an e-mail. "I'm having a very hard time with it, but I will move on." Still, even Doug knew that North-Linn had just completed a season for the books. The future, even without Dan, looked bright.

At Linn-Mar of Marion, the mood also was upbeat. In the first year after Jay, the Lions sent five wrestlers to Des Moines, only one of them—Matt McDonough—a returnee from the year before. McDonough battled through the 3A bracket at 112 pounds to capture his first state title, becoming only the fourth individual champion in school history. Jay's gradually appreciating assessment of Matt as a freshman had proved spot-on; in his sophomore season, Matt was stronger, more assured and consistently tenacious. But Doug Streicher had other reasons to be pleased: Jason Nelson made a surprise run at 152 pounds that resulted in a second-place finish; Wes Shetterly took sixth at his weight class. Linn-Mar, after four years of being known for Jay's exploits, was producing good wrestlers up and down the scale.

By all accounts, it had been another solid wrestling year for the high-schoolers in eastern Iowa. Of course, it couldn't compare with 2005, when that bumper crop of talent had come blasting through. That group was epic. It would be impossible to re-create that kind of magic. Anyway, they were long gone.

So it seemed.

• • •

When the Iowa wrestling world came unhinged in the spring of 2006, it did so in the manner Hemingway once suggested of the man who went broke: gradually and then suddenly. The Jim Zalesky years at the University of Iowa had built up this pressure, season by season, championship aspiration followed by NCAA disappointment. Recriminations flew among the bickering faithful, with many calling for Zalesky to go. The ghost of Gable, and all that winning, seemed to hover everywhere. It was finally too much.

Zalesky's team had rallied from a lackluster season the year before to finish second at the NCAAs in the spring of 2004, giving rise to the optimism that Iowa might prove strong enough to rebuild itself from within. Two winters later, that belief was almost fully diminished. Iowa finished the 2005–06 regular season with a 10-7 dual record, absorbing its most defeats in nearly forty years, and the Hawkeyes limped home a distant sixth place at the Big Ten Conference championships, which many Iowans interpreted as a rebuke either of the talent Zalesky had picked for his team or of his ability to coach it. A fourth-place finish at the NCAAs, at which the Hawkeyes crowned no individual national champions for the second straight year, confirmed things: Iowa no longer was perceived as an automatic threat to win. Something had to be done.

Still, it took an almost staggering turn of events for things to eventually blow apart the way they did. A job opening had been created at Ohio State, and rumors were flying around the national wrestling community as to who might be recruited to it. Two of the names near the top of the list were Cael Sanderson, the Iowa State assistant, and Tom Brands. Among the Iowa faithful, the notion of Ohio State taking its program to championship heights on the back of Sanderson or Brands was too much to bear, and it prompted a seismic shift. On the same day in March, Iowa fired Zalesky with a year remaining on his contract, and Iowa State University announced the surprise "retirement" of longtime coach Bobby Douglas. It was a one-two punch unprecedented in the annals of the sport in the state—and it was a direct response to the perceived outside threat. For Iowa State, moving Douglas aside meant creating room to immediately anoint Sanderson as the coach and the recruiting face of the program, and to get him away from Ohio State's clutches. Iowa's interest in Zalesky's successor lay a bit farther east.

For Tom Brands, Iowa's offer to have him return as head coach was to be one of the few automatic decisions of his life. This was the no-brainer about which he had always dreamed. Zalesky, in the end, had been the guy who couldn't measure up to Gable's stature; Brands would be the coach coming in to help fix all that, the one coming *after* the one who followed the legend. And whether or not anyone wanted to admit it, the bar had been lowered: Still just 37, Brands was taking over an Iowa team coming off a lousy dual season, a bad conference tournament and also-ran status at the NCAAs. He was viewed, almost immediately, as an answer. It was what he had always wanted to be.

After a cursory search period, Iowa athletic director Bob Bowlsby offered Brands the job in the late spring of 2006, and Brands needed about three seconds to know he'd take it. Shortly thereafter, the lives of his freshman class of wrestlers changed forever.

Prior to Brands's arrival in Blacksburg, the Virginia Tech wrestling program occupied no space on the national landscape. Brands being there, winning the ACC title in his first year and landing such a prized recruiting class changed that. The university had made commitments to Brands to upgrade facilities and improve the wrestling program, and Brands in turn had brought his considerable national pedigree to a place that was ready to be recognized. It seemed like a decent enough marriage, but the divorce was a wicked one.

After coming to grips with the fact that Brands had the contractual right to end his Virginia Tech tenure early and return to Iowa, university officials decided to play hardball. They couldn't keep Brands, but his recruits wouldn't be getting off so easy. Tech officials were determined not to see their program slip back into irrelevance after having come so far so quickly, even if, as athletic director Jim Weaver noted, they had not realistically expected Brands to be with them more than, say, three to five years. In one fell swoop, the school refused to allow Jay, Dan, Joey, Brent Metcalf and T. H. Leet "open" transfers to Iowa, meaning that if the wrestlers wanted to follow Brands to Iowa City, they would have to give up a year of NCAA athletic eligibility to do so. Thus, despite having just completed redshirt seasons, the boys found themselves likely to be able to wrestle only three years—unless they were to stay at Virginia Tech, a program they never would have considered were it not for Brands's presence there.

It would have been a surprising move by itself, simply because of the school's history of having granted such waivers in the past, something athletic programs have the leeway to do in non-revenue-producing sports such as wrestling. But it was especially stunning to the wrestlers in light of the events of October 15, 2004. On that day, in a meeting attended by Jim, Carol and Jay Borschel, Dan LeClere, Joey Slaton and Joey's father, Weaver told the Iowans that they would always be free to transfer out of Virginia Tech—"at any time, for any reason," Jim Borschel remembers—without penalty or loss of eligibility. It was clear to them that Weaver understood the boys were considering his university strictly because Tom Brands had come there to coach, and he was willing to offer the athletic immunity in order to secure their letters of intent. The boys could leave if they wanted to. That was the deal.

That's how the parents and the wrestlers recalled the day, and the meeting. It was one of the reasons they gave, individually and collectively, when I asked them in the winter of 2005 about their decisions to leave Iowa and drive fourteen hours to Blacksburg to attend college. For the wrestlers to commit there, and for the parents to be willing to see their sons leave home, they wanted to be sure that if Brands left Virginia Tech, the wrestlers would be free to follow him without punishment. Weaver, they say, assured them such was the case. And that assurance was one of the reasons—the chief reason, in fact—that the wrestlers gave in the spring of 2006 as the basis of their appeal, when they asked a university review panel to overturn the athletic department's decision to blanket-deny their requests to be released from scholarship.

At the in-house appeals process, however, Weaver said he could not recall having had such a meeting, and certainly couldn't recall having said anything regarding an unconditional release for the wrestlers—or for any athlete, for that matter. With only the athletes permitted to speak at their appeals, their parents reduced to sitting mute behind them in the hearing room, the questions from the university panel quickly turned away from Weaver's words and toward Brands. It became clear to Jay, Dan and Joey that the review board was more interested in whether Brands had tried to recruit them to Iowa—before formally accepting the Hawkeyes' coaching offer—than in what Weaver did or didn't tell them before they signed. (No such recruiting occurred, they say.)

In the end, it was a tack that succeeded mostly in making Virginia Tech look small. Brands didn't need to say a word to any of the Iowa boys, nor to Metcalf or Leet. He knew they had come to Blacksburg to wrestle for him, and he believed they would follow him wherever he went. His selling job on the boys had been accomplished more than a year earlier. He only needed to confirm that he was headed to Iowa; his relationship with the wrestlers and their families would take care of the rest.

Still, the university had parchment on its side. Under no set of NCAA guidelines was Virginia Tech required—or even much encouraged—to grant an open release to any athlete. Beyond that, the letter of intent that athletes sign when they commit to a program specifically recognizes that they are signing with the university, not a particular coach, and that coaches come and go, as coaches are wont to do. Under the rules, Tech was well within its rights to tell the wrestlers, "He can go. You stay." And so, it did.

From his new perch in Iowa, Brands alternately fumed and suffered. He felt responsible for bringing the recruits to Virginia Tech and angry that, in his view, school officials were blocking clean exits for the five of them as a way of getting back at him for bailing out when the Hawkeyes came calling. He also knew he was helpless to do anything about it. Absent definitive proof of what happened in the meeting with Weaver, the boys were left to make their own decisions. They could remain in Blacksburg and begin competing immediately for the new regime at Tech, at full or nearly full scholarship, under a longtime Virginia high school coach who was hired to replace Brands. Or they could transfer to Iowa, sit out a season without scholarship, and wait for the 2007–08 academic year—some two and a half years removed from their high school glory—to actually compete again under school colors.

It was no contest. Every one of them chose to transfer to Iowa, even if that meant losing a year of official college competition. For Jay and Dan in particular, it was time to go home.

And so it was that, in the fall of 2006, Jay Borschel found himself on the campus of Iowa University, having come full circle. Dan LeClere was there, too, and Joey Slaton. They would be joining Ryan Morningstar and the other Iowa wrestlers back in the room in which they had grown up together. And they would be doing it in some famous company: As one of his first acts as the Hawkeyes' new head coach, Brands had reached out to Dan Gable, asking him to come back into the program on an active basis—in the wrestling room, as an assistant coach. Gable, to the approval of virtually the entire state in which he made his name, agreed.

So Gable was back, and Brands was back. The old Iowa feeling began creeping into the conversation, the sense that maybe things for the wrestling program could be on the upswing again. Jay and Dan were going to be a part of that. Of course, nothing was going to be clean, or easy. After dealing with their outrage over the way the five wrestlers had been treated by Virginia Tech, many of the posters on the Iowa wrestling fan sites acknowledged a deeper belief that both Borschel and LeClere were long shots to crack the starting lineup even if granted a full release. Recent results notwithstanding, the Iowa fans still felt their roster was talent-rich, and not even four-timer status was going to alter that reality.

No, many of the posters agreed, Jay and Dan might have just traveled a long way back across the country in order to sit on the bench come dual time in Iowa City. The boys were now trying to raise themselves to the level of the elite in the country, and it wasn't going to be automatic just because they were from here, or because they happened to be Tom Brands's guys. After all, talent can be overrated, and you never know about a high school kid as a college wrestler until—well, until you know. Jay and Dan hadn't yet proved a thing. The score was 0-0, the competition this time was the big boys, and doubts already were being raised.

You could say it was just about perfect.

Acknowledgments

When David Hirshey, my editor at HarperCollins, was approached with the idea that became *Four Days to Glory*, the one question he didn't ask was why it should be a book. From the beginning, David intuitively understood the linkage between sports and small towns, and he was as interested as I in what lay behind the doors of the houses in middle America. In so many ways, this project reflects his vision of the story and his passion for words, and I am deeply indebted to him.

Bob Mecoy at Creative Book Services provided constant support, critical feedback and exactly enough fanatical encouragement to see the thing all the way through. Nick Trautwein edited with gentle good humor and consistently sharp insight. Ryan Doherty was critical in the late stages with his energy and organization. Thank you, one and all.

This book would not have been possible without the generosity of Jim and Carol Borschel and of Doug and Mary LeClere, who opened their hearts and their homes and allowed me into their families' lives at a time when they already had plenty to keep them busy. Thanks also to Hannah Borschel, Michael LeClere, Nick LeClere and Chris LeClere.

Jay Borschel and Dan LeClere, champions both, demonstrated remarkable grace and tolerance throughout, particularly upon being questioned for the third, fourth or fifth time in any given day. They have my appreciation and my admiration, as do their coaches, Doug Streicher and Brad Bridgewater.

In Iowa: Kevin McCauley, Bud Legg, Jeff Nelson, Mike Mc-Donough, Tom Brands, Mike Chapman, Kyle Klingman, Mike Fisher, Dan Gable, Pablo Ubasa, Jim Zalesky, Larry Henderson, Jason Haag, Curt Hynek, CJ McDonald, the Marion Maid-Rite Café and that used CD shop over by the mall off Collins Road.

For help unwittingly supplied: Brian Brown, Bruce Schoenfeld, Donald E. Wood, Shelly Wood, Barry Lorge, Bob Wright, Michael "Duke" McIntyre, Murph and Chris, Jim, Blake, Kevin and Mitch, the good folks at the Sacramento Bee, and countless others who volunteered good wishes and belief at precisely the times they were needed. Much love to big brother Steve and sister Kay; to my mother, Rachel; to Fitz; to my father's memory; to legions of Costellos, Kreidlers, Woods, Janssens, and FitzSimonses everywhere; and to our enduring friends. You know who you are.

Sincere thanks to Jeff Nicholson for the office space.

This book is lovingly dedicated to Colleen Costello-Kreidler, Patric Kreidler and Ryan Kreidler, for their unswerving loyalty and nearly limitless patience. You are my finalists.